THE MAKING

OF A SPY

By Jay M Johnson

Printed in the United States of America

ISBN-13:978-0-9981417-1-8

10 9 8 7 6 5 4 3 2 1

EMPIRE PUBLISHING

www.empirebookpublishing.com

Acknowledgements

Special thanks to my mother, Nedra Johnson and to my friend, Bob Sovey. Their stories inspired this book.

Contents

THE MAKING OF A SPY

Preface

Although occurring during a well-known period of history, this book is entirely a work of fiction. Time line, locations, characters, and events have been modified, as needed, to fit the created story line.

Isiac: The Early Years

Michigan, March 1925

Hannah Kalway could hear Dutch barking. It didn't mean much. Dutch always barked. But it brought back memories. She could still hear and would always remember, "Dit down Dutch," the first sentence Isiac had ever spoken. She sat at her small table in her small kitchen in her small house. It wasn't originally a small house. It was a small garage converted into a small house.

The plan was to build a new house on their lot in Lincoln Park, Michigan, a suburb on Detroit's southern border. (Lincoln Park is often referred to as "Downriver" because the Detroit River runs from north to south.) But as often happens with plans, this one didn't quite work out. NOT EVEN CLOSE!

The garage had been completed before the house construction had begun. Then, without warning, Elmer, Hannah's husband, left her with a 5-year-old, a 1-year-old, and 7-months pregnant. Thinking of things that could have been, things that should have been, Hannah's mind snapped back to reality.

Her German heritage and strength of character dismissed the "what ifs" and the negatives. She had no husband, no money, and no job. But she had a place to live. Her father and 2 of his friends, by putting in electricity, plumbing, and a coal furnace, were able to convert the garage into a house in a little over six weeks.

Now she needed to concentrate on supporting her family. She was determined. She could do it! Hannah already had several offers for both house cleaning and sewing. She could do the sewing at home, and take Lauretta with her when she went to clean houses. Isiac was starting kindergarten this fall; so, until then, he could stay with his grandparents when she had to work.

Hannah had no car, so she had to limit her house cleaning to areas that were within walking distance. She already had six houses that she cleaned every other week and two that she cleaned once a month. A good start, but searching for a full-time job was her real priority.

May 1925
Hannah has a healthy baby boy and names him, Jay.

August 1925
Hannah couldn't believe that her Isiac was going to start school in less than a week. Isiac needed a haircut.

Hannah had no problem letting Isiac walk to the barber shop by himself. It was only three blocks away; and in less than a week, he'd be walking twice that distance to school.

Isiac walked the three blocks to the barber shop. He entered by the back door, as instructed by his mother, to wait for his turn. Isiac could hear the customer in the other room talking with the barber. Isiac's head jerked up. He didn't need to peek around the corner. He knew that voice. It was his father.

"What's new," the barber asked?

"My last haircut," Elmer Kalway answered with a smile. "I'm moving to the north side of Detroit. I got a new job. It pays big bucks!"

"Congratulations, Elmer," the barber said. "I'll bet your family is excited."

Fortunately for Isiac, he couldn't see the slight frown on his father's face that was quickly followed by a big smile, as his father continued, "No, it's just me. No kids. No family."

Isiac quietly left through the back door. "No kids. No family." Isiac would never forget those words.

September 1925

Hannah smiled as she got off the bus on Fort Street. On the 15-minute walk home, she reminisced. Baby Jay born in May, Isiac started school this month, and she finally found a job. Whether or not it turned out to be a good job didn't matter. It was the job she needed to take care of her family. And she would continue to do sewing and cleaning. Every dollar counted, and she said out loud, "Family is everything."

Hannah was now officially a nurses' aid at the Veteran's Hospital in Dearborn, Michigan. She could make it to work in a little over an hour, but she had to change buses once, on the way. Hannah's parents had been watching the kids for the past two weeks, but, starting next week, Hannah had arranged for Mrs. Tuttle, the neighbor across the street, to watch the kids. Her Kids! Isiac, Lauretta, and Jay.

October 1926

Isiac, six years old now, had turned out to be a big help for his mother: doing chores, running errands, and helping with his younger sister and brother. In first grade now, Isiac was like a sponge, he wanted to learn everything.

When Isiac got home from school, there was a note on the table, in German:

"Kaufe Lebensmittel"
(Buy groceries)

Attached to the note was a list, in English, and next to that, a stack of 8 quarters.

Howard's store was just across the street from Isiac's house on the corner of Fort and Mayflower. Before he entered the store, Isiac heard someone shout, "Hey, Isiac!"

Isiac turned and saw three older boys, 3rd Graders that he recognized from school.

"What are you doing, Isiac," one boy asked?

"Shopping for my mother," Isiac answered.

"Come here for a minute," the same boy continued, "I want to show you something."

Isiac started to follow the boys around the corner, and, out of nowhere, a fist connected with Isiac's eye. Isiac's hands started to come up, but before he could defend himself, the other two boys knocked him down and grabbed his money.

"Hey," someone shouted, "What's going on?" It was Isiac's neighbor, Mr. Konno, who had just rounded the corner.

Isiac was quickly on his feet and could hear the boys laughing as they ran away.

Katsumi Konno saw despair in Isiac's eyes, but only for a moment, and then a spark of anger, again, only for a moment. Well, actually, Katsumi only saw those emotions in one eye. The other eye was already getting puffy and starting to close.

The emotional self-control that Katsumi saw in Isiac's one good eye was one of the three traits, the other 2 being discipline and determination, that Katsumi tried to instill in his students. And Katsumi could see that Isiac already had that.

"Isiac has potential," Katsumi thought. Then, out loud, "You're going to have a nice black eye, Isiac."

"I don't care about the black eye," Isiac said. "They took my money, and I was supposed to buy groceries for my family."

"Dedication to family," thought Katsumi, another admirable trait in such a young boy. "Do you know who they are, Isiac," Katsumi asked out loud?

"YES," answered Isiac, "And I'll get my money back."

"First, emotional control, and now such determination. Another amazing trait for such a young boy," Katsumi thought. Then he asked, "How old are you Isiac?"

"I'm six years old."

"How much did they take?"

"Two dollars."

"I can give you two dollars, Isiac, so you can buy your groceries."

Isiac shook his head no. "My mother says we never take charity."

"I see," Mr. Konno said. Then he asked, "How about a loan?"

Another negative head-shake.

Katsumi was silent for a moment. "I have an idea, Isiac. You know that I teach Judo in my basement."

Affirmative head-shake.

"I could use some help in my Judo training room. Are you interested in a job after school?"

Isiac stood a little straighter, but he made no reply.

Katsumi continued, "If you work for four days after school, for 2 hours each day, I can pay you 50 cents per day. Do you know how much that adds up to, Isiac?"

"Yes, sir. Two dollars," Isiac answered.

"Are you interested in that, Isiac?"

"Yes sir," Isiac answered.

"Let's shake on it," Mr. Konno said.

And they shook hands.

"Now, if I give you two dollars, it will be an advance on your pay," Mr. Konno said. "That's not charity, and that's not a loan. And you can still buy groceries. Is it a deal, Isiac?"

"Alright," Isiac said, and then he reached out to accept the two dollars that Mr. Konno handed him.

Four days later...

"You've been a big help to me, Isiac," Mr. Konno said. "I wonder if you'd be interested in working for me once in a while. I can only pay you 10 cents per hour, but I'd be willing to teach you Judo and how to speak Japanese."

Isiac didn't answer right away, but Katsumi could see a spark of interest. After a few moments, Isiac responded.

"Yes, Mr. Konno, I'd like to work for you, and I'd like to learn Judo and Japanese."

Isiac was unaware of how this arrangement would affect the rest of his life.

1926-1930

Isiac continued to work for Mr. Konno, but he spent his summers with his grandparents on Stoney Point, which is located on the west shore of Lake Erie. Isiac was always on the water or in the fields, forests, and marshes that bordered the lake. That's where Isiac learned to fish, hunt, trap, and track.

By the time he was ten years old, Isiac could drive his grandfather's Ford Model A. Lockeman's Hardware and Boats, in Detroit, became a dealer for Johnson Outboard Motors in 1925. Isiac's grandfather purchased a 6-hp outboard motor from Lockeman's, and Isiac could operate his grandfather's small wooden boat, with the 6hp Johnson outboard, better than most adults.

June 1930

Isiac's grandmother often sent Isiac to the German butcher shop to buy meat. On those trips, Isiac always took something to sell: fish, rabbits, squirrels, muskrats, or other small game. Isiac always cleaned the game first. He got a better price that way. Isiac was good with a knife.

Because of his skill with a knife and because he could speak both German and English, Otto Keller, the owner of the butcher shop, hired Isiac to work part time. Isiac, now ten years old, continued to improve his skill with a knife. And his skill in sharpening knives soon became evident. Some of Otto's customers started bringing their knives for Isiac to sharpen.

Isiac's sister and brother were both in school now, and expenses were rising. Selling fish and game, working at the butcher shop, sharpening knives, and still working for Mr. Konno, Isiac was becoming very creative in finding ways to earn money.

Isiac: The Middle Years

June 1931

Fritz Heimlich was a year younger than Isiac. He lived in Stoney Point not far from Isiac's grandfather. Sometimes, Isiac and his grandfather would take Fritz fishing with them. Fritz's family was also of German decent, so the boys frequently spoke German together. After one such fishing trip, when Isiac and his grandfather brought Fritz home, Fritz's father, who was standing outside, walked over to greet them.

"Thanks for taking Fritz fishing with you today," Mr. Heimlich said.

"Our pleasure," Isiac's grandfather responded. "He's a good boy like my Isiac."

"Isiac," Mr. Heimlich asked, "Did Fritz tell you I bought him a new .22 rifle?"

Isiac nodded yes.

"You know, I'm not much of an outdoorsman. I was wondering if you guys could take Fritz with you, sometime, and teach him to shoot his new rifle."

"I have no problem with that," Isiac's grandfather responded, "But Isiac often goes by himself, so it's up to him."

"OK," Isiac said.

The boys spent most summers together after that.

July 1931

Swan Creek enters Lake Erie just north of Stoney Point. Just south of the mouth of the Detroit River, the Huron River enters Lake Erie forming an expansive marsh, Mouillee Marsh. Between the two is Estral Beach. Behind Estral Beach, there is nothing but farms, fields, marsh, and forests. The only way to get to Estral Beach is by a 2-mile long dirt road.

Access by water is much easier. Almost everyone who lives there has one or more boats. Duck hunting and fishing are a big part of the culture there. And let's not forget Bootlegging. Canada is less than 10 miles away by water.

Deke Stovey owned the only two businesses on the beach, a grocery store and the "Hotel." It was a bar and a hotel, before prohibition, and a gathering place for all the local residents. Deke knew everyone.

Standing on the porch of the hotel, Deke saw Isiac enter his ice house with a bucket of perch. Deke knew Isiac well. Deke knew that Isiac was always trying to get fish and game to provide food for his family and to sell for extra money, so he let Isiac store his fish and game in his ice house. And he let Isiac park his grandfather's car behind the bar; I mean the "Hotel."

No, I guess I really did mean the bar. The "Hotel" functioned as the local "blind pig."

A few years ago, the Purple Gang made a visit and checked out the "Hotel." When they found only one barrel of beer and when Deke told them he only sold one or two barrels of beer a week, they decided he was too small to deal with. If he had run a larger operation, the Purple Gang would have forced Deke to buy his liquor from them. Good thing they didn't know there was a cellar under the grocery store because it was filled with a dozen barrels of beer and over 20 cases of whiskey. And that's not counting the booze that was still in his boat house.

As Isiac left the ice house, Deke called him over.

"Isiac, word has it that you can handle just about any boat," Deke said.

"Yes, sir," Isiac responded.

"Have you ever gone for a ride in a speed boat," Deke asked?

"No, sir."

"Isiac, you can call me Deke."

"Yes sir, Deke."

Deke couldn't help but smile. Isiac was different, that's for sure, still a boy, but acting like a man. The other boys noticed, too, because they never bothered Isiac, not even the older boys.

"Isiac, I'm taking the speed boat for a ride. Would you like to come," Deke asked?

"Yes sir, Deke," Isiac answered.

"Just Deke will be fine."

Isiac nodded, "And you can call me Bud, that's what my family and friends call me."

Deke had a Chris Craft with a 6-cylinder Packard engine. Deke drove slowly down the canal until they entered Lake Erie.

"Hold on, Bud," Deke said, "I'm going to open her up a little."

"How fast can it go," Bud asked?

"About 45 miles per hour," Deke answered.

"How fast can it go when it's fully loaded," Isiac asked?

"This boy is very smart. He knows what I use this boat for," Deke thought. Then he said, "It will go over 40 when fully loaded, Bud. Would you like to drive?"

"Yes, Deke."

"What do you know, no sir this time," Deke thought.

Bud drove for over an hour as instructed by Deke: starting, stopping (boats don't have brakes), different speeds, gentle turns, sharp turns.

Back at the dock, Deke said, "Come back on a windy day, Bud (Lake Erie is notoriously rough), and we'll see how you handle the boat in rough water."

13

"OK, Deke," Isiac said.

Deke had several men that operated his boats, but by the end of the summer, Bud was by far the best.

April 5, 1932

Deke was sitting on the hotel porch holding Bob, his 2-year-old son when Isiac walked up.

"Hi, Deke."

"Bud," Deke said, "I'm going fishing on the Canadian side, tomorrow. Would you like to come?"

"Sure," Bud answered, "What time?"

"Eight in the morning. Meet me at the dock," Deke replied.

"I'll be there," Bud said.

April 6, 1932

The next morning, they left the dock with Bud driving.

"Where to," Bud asked?

"Head toward the Detroit Light House, and then toward the north end of Bob-lo," Deke answered.

The giant roller coaster could be seen from quite a distance away. Although the amusement park wasn't open yet, as they got closer, they could see a few people moving around. They were getting the park ready for its opening next month.

From where they were anchored at the northeast end of the island, they could see the Bob-lo dock. They watched as the ferry from Amherstburg brought another load of equipment and more workers to the island. Looking in the other direction, Bud could see the Calvert Distillery on the opposite shore.

"A sign, maybe," Bud wondered?

At 10 AM, exactly, another boat pulled alongside, and the driver grabbed the gunnel of Deke's boat.

"How are they biting, Deke," the man asked?

"I'd say over 50, Wayne," Deke answered.

"Good," Wayne replied, "Who's your friend, Deke?"

"Wayne, this is Isiac."

"Deke, I've got a present for you if it's alright," Wayne said.

"It's alright; Isiac knows the score, Wayne."

Wayne nodded and handed Deke a bucket with a bag in it. It wasn't hard for Isiac to tell that the bag contained a bottle.

"Good luck fishing," Wayne said as he shoved off. "Gotta go to work."

After Wayne started his motor and headed back to the Canadian shore, Deke said,

"Wayne works at Calvert Distillery, Bud."

Maybe a sign? No, Bud was sure you could take away the 'maybe.' After about an hour, with another dozen perch in the bucket, Deke said,

"Let's head back. It will give you time to clean fish so you can have fish for dinner. I know how much your grandfather likes to eat perch."

Bud pulled the anchor, and with Bud driving again, they headed back to Estral Beach.

"Do you think you could find this spot again, Bud," Deke asked?

"I've fished here with my grandfather before," Bud replied.

"Good," Deke said.

The wind picked up, and the ride back was pretty rough. Deke noticed that Bud was superb at reading the waves. He angled into them so that he kept part of each wave under the bow until the next wave arrived. That prevented the bow from crashing into each wave. Not only did that give a drier and more comfortable ride, but it also allowed more speed. Bud knew that the shortest distance between 2 points was a straight line. But he also knew that the shortest time between 2 points is not always a straight line, especially on the water.

After entering the calm water of Swan Creek, Deke said, "You handled that crossing very well, Bud. Do you think you could do it again by yourself?"

"Are you asking me to drive for you, Deke," Bud asked?

"Yes, I am, Bud, but you know it could be dangerous."

Bud shook his head yes. Bud's intuition was confirmed. The signs had now moved from 'maybe' to 'absolutely.'

"Think it over, Bud. You'd have to do it at night," Deke cautioned.

"I've driven in the dark lots of times, Deke," Bud reassured him.

"I know you have, Bud," Deke said, and after Bud's perfect landing at the dock, Deke continued, "After you're done cleaning fish, come by the house, and I'll give you the details."

"Do you want some fish, Deke?"

"No, Bud, you keep them all."

On the way back to his grandfather's house, Bud rehashed what Deke told him.

"Go to the same spot and anchor. Be there no later than 4 PM. Catch some fish. Wayne will be watching with binoculars. If no suspicious boats are around, he will drive by around 5 PM. Don't wave. Wait about 10 minutes. Then follow his path around the island. He'll be anchored off the southwest shore of Bob-lo. Pull alongside and change boats. Take your fish bucket with you and clean fish while you wait. Take a bag to put the cleaned fish in because there won't be room for the bucket on the way back. Just leave the bucket in Wayne's boat. Maybe I'll get another bottle in it when Wayne returns the bucket."

"Wayne will take my boat and load it up with cargo and secure the cargo just in case it gets rough on the way back. When Wayne comes back, he'll come down the west side of the island from the north. Wayne will have plenty of time to see if anyone is following him before he gets to you. If Wayne thinks he's being followed, he will continue around the island and make another pass. You are still in Canadian waters, and all you have in the boat is fish, so you have nothing to worry about."

"If Wayne doesn't show up by 10 PM, come home in his boat. If there is any kind of emergency before that time, Wayne's boat will be anchored close enough to shore that you will be able to wade ashore to Bob-lo and find a place to hide, if necessary. If you are not back by 2 AM, I'll come and get you with my other boat."

"When Wayne does arrive, if it's safe, Wayne will come to you, and you change boats. Then give him his envelope with his payment in it. Wait for him to pull anchor. When Wayne is about a hundred yards away, start following him slowly, with no lights. He'll go out about a mile into the lake. In a few minutes, Wayne will turn to the west, put his lights on, and, at full speed, head toward the American border."

"You continue slowly, southeast, and watch Wayne. If no one is following him, Wayne will turn his lights off. That will be your signal that it's safe. You can then turn south and open it up as much as conditions allow. You'll still be in Canadian waters. When you are about a mile south of the Detroit Light, head due west. That way, when you cross the border, you will be heading straight for Swan Creek."

"If you see three white lanterns close together, that means it's safe to come in. If you see a red lantern between 2 white lanterns, turn around and head back toward the Canadian border. After a few minutes, if you don't see anyone following you, turn off your motor and listen for a minute. If you don't hear any other boats, head toward Stoney Point, and I'll pick you up there. If, at any time, you do hear a boat approaching, head back across the Canadian border. Wait for an hour or so, and then repeat the procedure."

19

Bud was learning the importance of plans and contingency plans and contingency plans for contingency plans.

April 12, 1932

Bud had just returned from his first bootlegging run, and everything had gone smoothly. On the way to his grandfather's, Bud thought about the 5 dollars in his pocket. As long as I don't say where it came from, Mom will be happy.

Eventually, Bud would become very good at keeping secrets. And he learned that there are times when the lines between right and wrong blur a little; and you need to bend the rules, just a bit, in order to survive. During a depression, when your family is struggling, was one of those times.

April 19, 1932

After another successful run across the river, Deke handed Bud another 5 dollars.

"Come in the kitchen, Bud," Deke said. "I have a bonus for you."

The kitchen was in the back of the bar. Hazel, Deke's wife, did the cooking there. And there was no better cook on the beach. Hazel liked Bud. She always seemed to find enough food to feed Bud when he was around.

"Hazel's food is a bonus," Bud thought, as he walked into the kitchen behind Deke. And, sure enough, there was a plate of food waiting for him on the table. Next to his plate was a bowl of dog food. Bud sat at the table, but before he could take his first bite, Hazel said,

"Don't you think you should feed your dog, first?"

"I don't have a dog. Dutch died two years ago," Isiac responded.

"She means your new dog, Bud," Deke said as he reached out the back door of the kitchen and pulled on a dog leash with a beautiful 3-month old Black Lab on the other end.

Bud and his new dog were immediately rolling around on the kitchen floor. After a minute or two, and in between the barking and laughing, Hazel interrupted the play.

"It's time for the two of you to settle down and eat."

And Bud did feed his dog before he began on his own plate of food.

May 1, 1932

Bud and Peg, walking around the neighborhood, had already become a familiar sight. Although Bud knew that, at three and one-half months, it was still too early to begin the serious training needed to teach Peg to hunt, he also knew that it wasn't too early for Peg to learn when she was being trained. Right now, Peg was still full of curiosity; and because Bud didn't want to discourage that, he kept the training sessions short.

Peg understood the common commands: COME, SIT, DOWN, HEEL and STAY. In a quiet place, with no distractions, Peg heeled perfectly without a leash. But Bud was still using the leash for reinforcement when he took her into new areas with new stimuli. Bud used short tugs on the leash to remind Peg that, although she was expected to be aware of her surroundings, she could not let anything interfere with her heeling or other commands.

June 1932

Fritz was leaving the back door of the butcher shop carrying two, empty 5-gallon buckets, one in each hand. He and Bud had just dropped off over 100 silver bass and eight walleyes. Bud was still inside. Fritz saw four older boys approaching and could immediately tell that they were looking for trouble.

"Hey, look what we have here! A Stoney Point Sissy," one of the boys said, as they moved toward Fritz. They all started laughing when the closest boy gave Fritz a shove.

"Leave him alone," Isiac said, as he opened the butcher shop door and walked outside.

"Another sissy," one of the boys said. "Or maybe he thinks he's a tough guy. You looking for a fight, tough guy?"

"No," Isiac said, "It wouldn't be a fair fight."

"You're right about that," the biggest boy said. "We'll kick your butt and send you home crying."

"No," Isiac said, "I meant there are 2 of us and only 4 of you. You better get some more help or just walk away.

"Oh yeah," the biggest boy said as he moved toward Isiac and cocked his fist.

Suddenly, the "tough guy wanna-be" was on the ground. And then a loud "BONG" was heard. While Isiac was flipping the first boy, Fritz banged one of the other boys in the head with one of his buckets. Now there were two boys on the ground. Then all 4 "tough guys" were running away. Two of them were way behind the other two because they had to get up off the ground before they could start running.

It didn't take long for word to spread. It soon became common knowledge. Leave Fritz and Isiac alone.

July 15, 1932

Now that Peg was 6-months old, Bud became more serious with her training. Peg now heeled perfectly without a leash, even when distractions were present:

other people, other dogs, squirrels, it didn't matter. Bud had switched to a rubber training dummy with feathers tied to it. Now, when Peg was completing a retrieve, as she moved toward Bud, she passed him on his left side, immediately circling behind him and sitting on his right side, touching his leg and facing forward. There, she would hold the training dummy until Bud said GIVE.

Preparing for the next training session, Bud was in the shed behind the house with Peg and his little brother, Jay. Bud was letting Jay help him make a new training device. Bud had given Jay a hammer and some finishing nails. Jay was pounding the nails into a foot-long piece of one-by-one pine. The end of each nail protruded slightly from the other side of the board.

"This board looks like Mom's pin cushion," Jay said.

"Exactly," Bud said.

"But won't that hurt Peg's mouth," Jay asked?

"Peg is smart. Hopefully, it will only hurt her once. She will quickly learn to pick it up softly. Do you remember the ducks that Fritz and I brought home last season when we hunted with Mr. Nagy," Bud asked?

"You mean the ones that had the breasts all chewed up by his dog," Jay asked?

"You do remember," Bud said.

"Are we making this, so Peg won't chew up our ducks," Jay asked?

Again, Bud said, "Exactly."

August 1932

By the end of August, Bud had Peg retrieving pigeons. He had practiced with her in the thickest part of Mouillee Marsh. Peg had an excellent nose. Sometimes it took her a while, but she almost always found her bird. Bud also trained Peg in the wooded areas around Mouillee Marsh, and in the soybean and corn fields of nearby farms. Peg also knew how to handle herself in the open water of Lake Erie, even when it got rough.

September 6, 1932

It was still dark, and there were 5 of them in the duck blind with the decoys already set out in front. A group of millionaires owned most of Mouillee Marsh and had turned it into a private hunt club, so Bud and Fritz had to build their new duck blind on the edge of the marsh. They had worked on it for a good part of the summer. The blind was built on a small pothole that the boys had enlarged by removing some of the cattails. They entered the pothole by using their waders and dragging the duck boat along a muskrat trail that they also had widened. The blind was built on four posts with enough room underneath for the duck boat.

The rectangular blind had enough space for three people and two dogs. It had a bench to sit on with a roof that covered the back of the blind and the bench, leaving just enough room in front of the bench for them to stand and shoot over the front of the blind. The sides of the blind were open. Each side had steps and a dog ramp that ended in a flat area so the dogs could sit or lay down just outside the blind. This allowed the dogs to watch for ducks.

The top of the roof was level with the height of the surrounding cattails. This made it invisible to approaching ducks but still allowed the hunters to see all areas of the marsh with just their heads showing when they stood up. This way, they could scan the marsh for ducks, and then disappear by sitting down when ducks were spotted.

Fritz sat in the middle. Bud and Deke sat on the ends so they could handle the dogs. Peg sat outside the blind on the right side next to Bud. Being left-handed, Bud always sat on the right side of the blind. It is easier for a left-handed shooter to swing to the right. Deke was right-handed. Because he could swing his gun more easily to the left, Deke sat on the left side with his dog, Brownie.

About 10 minutes before shooting time, they heard the first shots from the marsh. In a few seconds, they heard more shots from the same direction. Deke looked at the boys,

"How much money do you boys have in your pockets?" he asked. "It sounds like the rich guys from the hunt club need new watches. They shot 10 minutes early. All their watches must have been broken. Maybe we should take up a collection and buy them new watches."

The sky was starting to lighten in the east, and Deke knew the boys enjoyed his humor by the smiles on their faces. Just then, three blue-winged teal landed in the decoys.

"Hold your dog, Bud. We still have 3 minutes before shooting time," Deke murmured.

Bud grabbed Peg's collar and gave her the STAY command. He could feel her excitement and knew Deke was right. It would be difficult for Peg to hold the STAY command for 3 minutes with three ducks swimming in the decoys. Deke's dog had enough experience to know that she needed to remain still until she heard the shooting start and heard the FETCH command, but, just to be safe, Deke held Brownie's collar, as well. While they waited for the eternally slow 3 minutes to pass, Deke spoke to the boys,

"This is a good situation to begin our hunt. Fritz, you are in the middle, so you shoot the middle duck. I'll shoot the one on the left. Bud, you shoot the one on the right. If we all shoot at the closest bird, we will all be shooting at the same duck while the other two ducks get away. Same thing when the ducks are flying, or when a large flock lands in the decoys. Mentally divide the flock into thirds, and shoot only in your section of the flock so that we never double up on the same bird."

"It's almost time. When I stand up, you boys get up slowly and pick up your birds. As soon as you have them sighted, say, 'READY.' As soon as you hear the third READY, open up."

With three dead ducks in the decoys, Deke yelled, "FETCH." Brownie was in the water immediately.

"FETCH," Bud yelled. And Peg was also in the water.

Bud watched Peg check out the decoys as she went by them. She was making sure they were the decoys and not real ducks. Brownie was already swimming back to the blind with a duck in her mouth when Peg reached her bird. As soon as Peg had the duck in her mouth, she also turned back toward the blind. Bud heard Deke and Fritz shooting at another group of ducks that were flying over the decoys, but he had already put his gun down. He was more interested in watching Peg make her first real retrieve.

That afternoon, as the boys were cleaning ducks, they rehashed the day's hunt.

"I can't believe Peg retrieved 13 ducks on her first duck hunt," Fritz said.

"I knew she was going to be a good dog," Bud said proudly.

"And she even found those two cripples that fell way back in the trees," Fritz said. "Did you train her to make retrieves that long?"

"She made long retrieves, but none that long," Bud answered. "Deke gave me Peg, and I think he was impressed with her too." After a pause, Bud spoke again, "I hope Hazel cooks up some ducks for supper, I'm starved."

"Why don't you take her some of the ducks that are already cleaned?" Fritz suggested, "Then maybe she will have them ready by the time we finish the rest."

"I like the way you think, Fritz," Bud said, as he put down his knife and washed the blood off his hands. And out the door he went, headed toward Hazel's kitchen, carrying six cleaned mallards.

When the boys finished cleaning ducks, Hazel was still working on supper, so the boys sat at a table in the back of the bar, each with a Nesbit's orange pop. They were listening to Deke telling the other hunters in the bar about their day's hunt.

"You limited out by noon?" the boys heard one of the other hunters ask.

"It was a quarter after 12," Deke said, trying to respond modestly. But he didn't fool anyone. He was proud of his two boys. That's what he had begun to call Bud and Fritz. If anyone mentioned Deke's boys, it was understood that he was talking about Bud and Fritz. Ironically, Deke called his 2-year-old son, Bob, "My little man."

"It wasn't hard." Deke was bragging now. "Tomorrow morning, I might even leave my gun home. I don't need it. You wouldn't believe how well an 11 and a 12-year-old can shoot."

But the other hunters did know. Everyone on the beach knew Isiac and Fritz. While Deke called them "his boys," everyone else on the beach called them "the marsh rats."

"And you should see that new dog of Bud's," Deke continued. "Peg is only 8-months-old; and on her first hunt, she retrieved 13 ducks."

"Deke must have been counting too," Bud thought.

"Do you think he'd sell that dog?" One of the hunters asked?

"I don't think anyone in this room has enough money to buy that dog," Deke answered.

"As usual, Deke was right again," Bud thought. "No one anywhere had enough money to buy his dog." Then Bud's thoughts were interrupted.

"Supper is ready," Hazel called from the kitchen.

After supper, as the boys were leaving the hotel, Deke said,

"Same time tomorrow."

January 1933

Isiac, now 13, found another job working at Andy's gas station. The gas station was on the corner of Fort Street and Detroit Street. All Isiac had to do was cross the field behind his house, then cross Detroit Street, and he was there. The walk only took 2 minutes, less than a minute if he ran. Andy didn't speak English very well, but he had made Isiac an offer he couldn't refuse.

"Have old car. Man no can fix. I buy cheap. I fix. I pay only little money, but you 13, you work for me, you drive old car." Andy then made back and forth motions with his hand. "Free gas," Andy added.

"Can I drive it to Stoney Point on weekends," Isiac asked?

"Where Stoney Point," Andy asked?

"Less than 20 miles south," Isiac answered.

"Yes," Andy replied. "But, more than 20 miles, you buy gas. You park in my garage when empty, outside when full."

Then Andy held out his hand, and they sealed the deal. Even though Isiac was only 13 years old, in addition to his weekly pay, Andy gave Isiac unlimited use of his old car. For a young boy, this was about as close as you would ever get to a dream job.

February 1933

Isiac was getting pretty good at reading people. When he walked through the snow to the gas station after school, he noticed that Andy looked nervous.

"What's the matter, Andy," Isiac asked?

"Family from Poland come to airport tonight. Road have ice. Me no drive on ice."

"What time," Isiac asked?

"Two in the morning," Andy said.

"I can drive you to the airport, tonight," Isiac said.

"You drive on ice," Andy asked?

"Last weekend, I went ice fishing. I drove on the ice on Brest Bay," Isiac answered.

"You drive my car on ice?" Andy asked with surprise.

"No, my grandfather's truck," Isiac said, and Andy's obvious relief made Isiac smile slightly.

"Good. You drive airport. Get family." Andy muttered as clearly as he could, unable to hide his excitement.

After his trip to the airport last night, Isiac was pretty tired by the time he got out of school and walked to work. And Andy could tell that Isiac was tired.

"You go home sleep," Andy said. "Come back tomorrow. Pay extra dollar this week."

As tired as he was, it was easy for Isiac to see the happiness radiating from Andy now that he was reunited with his family. Isiac understood the importance of family.

Andy was still beaming when Isiac got to work the next day. It didn't take Isiac long to figure out that it would probably be easier for him to learn Polish than it would be for Andy to learn English.

"Andy," Isiac asked, "Do you think you could teach me Polish?"

"You teach daughters English?" Andy said, answering a question with a question.

"Sure," Isiac replied. Then noticing that Andy didn't seem to understand the word "sure," he added, "Yes."

"Deal," Andy said with a smile. Another handshake followed. Not only was Isiac learning to become a mechanic, but he was also on his way to becoming quite a linguist.

March 1933

Hannah sat in the folding chair with Lauretta on one side of her and Jay on the other. There were over 60 people seated in the Goodell School gym. They watched as Mr. Konno's students put on a Judo exhibition. This was the prelude to the awards ceremony. You could hear and feel the excitement in the gym.

The ceremony began with awards being given to the youngest students first. The parents were all so proud of their children. As the ceremony was coming to an end, Mr. Konno announced,

"And now, our last award goes to Isiac Kalway."

Isiac bows.

Then, continuing to address the crowd, Mr. Konno said,

"At the age of 13, Isiac has achieved 'Shodan,' 1st degree black belt."

Then you couldn't hear anything but clapping and cheering.

June 1933

Isiac was a busy boy, trying to juggle driving for Deke, working at the butcher shop, working at Andy's gas station, and keeping up with his Judo. Isiac eventually had to cut back his hours at the butcher shop and Andy's.

July 1933

Isiac had no problems on his late-night boat rides to Canada, but, one night, just to be safe, Isiac anchored in Canadian waters southeast of the Detroit Light when he heard the sound of at least two high-speed boats. He waited almost 2 hours, making certain there were no boats in the area before he finished his run.

Deke was a little worried that night because the ATF Federal Agents were becoming more active in the downriver area. One of Deke's drivers had to dump a load of booze last week when he tried to come straight across the river, instead of taking the longer, but safer route by staying in Canadian waters until well into Lake Erie before turning West. That cost Deke a pretty penny, and he wasn't happy. That driver got fired. Isiac and Ed Miller were now Deke's only drivers, so Deke was making some of the runs himself.

November 1933

The Great Depression was getting worse. From 1929 to 1933 over 10,000 banks failed. The unemployment rate had jumped to 25%. Thirteen million American workers lost their jobs. More than half of all Americans were living below minimum subsistence levels. And Hannah Kalway lost her job.

December 1933

Prohibition ends.

June 1934

Isiac achieves, "Sandan," 3rd degree black belt, finishes 8th grade, and starts working full time at Andy's. Hannah is still without a job. She does some sewing, but the economy is so bad that people can't afford to have their houses cleaned anymore. Fortunately, Isiac is catching enough fish to feed his family. Yes, his family. Isiac is the head of the household now. He has been for quite a while. Isiac and his family are surviving, like so many other families, from day to day and from hand to mouth.

September 1934

Isiac has to quit school so he can continue working full time at Andy's. Family is everything.

March 1935

Isiac achieves "Yodan," 4th degree black belt, and is now fluent in Japanese. When together, Mr. Konno and Isiac only speak Japanese.

January 1936

Isiac, now 16, lies about his age and gets a job at Ford Motor Company in Detroit.

May 1937

Nedra Wigman and Pam Raleigh are best friends. Nedra lived on Progress in Lincoln Park. Pam lived on Detroit Street. Isiac's house was on Mayflower, across the alley and right behind Pam's. Bud had known the two girls since he was seven years old. Bud was two years older than the girls. The three of them had gone to the same elementary school together. Bud never paid much attention to them then, but now the girls were both 15-years-old. And it was hard not to notice Pam's fiery red hair and Nedra's beautiful long legs. Bud finally asked Nedra if she wanted to go with him and get an ice cream cone. That was the beginning.

August 1937

Due to the closeness between Bud and Fritz, and the closeness between Nedra and Pam, it seemed inevitable that Fritz and Pam would get together. And, at the end of summer, they did.

Isiac: All Grown Up

1938

Big life changes:

Isiac and Nedra are going steady.

Isiac achieves 'Shichidan' 7th degree black belt.

Isiac gets a job at the Chrysler plant on Jefferson Avenue in Detroit.

Isiac buys his first car, a 1936 Plymouth.

June 1940

Isiac surpasses his teacher and achieves 'Hachidan' 8th degree black belt.

July 11, 1941

The United States was the only major power that did not have an organized intelligence network. On July 11, 1941, William Donovan, a medal of honor soldier from World War 1, was named the "coordinator of information."

1941-The Best of Years

Hannah still lived in her little house on Mayflower. She was making preparations for tomorrow's Thanksgiving Day dinner. Her whole family would be there: Bud, Lauretta, Jay, and her new daughter-in-law, Nedra. Hannah thought about how fantastic this past year had been. Without a doubt, it was the best year of her life.

The Great Depression was over, and she had a new job working as a nurse's aide at Wyandotte Hospital. Wyandotte Hospital was much closer to home than the Veteran's Hospital had been. In the month of May, Bud and Nedra wed. In June, Bud and Nedra's best friends, Fritz and Pam, were married. Pam had been like a second daughter to Hannah. In August, Hannah found out that she was going to be a Grandmother. Nedra was pregnant. And so was Pam. Both babies were due in the spring.

1941-The Worst of Years

December 7, 1941

Japan attacks Pearl Harbor bringing the United States into World War 2. Japan also attacks the Philippines, Wake Island, Thailand, Shanghai, and Midway Island.

World War II

Shanghai, China December 7, 1941

Bai Lin and her cousin, Lu Ming, stood on the Shanghai wharf watching as Bai Lin's husband, Hai Lin, was preparing to deliver a cargo of rice to their warehouse in Hong Kong. It was light enough to see as the sun was just about to peek over the horizon. Bai Lin loved this part of the day. When she was a child, her mother had taught her to use the quiet, usually associated with this time of day, to reflect on all the goodness in her life before making plans for the rest of the day.

Suddenly, the peacefulness of daybreak shattered as smoke and flames erupted from the ships in the harbor. Several seconds later, Bai Lin heard the sounds of explosions mixed with machine gun fire. Where her husband's ship was floating so beautiful the moment before, she now saw nothing but burning debris scattered in all directions. Bai Lin immediately knew that she was now a widow. That was the last thought she had as the Japanese planes that bombed the harbor were now strafing the docks and warehouses.

As Lu Ming looked at Bai Lin, she saw the anguished look on her face just before Bai Lin collapsed. Blood was spreading across Bai Lin's chest and was coming from what was left of her once beautiful face as the machine gun bullets tore through her body. Most people on the docks were screaming and running in all directions as panic set in. Some people just stood there in shock. Their brains seemed unable to process what was happening or what to do about it.

But Lu Ming knew exactly what she had to do. Although Bai Lin had died before the thought of her children being orphans could form, that was Lu Ming's first thought. Lu Ming was also running now, but unlike many of the panicked crowd, she had a destination and a purpose. She headed for her cousin's house that was about a mile away. Bai Lin's 8-year-old daughter, Fang Lin, was there alone.

The panic spread from the harbor area to the entire city in a matter of minutes. Lu Ming alternated her running and walking as the circumstances dictated. She had to navigate between the fires and the surging crowds. Most of the damage was concentrated in the harbor area, but Lu Ming could see the results of the bombing scattered throughout the whole city.

When she reached Bai Lin's neighborhood, she saw people standing around looking confused or possibly in shock. Many people just stayed in their homes, peeking out windows and doors. At one of the houses she passed, the family was busy packing things into a cart. It was evident that they were planning to flee the city. That's what she was going to do as soon as she found Fang Lin. Lu Ming found Fang Lin hiding under her bed.

Lu Ming realized that a young woman and a child, traveling alone, would only invite trouble, so after packing as much as she and Fang Lin could carry, they joined a group of four families that were leaving the neighborhood. The group had asked other families to join them, but the other families refused, making it clear that they needed to stay to protect their property. How were they going to protect their property against determined looters or armed Japanese? Lu Ming had no idea.

December 8, 1941
The United States and Britain declare war on Japan. The United States declares war on Germany.

December 9, 1941
China declares war on Japan.

December 11, 1941
Japan and Thailand invade Burma.

Calcutta, India December 12, 1941

Chao Lin was proud that he and his entire family, having been born in Hong Kong, were British Subjects. His father, Hai Lin, and Shawn McGregor were partners. They owned an import/export company called the HSC Trading Company. Shawn McGregor had formed the company under British law, and the future looked bright. The company owned 3 warehouses: one in Hong Kong, run by his Uncle Guang Lin, one in Shanghai, run by his mother, Bai Lin, and one in Calcutta, run by Shawn McGregor. They also owned 3 ships.

After the bombing of Shanghai by the Japanese, the company's prospects were now uncertain. But more important, the whereabouts and condition of his family in Shanghai were unknown. Those thoughts were in Chao Lin's mind as he walked home from school. Chao Lin's father was at sea a lot, so Chao lived with Shawn McGregor in living quarters that had been constructed in the back corner of the company warehouse. By residing in the warehouse, the money they saved could be reinvested in the business. His uncle in Hong Kong also lived in the warehouse, but his mother and sister were currently renting a house in Shanghai. The warehouse in Shanghai was their newest acquisition, and the living quarters in the warehouse were not yet completed.

When Chao entered the warehouse and approached the living quarters, he could tell by Shawn's body language that something was wrong.

"Bad news?" Chao asked softly, knowing full well that the news was going to be bad.

Shawn shook his head, yes, but he didn't say anything. Shawn, still silent, was now shaking his head from side to side. There was no way he could soften the news for Chao. He finally ended his silence.

"Your father and mother were both confirmed killed in the bombings. Our ship sunk, and our warehouse destroyed."

Now it was Chao's turn to be silent. Shawn watched Chao trying to process the news. When Chao finally spoke, he didn't mention his father and mother.

"What about my sister?" was all he asked.

"Unknown," Shawn answered.

December 19, 1941

The United States draft is amended to "duration of the war" plus six months.

Calcutta, India December 20-24, 1941

The Japanese bombed Calcutta. Although Chao and Shawn were unhurt and the warehouse was undamaged, their ship in the harbor was sunk on the first day of the bombings.

Calcutta, India December 25, 1941

By Christmas day, the bombing of Calcutta had ceased. But the news was still bad. The British had surrendered in Hong Kong, and the HSC Company warehouse and their ship, the Green Goddess, were confiscated by the Japanese.

Calcutta, India December 28, 1941

Shawn McGregor, a former British naval officer, received notice that he was being called back to active duty and was ordered to report to the British Admiralty on January 4, 1942, for assignment. He and Chao Lin had decisions to make and not a lot of time to make them.

The HSC Trading Company now owned only a single warehouse in Calcutta and no ships. Without ships, the HSC could no longer conduct business. They decided to sell the warehouse. With the onset of the war with Japan and the uncertainty that it created, there was little interest in purchasing a warehouse unless you were willing to practically give it away. And that's exactly what they did.

Shawn found another trading company that had lost their warehouse in the bombings. And they needed one for the next shipment of goods expected soon. But they didn't have enough capital to buy the warehouse, let alone the merchandise it contained. But McGregor made them an offer that they couldn't refuse.

He would give them the warehouse and all the merchandise within for free. In return, when they sold the merchandise, they could keep 40% of the sale price but were required to deposit the rest, in equal shares, into his bank account, the one he was going to open for Chao Lin, and the HSC Trading Company bank account. All three bank accounts were opened in The Chartered Bank of India, Australia, and China. The Charted Bank of India, Australia, and China was incorporated in London. That provided more safety, stability, and liquidity than the other banks in Calcutta. Plus, the bank had offices in Hong Kong, Shanghai, and Calcutta, the same three cities where the HSC Trading Company had previously conducted business.

Shawn McGregor planned to keep 10 pounds sterling in the HSC company account to keep it active. He then divided the remaining company funds, 90 pounds, between himself and Chao. Also, Chao would be allowed to live in the warehouse until he was 18 years old. And Chao would be provided with a part-time job until he finished school. After that, if mutually agreed, Chao would continue to work for the company fulltime.

Calcutta, India December 30, 1941

Shawn McGregor, with all the legal papers signed and witnessed, made five copies. He kept a copy, gave a copy to Chao Lin, and another copy to the new owner, Mr. James. He also made four legally certified copies of the HSC Trading Company's incorporation documents, Chao Lin's birth certificate, and other documents that would prove that Chao Lin was a British Subject.

Again, he kept a copy, gave a copy to Chao Lin, and deposited a copy with the same bank in which they kept their bank accounts. All three bank accounts were created in British Sterling, just in case there was no India after the war. And the final set of papers was mailed to a bank in Edinburgh, Scotland where his family had banked for years.

Shawn McGregor was a cautious man. He had even included his and Chao Lin's fingerprints under the respective signatures on each document. He was going to war, and Chao-Lin was a young orphan boy alone in Calcutta. No room for carelessness!

Isiac and Fritz Enter the Army and the War Continues

Michigan, January 10, 1942

Isiac and Fritz are drafted.

January 12, 1942

Bud and Fritz sat in the Hotel having a beer with Deke Stovey. Peg was lying down next to Bud. Bud and Fritz had come to tell Deke that they had been drafted, and Bud wanted to ask Deke's permission to give Peg to his son, Bob. Deke agreed immediately.

"He should be home from school in a few minutes," Deke said. "He usually comes into the bar through the kitchen door to see what his mother is cooking. That boy is always hungry."

Bud and Fritz both smiled. They knew the almost magical attraction Hazel's kitchen had on people. A few minutes later, they heard the kitchen door open.

"Hi Bud, Hi Fritz," Bob said, with his mouth full of something from his mother's kitchen.

It was almost as if Bob and Peg both knew what was coming. Bob walked over to Peg, and she immediately rolled over on her back so Bob could rub her stomach.

Bud didn't waste any time. He wanted to get this over with.

"Bob, you and Peg worked well together in the marsh last fall. Fritz and I got drafted. I was hoping you could take care of Peg for me while I'm gone."

"Sure Bud, I'd like that," Bob replied.

It was going to be just as hard to leave Peg as it would be to leave the other members of his family. Harder, in fact; because of Peg's age, it was unlikely that he would ever see her again.

"Thanks, Bob," Bud said, as he shook hands with Bob and Deke. Then he bent down and said, "Be a good girl, Peg," as he rubbed her neck. When Bud looked into her eyes, tears formed in his own eyes. Then Bud stood up and told Peg to stay as he and Fritz left the bar. It was a quiet ride back to Lincoln Park.

Georgia, January 17, 1942

After medical exams, shots and more shots, paper work and more paper work, Isiac and Fritz were finally sent to Fort Benning, Georgia to begin basic training. Isiac and Fritz were assigned as "battle buddies." At this stage of their training, "battle buddies" was mostly an exercise in discipline. Each soldier was required to be with his "battle buddy" whenever he left the barracks, no exceptions. Later, "battle buddies" would take on a more important purpose. Always have your buddy's back. This would prove easy for Isiac and Fritz. They had been practicing that concept since they were kids.

January 24, 1942

Captain Russel was sitting at his desk when Sergeant Hanley came in.

"You wanted to see me, sir," the Sergeant asked?

"Sit, Sergeant," the Captain said. "How's training going?"

"As well as can be expected, sir," Sergeant Hanley answered.

"That's a safe answer, Sergeant," Captain Russel replied with a smile. "Everyone knows basic training is hard on new recruits. It was designed to be that way. But, with the recruits coming in faster than we can find and train new drill sergeants, I don't think the brass understands that you guys are being stretched to your limits, and even beyond."

There was no response from Sergeant Hanley.

"I have an idea I want to run by you, Sergeant, before I send it up the chain of command."

"Yes sir," Sergeant Hanley said.

"Keep your eyes on the new recruits," Captain Russel continued, "Let me know if you think any of them are qualified enough or show enough potential to help us train the next batch of new recruits. And let me know if you would feel comfortable having them help you train the new recruits. This is a big deviation from standard procedure. That's why I need your input, Sergeant. I'm looking at this as a temporary solution until more drill sergeants become available. I'll ask for your honest opinion in a couple of weeks."

"Yes, sir," the sergeant said.

"That will be all, Sergeant Hanley," Captain Russel said, ending the conversation. "Dismissed."

Calcutta, India January 25, 1942

It had been three weeks since Shawn McGregor had left. Chao had kept busy going to school and working in the warehouse, but this was understandably the most difficult time of his young life. He still had a few friends at school; actually, they were only acquaintances since he never associated with them outside of school. And Mr. James was friendly. But that could not fill the void that had formed within Chao Lin.

The effect of the war was changing Calcutta. People were worried. Would they be bombed again? Would they be invaded like Hong Kong? And as the uncertainty increased, so did the crime. New youth gangs were forming. Some cooperated with the already established organized crime organizations. There was competition among the gangs for new membership. The new Indian gangs were not interested in a Chinese boy, but the newly formed Chinese gang was. They knew that Chao Lin, as an orphan, would be a perfect prospect.

On his way home from school, Chao watched a group of 5 Chinese boys, of various ages, approaching him. Chao knew what was coming. Upon arrival, the oldest boy addressed Chao in Chinese.

"Chao Lin, you are an orphan. Tomorrow, you will become part of our family, the Black Vipers. You will be joining three others as new brothers in an initiation ceremony behind Din Cow's place. Do you know where that is?"

"Yes," Chao Lin answered.

"Be there tomorrow at midnight," the obvious leader of the group said. "And don't be late. Don't make us come looking for you. And don't make any plans for afterward. We'll take care of that."

Chao bowed slightly, indicating his acceptance of their offer of brotherhood in the Black Vipers. It wasn't an offer; it was a mandate. Chao stood there watching as the boys left to continue their search for new members. Chao knew that the Black Vipers were trying to model themselves after the Triads in China. That meant death for anyone foolish enough to defy them. Chao Lin was no fool, but he would never become a Black Viper. Someday, after the war, he was going to be a seaman and a trader like his father.

Chao immediately began considering his options, but one thing was sure; he was leaving Calcutta. A plan was forming. A new chapter of his life was about to begin. On the way back to the warehouse, Chao stopped at the bank and withdrew 40 pounds, leaving his account with a balance of 5 pounds. He was young, but he was about to begin the life of a trader.

When Chao reached the warehouse, he told Mr. James about his meeting with the Black Vipers, and that he planned to leave Calcutta shortly after nightfall. Mr. James' initial objection subsided after Chao explained that, if he stayed and didn't join the Black Vipers, he would probably be killed, severely beaten at least. And it was very likely that they would also burn down the place where he lived. They liked to set examples. After Chao had explained his plan, Mr. James said that he would help in any way he could.

"Can I keep my father's things stored in the warehouse," Chao asked? "I intend to return for them someday, or else send for them. When, I don't know."

"I'll keep your father's things for you, Chao. Don't worry," Mr. James answered.

With that settled, Chao began to pack. He had a nice sea chest that he used when he traveled aboard ship with his father, but that was too heavy to carry. He also had a suitcase that had belonged to his father, but that would attract too much attention. And it would not fit with the image that he intended to create: a poor, wandering orphan boy. Chao found a large empty burlap sack in the warehouse that would fit perfectly with his newly created image. And he began to pack.

The first thing he put in the burlap sack was a seaman's bag that had belonged to his father. The seaman's bag contained a good set of clothes. He might not always want to play the part of a bum. Chao Lin's father had been a tall man, over 6 feet. At the age of 13, Chao was already five feet seven inches tall and weighed 145 pounds, with more growth sure to come as he approached manhood. But when the burlap sack was filled, Chao could barely lift it. There was no way he'd be able to carry it more than a few steps, so he emptied it and started over.

Now he made three piles: a "necessary" pile, a "maybe" pile, and an "I can leave behind" pile. He knew that he had to keep sorting until the "I can leave behind" pile was larger than the other two piles. Again, he started with the seaman's bag; but this time it contained a good pair of shoes, in addition to a good set of clothes. Then he put in another pair of shoes and another set of work clothes. Next, he put in an adjustable wrench and a hand drill, both wrapped in a light jacket. On top of that, he placed his father's telescope wrapped in a blanket. Then came two pans, one that fit inside the other. Inside the pans was a small bag that contained a fork, spoon, toothbrush, small mirror, a box of matches, pencil, and paper, needle and thread, and a ball of string. On top of that came another bag, slightly larger, that contained his wool cap, a heavier ball of twine, fishing line with an assortment of hooks, two pairs of gloves and four water bottles. The next and final bag was filled with non-perishable food.

This time, Chao Lin could lift the bag with one hand, if necessary, but he wasn't done packing yet. In a waterproof carrier that his father had used when traveling at sea, Chao put his money and valuable papers. It was a thin pouch that had a strap that fit around his neck with another strap that could be worn around his waist, like a belt. Chao could wear the pouch under his shirt, either on his stomach or on his back.

Chao then wrapped an eight by 10-foot tarp around his bag and secured it with a 25-foot piece of rope. He tied several loops in the rope so that he could carry the bag by hand, over his shoulder, or on his back. He put his father's rain slicker in another bag that had a draw string at the top to keep it closed. That, he attached to one of the loops that he had just tied in the rope that secured his pack. That would give Chao easy and quick access to his rain slicker if storms developed unexpectedly.

Chao Lin smiled for the first time in a long time. He saw a pattern developing here.

"Maybe, Chao the bagman should be my new name," he thought, "I'm not done packing yet, and I've already used six bags."

Then Chao turned serious again. He rolled up both pant legs. On his left leg, he strapped an ankle holster that contained his father's loaded .41 Caliber 2-shot derringer. The holster had four shell loops. They were also filled. Chao put a small, zippered leather pouch containing extra shells in his pocket. Chao filled another identical zippered pouch with steel ball-bearings for his sling shot. He put that in his other pocket. His sling shot was put in his back pocket. On his right leg, Chao strapped a sheath containing a fillet knife with a 7-inch blade. Chao had often used this knife to clean fish on his father's ship.

When he was done packing, Chao cut off the handle of a broom to use as a walking stick. Then he cut off a 7-inch piece from the rounded end of the broomstick and drilled a hole into each piece. Chao then removed the handle from a screwdriver and pounded the screwdriver into the hole at the end of the broom handle. Placing the shorter 7-inch piece with the rounded end over the screwdriver, Chao now had a newly created spear that looked like an ordinary broom handle.

Just below the screwdriver, Chao drilled a larger hole completely through the broom handle. Through this hole, he inserted a one-foot wooden dowel that could slide in and out freely or be tied in place to convert his walking stick into a handle, when necessary. At the other end of the broom handle, Chao drilled 2 holes completely through the broom handle about 8 inches apart. With his adjustable wrench, he removed 2 metal brackets from a book shelf. Chao then used a nut and bolt to attach the brackets to each side of the broom handle through the upper hole. He placed another wooden dowel through the bottom hole and bolted the other end of the metal brackets to each end of the dowel, forming a triangle.

At each of the bottom two corners of the triangle, Chao attached a wheel that was about 6 inches in diameter. He now had a primitive 2-wheel cart to help him transport his gear, or he could remove the wheels and have a walking stick with a spear at the end.

Finally, Chao used a short piece of metal to protect the end of his walking stick from splintering. And his new invention was complete. As Chao was admiring his newly created cart, a machete, hanging from the wall by a leather strap, caught his eye.

"I almost forgot about the machete," Chao said out loud. "That would have been a terrible mistake."

By this time, it was dark, and Chao was almost ready to implement his escape plan. The last thing he did was to lift his pant legs and tie thick pieces of newspapers over each knee forming primitive knee pads. He put on a pair of gloves, also stuffed with newspaper. With Mr. James on Chao's left and his foreman on Chao's right, they were ready to rehearse for the coming show. The two men, forcefully, but carefully, threw Chao Lin so he would land on his padded hands and knees. The rehearsal was successful.

There were already several people in the street when Mr. James turned on his outside floodlight. The show was about to begin, and to make sure that he had a good-sized audience; Mr. James intended to put on quite a show. It started with Mr. James yelling at Chao Lin. It didn't take long for people around the warehouse to move closer to see what all the commotion was about. Then, when everyone in the street was watching, Mr. James and his foreman dragged Chao Lin out of the warehouse.

"Don't you ever come back here you dog turd," Mr. James continued to yell as they threw Chao Lin into the street. "Run away to sea and sink like your father."

Chao Lin landed on his hands and knees, as practiced; and then, with a quick but planned collapse, fell to his stomach. Chao Lin made loud whining sounds mixed with sobs as he slowly got to his feet. Then, as planned, each man threw a short piece of 2-by-4 at Chao Lin and laughed as he ran away.

"What a baby," Mr. James yelled after the retreating Chao Lin.

As the men continued to laugh, some laughter started coming from the spectators as well. Finally, they reentered the warehouse and turned out the outside light. The show was over.

After everything had settled down, Chao Lin slipped quietly back to the darkened warehouse, grabbed his gear, and just as quietly slipped away. And his new life began.

January 26, 1942

Chao Lin walked north through the city. His idea of an exciting adventure changed to one of shock as he moved out of the warehouse district and into the slums of Calcutta. His decision to carry all his gear so that he could move more quietly now turned out to be wise for another reason. Without his cart, it was easier to navigate around the bodies lying in the street. At first, Chao thought that they were just sleeping. And some were, but many were dead, and many appeared to be near death. Chao moved to the side of the street as a truck went slowly down the street, periodically stopping to pick up the dead. With daylight still hours away, the truck was already almost half full. India was starving.

Recent crop failures had caused a famine. And, because of the war, the food from Australia that typically would have been used to relieve the famine was being diverted for use by the British troops, instead.

As Chao approached the railroad station, he decided it would be safer to give it a wide berth. He waited until he was well past the station before he circled back to the tracks that led to Goalundo. Chao wasn't the only one using the railway as a roadway. For reasons known only to themselves, as many people were moving south as were moving north.

With the coming of daylight and the presence of other travelers, Chao felt a little more secure. Chao was tired after his long night. Although he was used to hard work, carrying his pack used different sets of muscles. And his shoulders were sore where they came into contact with the ropes that secured his pack to his back. Chao moved off the path that followed the tracks looking for a quiet place to rest. When he found one, he took off his pack, sat down, leaned his head against his pack, and closed his eyes.

Chao heard crying. He thought he must be dreaming about his staged exit from his warehouse home. As he became fully awake, Chao realized that the crying was real, not the pretend crying of the day before. Not far away, Chao noticed a young boy sitting on the ground with his arm around a dog. Sitting up slowly and speaking softly, so as not to startle the boy, Chao said in Hindi,

"What's the matter young one?"

"I have to sell my dog for 10 rupees or trade her for food," the boy said, "Or my parents are going to eat her. And no one will buy her because they don't want to feed her." Then the boy started to cry again.

Chao noticed that the boy was about the same age as his sister. That distracted him for a moment. He still didn't know if his sister was alive. But he would continue to believe that she was unless he found out otherwise. Refocusing on the boy, Chao asked,

"What's your dog's name?"

"Lena," the boy said between sobs.

"Would you sell her for 8 rupees," Chao asked?

The boy stopped crying but shook his head no.

"You're a tough trader," Chao said. "I will buy your dog for 10 rupees if you share my lunch with me."

The boy nodded his head, yes, as he and his dog moved next to Chao and sat down. It was easy to see how much the boy loved his dog. And that gave Chao an idea. As the three of them ate lunch, Chao asked the boy,

"Will you keep Lena for me while I'm traveling?"

"No, you have to take her with you, or they will eat her next week," the boy said, and then he started to cry again.

After lunch, the Indian boy left with a full belly and 10 rupees, sniffing, but no longer crying. Chao, now feeling safer, decided to put his cart together. His shoulders could use a break from the load they had been carrying. With his new dog, Lena, on a short lead, Chao returned to the path alongside the tracks.

Although Lena was in between a medium and large sized dog, she was skinny, between 40 and 50 pounds, Chao guessed. He needed to fatten her up a little. Lena had short hair and was mostly black. She had a small white spot above each eye and a narrow white blaze down her chest. Her two hind feet had white tips. Chao was no longer alone.

Chao could tell Lena was a young dog, maybe not even full-grown yet. He began her training as soon as he returned to the tracks. He pulled his cart with his right hand and held Lena on a short lead with his left hand. If Lena moved too far to the side, fell behind, or pulled ahead, Chao would say HEEL and give a tug on the rope until Lena returned to her proper position, with her right shoulder almost, but not quite, touching Chao's left leg. Each time Chao stopped, he would say SIT as he pulled up on the rope and pushed down on her rump at the same time.

Calcutta, January 27, 1942

When Chao Lin didn't show up for the initiation, the same five boys came looking for him. When they heard about Chao Lin's undignified exit, one of the boys asked, "Should we look for him at the docks?"

The oldest boy shook his head, no, then said,

"There's no place for a crybaby in the Black Vipers. If we brought him back now, we'd be the ones laughed at, not him."

And the only five members of the Black Vipers who knew Chao's name decided it would be better for them if they just forgot about him. And they did.

India, February 1, 1942

Chao did not want to keep Lena always tied to a lead, so he was watching for an isolated spot where he and Lena could be alone together. Chao spotted a hilly, non-cultivated area that was over 2 miles from the tracks. Since no trail led in that direction, Chao was hopeful that he would find the isolation he was looking for.

Chao took his cart apart and headed into the brush with everything on his back. As Chao moved away from the low area around the tracks and approached the hills, the ground started to rise gradually. In this area, the brush was thinner, and it was easier to move. And still no trail. That was good.

Chao had been walking for over an hour when he finally reached the base of the hills. In a notch between 2 hills, Chao found a small clearing that was surrounded by small trees and brush. The clearing, which was invisible from the tracks, was a small level area next to a mostly dry rocky channel that carried runoff when it rained. Large boulders, which had rolled down the hillside, were scattered around the clearing. Chao found a spot where three stones laid against each other.

The two bottom boulders were side by side with the third boulder balanced on top and against the base of the hill forming a narrow space, about 8 feet wide, that ran from the base of the hill for about 20 feet. The boulder on top acted as a roof and covered about half of the area between the bottom two stones. Chao had found a perfect place to camp.

For safety, Chao had previously camped near other travelers. Now, however, Chao unrolled his tarp; and he and Lena spent the night together, their first night alone, in their new camp.

February 2, 1942

Chao got up and fed Lena; then, after he finished his breakfast, it was time for Lena's next test. Chao poured water into one of his pans. Then he removed the lead from Lena's neck. Away she went! Back and forth, across the clearing, around the boulders, into the trees, out of the trees, and when she wasn't running, she was sniffing everything. Ten minutes later, with her tongue hanging out and panting, Lena returned to the pan of water, emptied it, and then curled up next to Chao. That moment provided a much-needed lift to Chao's spirit.

After Lena had caught her breath, Chao gave her some more water and a biscuit. Then, as he walked away from her, Chao called,

"Lena, HEEL."

Lena immediately moved to Chao's left side and matched his pace. Chao heeled Lena around the campsite: turning right, turning left, slowing down, and speeding up. Lena followed Chao's every move. Each time Chao stopped, Lena would sit and look at him, as if asking, "What next?"

At the end of the training session, Chao stopped; and when Lena sat, Chao grabbed her by the neck with both hands and playfully shook her saying "OK" to release her. Then Chao jumped up and darted from side to side signaling that it was time to play. Chao and Lena spent the rest of the day exploring the area: sometimes heeling and sometimes apart, but never very far apart and always within sight of one another.

The STAY command was next. Chao used his voice and a hand signal. Every time he said "STAY," he would push his open palm toward Lena. When she started to move toward him, Chao would repeat STAY and the hand signal, as he physically returned her to her sitting position. Eventually, Chao was able to enforce the STAY command by leaning forward (a sign of aggression) and extending his hand like a stop sign when he said "STAY." Then Chao would take a step back, bend down, and with his arms extended toward Lena, he would say "COME." Chao kept repeating this procedure, gradually increasing both the time and distance between the two commands. Lena quickly learned the STAY and COME commands.

After some play time, Chao and Lena had lunch and took a short nap in the shade. After his rest, Chao decided that he would try to teach Lena to FETCH. The first thing he did was grab a stick and start playing tug with her. Lena liked that game. Chao used the word, PULL, to initiate the tug game. Sometimes Chao would release the stick letting Lena win. And sometimes Chao would hold the stick with one hand and put the index finger of his other hand into Lena's mouth at the joint of her jaws. This forced her to open her mouth at the same time that Chao issued the GIVE command. Then Chao would give the stick back to Lena and begin the game of tug again, only now GIVE was also part of the game.

Eventually, Chao added a new element to the game. Now, each time Lena gave him the stick, he would throw it and say FETCH. Chao knew that Lena would have to bring the stick back if she wanted to continue playing the game of tug. And she did. Eventually, Chao added SIT and GIVE at the end of each retrieve.

That evening, as Chao watched the flames of the fire he had built, he thought,

"This was a good day and this is a good place. I wonder how long we could stay here?"

And he began to calculate: enough food for 10 days, but only enough water for half that time. They would stay until they were down to one day's water, he decided. Then they would continue on their journey.

February 3, 1942

In the twilight time between sleep and being fully awake, Chao had thoughts of food and water and Lena and snakes. With the thought of snakes, Chao instantly became fully awake. There were so many deadly snakes in India! He needed to train Lena to stay away from snakes. His next thought was, "And we can eat snakes." Just that quickly the day's plan was made.

After breakfast and after playing with Lena and reviewing commands, Chao took his hand drill out of his pack and his machete out of its sheath. Time to create a new weapon. The machete had a hole drilled through the end of the handle with a leather strap tied through the hole forming a loop. His father had used the loop to hang the machete from the warehouse wall. The steel blade, which was about 14 inches long, extended another 6 inches into the handle and was riveted in place. Just past the part of the blade that was riveted in the handle, Chao drilled another hole.

The two holes in the machete handle were closer together than the two holes at the bottom of his walking stick. Since the holes in the machete handle did not line up with the holes in the bottom of his walking stick, Chao measured the distance between the holes in the machete, and drilled another hole in the bottom of the walking stick so that the bottom 2 holes in his walking stick lined up perfectly with the holes in the machete handle.

Chao looked at all the holes in his walking stick and thought,

"First, I'm a bag man; now it looks like I'm becoming a holy man."

"A wandering holy man in India," Chao said out loud and laughed. He was regaining his sense of humor.

Chao then put his wheel bolts through the machete handle and used his adjustable wrench to attach the machete to his walking stick. Chao then removed the cap that covered the screwdriver at the other end of his walking stick. Now, not only did he have a lunging spear, but he had a slashing spear, as well.

Chao called Lena and put the lead around her neck. Then he tied a 10-foot piece of rope to the end of the lead. Her next lesson required that she be allowed to get farther away from Chao. They were going snake hunting. There were a lot of snakes in India, and Chao couldn't identify very many of them. But in India, as soon as children are beginning to walk, one of the first things they are taught is to identify the poisonous snakes: King Cobra, Daboia, Saw Scaled Viper, and the Common Krait. These, Chao knew well and intended to avoid during Lena's training period.

Chao had already seen snakes in the area. Morning was the best time for snake hunting. After a cool night, the snakes liked to lay on the rocks that were absorbing heat from the sun. This helped the snakes regulate their body temperature. As the day progressed, the snakes retreated to the cracks between the rocks and other shaded areas.

The first snake they saw was a safe one, and Lena's training began. Chao pointed out the snake to Lena and released the lead but held on to the attached rope. As Lena lunged toward the snake, barking, Chao pulled on the rope and yelled "NO," as he pulled Lena back to his side. Chao then heeled Lena a little closer to the sunning snake that was now aware of their presence and hissing. Chao stopped, and Lena sat. Chao again said, "OK." Lena again charged the snake and this time Chao pulled so hard that Lena nearly turned a backwards summersault when he yelled, "NO." By this time, the snake had enough of these disturbing creatures and disappeared into the rocks.

They repeated the process with the next snake they found. When they approached the fourth snake, Chao said "OK," and Lena took several slow steps toward the snake, growling, but stopped before she reached the end of the rope. Chao smiled. He had a smart dog. Chao didn't yet realize that he had a natural ability for training animals.

Chao wanted to find one more snake before it became too hot, and the snakes retreated into the shade. And he found one quick enough, but he passed it by; it was a Saw Scaled Viper, and Chao wanted a little more training before approaching one of the poisonous snakes.

The next snake Chao and Lena saw was non-poisonous, but it was a big one, over 6 feet long. Chao removed the lead from Lena's neck and told her to STAY. As Chao moved away from Lena, he continued to glance back at her every few seconds. When Chao was about 15 feet away from Lena, he again gave her the hand signal for STAY. Lena was still in the same position as Chao continued to move slowly sideways, careful not to get any closer to the snake. The snake now had 2 potential enemies to watch. Now Chao began angling closer to the snake. A direct approach is immediately perceived as a threat, but an angled approach forces any animal to decide whether a potential threat is advancing toward it or is just passing by. With Lena still holding her position, Chao again gave her the hand signal for STAY.

Chao's father had taught him that chance plays a major role in everyone's life, but with anticipation and planning, you can avoid many problems before chance has the opportunity to interfere. Chao knew exactly what he was going to do. He was going to change direction and move slowly but directly toward the snake. If the snake held its ground, Chao was going to cut off its head. If it attacked or retreated, he was going to cut it where ever he could. Then he would immediately return his attention to Lena to see if his sudden action caused her to react.

A quick glance showed Chao that Lena was not moving. Chao was so close now that the snake decided to threaten Chao instead of retreating. That's what Chao was hoping for, and with a quick downward motion of his walking stick-machete, he cut off the snake's head. Turning his attention immediately back to Lena, Chao saw that Lena had jumped to her feet and moved several steps forward. A loud "NO" and then the SIT command returned Lena to her sitting position. As Chao let the headless snake thrash, he moved to within 5 feet of Lena and stopped. He could see her excitement, feel it almost, but she remained sitting.

Chao then gave the command, HEEL, and Lena quickly moved to his side and sat down. Chao heeled Lena closer to the snake, with Lena between him and the snake. Whenever Lena's curiosity drew her toward the snake, Chao yelled "HEEL," keeping her close to his side. Chao heeled Lena back and forth and around the snake until she heeled without him having to repeat the command. Chao was careful never to get closer than 10 feet from the snake. He was showing Lena the boundaries of how close she could get to a snake.

Finally, Chao and Lena started back to camp with the snake in an empty sack.

"Now I have a hunting partner and enough food to fatten her up," Chao said to himself.

Looking up, Chao could see the sky darkening. He and Lena had found a way to increase their food supply, and it looked like their water supply would also soon be increased. Hurrying back to camp, the first thing Chao did was to get the water bottles and pans out of his pack and give Lena a drink. Now that there was no question that a storm was coming, Chao set out his 2 pans and was ready to catch rainwater.

The storm hit with a wallop. Chao could hear the water hitting the bottom of his pans. Shortly after that, he saw water begin to flow down the small channel between the hills. Chao quickly realized he could catch more water and catch it more quickly from the small channel. He took the largest pan and began to catch water as it flowed around a large rock. By moving some small rocks from the side of the large rock, he made the channel around the large rock a little bigger. Then he removed some rocks from the bottom of his little channel, making a depression big enough for his pan to fit. With the pan now below the level of the water flowing around the rock, Chao's newly created waterfall filled his pan in a few seconds. Within minutes, Chao had all of his water containers filled, wishing he had more, but realizing that, while traveling, the weight of additional water would be prohibitive.

If he and Lena were going to stay here a while, he would have to figure out a way to increase water storage; that would be tomorrow's plan. And that's what Chao was thinking when he finally fell asleep.

February 4, 1942

Chao had 2 small snakes in his bag, plus, he had meat left over from the snake he killed yesterday, more than enough food for the day. The ground was so porous that most of the water from yesterday's rain had already soaked in, but Lena was still able to find a few spots in the small channel where she could get a drink.

As Chao watched Lena drink, his thoughts returned to the problem of water storage.

Before they left this morning, Chao had scooped out a small depression in the sand. Chao pushed part of his rain slicker into the hole, and then poured water into it. Then he placed a flat rock over the waterhole and folded the rest of his rain slicker over the rock. Chao placed another flat rock over his rain slicker, both holding it in place and forming a seal, of sorts. If the slicker still held water when they returned, Chao had an idea of how to make a larger and more stable water storage container.

Chao began to pick up small stones that would fit in his sling shot. He was about to become a bird hunter. He decided to save his ball bearings. He might find a better use for them in the future. There were a lot of birds in the area, and they didn't seem to be very fearful. He got within 20 feet of a bird perched on a low tree branch and fired. He missed. By the time Chao had used all of his stones, he had managed to hit only one bird, and it was still able to fly away. It didn't look like Chao was going to become a bird hunter any time soon, so he decided to change plans. He would become a bird trapper instead. How to build a bird trap occupied Chao's thoughts as he and Lena headed back to camp.

By the time Chao and Lena returned to camp, Chao knew how he was going to make his bird trap. But first, he checked to see if his rain slicker still held water. It did. With that good news, Chao was ready to begin his construction project, making a bird trap.

Chao removed his machete from his walking stick and wandered about searching for small straight branches about the same diameter as his broom handle. He found and cut four suitable branches, one for each side of his trap. He made each branch 6 inches longer than the planned size of the trap. He then placed the 4 branches on the tarp, forming a square, with about 2 inches of the tarp outside of the square. Chao then used his ball of twine to tie the 4 branches of his square together at the corners. He used more twine to secure the tarp to the corners of his wooden frame. Chao then took his now somewhat smaller ball of twine and tied it to one corner. Letting the ball of twine unroll, Chao walked to the center of the tarp, raised his hand with the twine above his head and cut it there. He repeated this procedure for the other 3 corners. Next, Chao found a short piece of wood that was twice as thick as his frame and had a fork on one end. To the forked piece of wood, Chao tied the loose ends of the twine that were attached to each corner of his frame.

Chao then tied one end of his rope to the forked piece of wood, and threw the other end of the rope over a low tree branch. Pulling on the rope, Chao lifted his trap off the ground. It looked like a dip net that fishermen use to catch fish, minus the holes. Only fishermen use their net to catch fish by lifting it up. Chao was going to use his trap to catch birds by letting it drop. When Chao released the rope, the trap fell to the ground. Now, 2 big questions arose: could he lure birds under the trap, and would the trap fall fast enough to catch them?

Early that evening, with Lena on her lead, Chao went to the edge of a stand of small trees looking for a place to set up his trap. He had seen birds in this area each evening. They were hunting for bugs. With the trap hung from the bottom branch of a small tree and with Chao holding the end of the rope that held his trap in place, Chao and Lena moved behind a rock to hide. The rock was right next to the tree holding his trap, and it was a little less than waist high. When Chao sat up, he could see the ground beneath the trap with just his eyes showing above the rock.

And they waited. As in previous evenings, the birds started landing to begin their search for bugs. And the birds were everywhere, except under the trap. But Chao was patient. Eventually, in search of virgin bug territory, some of the birds began to move closer to the trap. Eating bugs as they walked, 2 birds finally walked under the trap. But Chao still waited. When 8 birds were under the trap, Chao released the rope and let it drop.

Chao ran to the trap and fell to his hands and knees. Using the palms of his hands, he slapped down at any part of the tarp that showed movement. When all movement ceased, Chao returned to the rock and released Lena. If any of the birds tried to get away, Chao would use it as a training session. Chao reached under the tarp and pulled out the first bird he could find. It was dead. Chao let Lena sniff it and then put it into his bag. Chao repeated that 3 more times. With 4 birds now in his bag, Chao completely lifted the tarp. Two of the birds had been sitting still, but when the tarp was lifted, one flew away, and the other one tried to run away.

"FETCH," Chao said, and Lena caught it before it could scamper away.

Lena brought back the bird and sat at Chao's side, waiting for him to take it from her mouth, just as they had practiced with the stick.

February 5, 1942

After a big breakfast, Chao and Lena still had a lot of food left over. Then it was time to play. In just a few days, a strong bond had formed between Chao and Lena. Lena was a young dog, and Chao could tell that Lena had never before been provided with so much food. Chao wondered if it was him, or the food that he provided for her, that had created such a close relationship between them in such a short time. As Chao began to better understand the human-dog relation, he would soon realize that it was him.

After playtime, Chao took time to review and practice all the new commands that Lena had learned. This eventually became a daily routine. With the amount of food that they had accumulated, and confident that they could catch more when necessary, they started on their morning snake hunt with it as a secondary objective. If they could find a snake or two, they would take advantage of the opportunity, but their primary goal for today was to create a water storage system. Chao intended to create his envisioned water storage system under the rock roof of his camp; but first, he needed to find the material he needed.

He was looking for a large log that was not too heavy to carry or drag back to camp. He planned to hollow out the log and use his rain slicker to line the hole he created, forming a primitive barrel. It would take some work, but Chao felt that it was a much better idea than using his rain slicker to line a hole in the sand. A log that was beginning to rot would be best because it would be easier to remove its center. It would also be easier to cut to a length that he could carry back to camp.

So far, in his explorations around the camp, Chao hadn't seen any trees or logs that were large enough in diameter for his purpose. He would have to explore areas farther from the camp. Chao had a medium-sized snake in his bag. That would provide lunch if his search took that long.

Chao started up the hill that formed the left side of the notch that sheltered their campsite. It was the smallest of the 2 hills, but high enough to give Chao a good view of the surrounding area. Even though the hill wasn't very steep, Chao decided it would be a lot easier to angle his way up instead of trying to walk straight up to the top. A 10-minute hike brought him to the top of the hill. Looking back, Chao could see the railroad tracks. In the other direction, as far as Chao could see, there was nothing but more brush covered hills. There was no cultivated land in sight.

At the base of the far side of the hill, Chao saw some larger trees. They didn't appear to be as large in diameter as he hoped, but things always look smaller at a distance. And they weren't very far from camp. That was good. Besides, he could always hollow out a longer section of a log that was less than the desired diameter, making a barrel that was smaller in diameter, but taller. With that problem solved, Chao started down the hill.

The fallen trees were all about the same diameter, so Chao decided to look for one that was rotten enough to hollow out easily, but not so rotten that it wouldn't retain its outer integrity. He found the one he wanted and started to work. He used his machete to chop off the rotten end of the log until he reached a point where it was still rotten on the inside but hard on the outside.

Then Chao laid his rain slicker next to the log, with the center of the rain slicker, at the end of the log. This allowed him to estimate how long to cut the log so that the middle of the rain slicker would reach the bottom of his soon to be barrel, and still leave the hood to form a top.

Chao marked the log at the spot where the rain slicker ended and then added 4 more inches to form a sturdy bottom. In order to cut the log, Chao would have to cut it at an angle. That would form a notch. Chao had to carefully estimate how wide of a notch would be needed to sever the log. He then made his cut far enough down the log, so that, the ever-widening notch would not cut into the part of the log that would eventually become the bottom of the barrel.

The log was about 18 inches in diameter. Before he began cutting, Chao lifted the end of his chosen log and placed another branch that was about 4 inches in diameter, beneath it. This lifted the piece he intended to take back to camp off the ground. And Chao began his attack on the log with his machete. The section of log that Chao was cutting was not as rotten as the end. But, because it was starting to soften just a little, it didn't take long for the notch to reach the middle of the log. Chao didn't intend to cut all the way through the log; only far enough, so that, when he jumped on the end, it would break. When the notch was about 6 inches past the center of the log, Chao put down his machete and jumped on the end of the log to see if it would break. It did.

Chao lifted the end of the log to see if he could carry it back to camp or if he should hollow it out here. It was only mid-morning, so Chao decided to do both. He would trim the broken end and start to hollow out the other end until noon, and then eat lunch. After lunch, he would carry his half-made barrel back to camp and finish it there. But first, he played with Lena for a few minutes.

That afternoon it rained again, and Chao was able to top off his water supply. With his barrel only partially completed, Chao hoped that these afternoon rain showers were part of a pattern that would continue. Even though Chao took periodic breaks to play with Lena, by dusk, he had hollowed out over 3/4 of the barrel.

February 6, 1942

After breakfast, and after playtime and training with Lena, Chao started working on his barrel. Because of the softness of the wood, progress was more rapid than expected. In less than 2 hours, Chao reached the desired depth for his barrel. He then began smoothing the inside of his new barrel.

With his rain slicker unzipped, it completely lined the now smooth interior of the barrel. The hood fit perfectly over the barrel, as planned. Finally, Chao dug a hole in the loose sediments under his camp roof. He made the hole deep enough, so that when he placed the barrel in the hole, only 6 inches of the barrel extended above the ground. He packed sediments around the barrel, filling the remaining part of the hole, and his new water storage system was complete.

It rained again that afternoon. As Chao held his rain slicker in the rain to rinse it off before placing it in the barrel, he had a new thought. His barrel will be watertight without using his rain slicker as a liner. Instead, Chao replaced his rainslicker in the hole that he had previously created to test it. Now, in addition to his new rain barrel, he had just created a new drinking hole for Lena. That doubled his water storage system. Chao had just learned another valuable life lesson; even good ideas can sometimes be improved. In a safe place, with a full rain barrel and a drinking hole for Lena, and with full stomachs of their own, Chao and Lena drifted off to sleep.

Georgia, February 14, 1942

Isiac's company began training in hand to hand combat. At first, it looked like it was going to be a session of how quickly the sergeant could put each man down. Most men went down almost immediately. During the training, Captain Russel came in.

"Take 5 men," he said, and called the sergeant over. "Any potential trainers in this group, Sergeant Hanley?"

"Yes sir," Sergeant Hanley answered. "I wouldn't hesitate to have Kalway and Heimlich help me with rifle training. Word has it that they both have been shooting since they were kids."

"They still are practically kids," the Captain thought, then he said,

"Good. I wanted to make sure that we had some actual candidates before I ran it by the colonel. If the colonel OK's the plan, you can give the other drill sergeants a 'heads up' and have them start watching for other potential candidates. Any thoughts, Sergeant?"

"Just one, sir, and it is also a deviation from standard procedure," Sergeant Hanley answered.

"Let's hear it, Sergeant," the captain said.

Sergeant Hanley then explained his concern and offered a solution,

"After 10 weeks of basic training, the men learn how to take orders, but not how to give them. A promotion might give them the confidence and the authority they would need to deal with the new recruits."

"Duly noted, Sergeant. I'll pass that on to the colonel for consideration. Continue with your training, Sergeant. I think I'll stay and watch for a while."

"Yes sir," Sergeant Hanley said, then to his men he said, "Break's over. Williams, you're next."

And down went Williams.

"Heimlich, you're next," the sergeant said.

As Fritz approached the mat, he was thinking,

"The sergeant is calling the men in order and with the battle buddies back to back. That means that Isiac is next."

Then Fritz focused on a more immediate concern,

"I should try to stay away from the sergeant as long as possible, or maybe not."

When Fritz stepped onto the mat, he did something none of the other men had done. He charged the sergeant. With his momentum, just before reaching the sergeant, Fritz was able to slide under the sergeant's grasp, and with a leg sweep that Isiac had taught him, bring the sergeant to the mat. The sergeant was up quickly, but he was obviously stunned; and he couldn't decide if he was angry or pleased. The teacher in him made his decision, and he chose pleased.

"Nice move Heimlich," the sergeant said, and then he went back to work.

"I think now is the time to keep my distance from the sergeant," Fritz thought, and that's what he did for over a minute. Twice, the sergeant got his hands on Fritz, but Fritz was able to break free. But not the third time, and down he went.

As the sergeant reached down to help Fritz up, he said, so all could hear,

"It looks like Heimlich is the toughest one in this group. I can train this boy. I don't know about the rest of you bums."

"My fame will be short-lived, Sergeant," Fritz said softly, as he moved off the mat.

"Quit your mumbling, Heimlich, and go sit down," Sergeant Hanley said, ignoring Fritz's remark. Then the Sergeant said, "Kalway, you're next."

"Yes, Sergeant," Isiac said.

As Isiac stepped onto the mat, Sergeant Hanley said,

"Let's see if you are as tough as your buddy."

The Sergeant moved toward Isiac. And then it was over. The Sergeant was on his back and in an arm-bar.

"What the Hell," Sergeant Hanley said, as he tapped out.

"Take 5 men," Captain Russel said as he again conferred with Sergeant Hanley, "What was that, Sergeant? A fluke?"

"Sir, I've never experienced anything like that before, but I can tell you it was no fluke. That boy knew exactly what he was doing."

"Keep an eye on both Kalway and Heimlich," Captain Russel said. "It looks like we may have lost a rifle instructor and gained a 'hand-to-hand' instructor. Keep me posted."

February 22, 1942

The U.S. War Department approves road construction in Burma.

March 1942

Britain wanted to concentrate the war efforts in Burma to protect India. America, believing that a million-man Chinese army would hold the Japanese army in China, sent money to Chiang Kai-Shek. The Chinese army was poorly equipped. Chiang Kai-Shek knew his army could never defeat the Japanese in China, but he took the money anyway. Instead of training and arming his troops, he used the money to feed his troops and kept most of them in reserve. When Chiang Kai-Shek finally did send 2 of his armies to Burma to fight with Stillwell, they were destroyed by the Japanese. Stillwell barely escaped, by foot, to India.

March 4, 1942

The U.S. Army Services of Supply is established and sends engineers, equipment, and support personnel to India to work on road construction in Burma.

Burma, March 8, 1942

The Burmese Army is defeated, and the Japanese capture Rangoon. The Burmese government is in disarray, and some of the Burmese Army defects to the Japanese.

India, March 9, 1942

Chao and Lena returned to the railroad tracks. After Chao had assembled his cart, they continued their journey to Goalundo. His time spent at the camp with Lena helped Chao adjust to the loss of his parents. He was no longer alone now that he had Lena. His time spent at the camp also gave Chao confidence that he and Lena could survive on their own, if necessary. And Chao felt that he had an insurance policy, of sorts. He and Lena could always return to the camp if the need arose.

Chao and Lena had lived at the camp for over a month, and life had been good. They had plenty of food and water, and the decision to leave had not been an easy one. But Chao knew that it was time.

While at the camp, Chao had devised a way to increase his food supply without spoilage. He kept it alive. The movement in the 2 food bags, attached to his cart, attested to that. One bag contained birds that he had trapped but not killed. The other contained live snakes that Chao learned to catch with a forked stick instead of chopping their heads off with his machete. Experience showed that the snakes could stay alive for quite some time while in the bag. Not so for the birds. Because the birds seldom lasted for more than a day or two, Chao planned to eat them first.

Before nightfall, Chao reached a settlement that had developed where a bend in the Ganges River was near the tracks. There, Chao was able to purchase rice, bread, salt, and a few cans of fruit. There were over two dozen people who had set up camp next to the tracks, just outside of the settlement. Some were obviously other travelers, but some looked like they had been there for a while and were attempting to make the camp a permanent home.

Before the camp quieted down for the night, Chao started talking to two boys not much older than him. They were traveling together and were headed to Goalundo in search of work on the docks or the barges. When Chao told the boys that he was also following the tracks to Goalundo, the 3 of them agreed to travel together. The boys then told Chao that they knew of a short cut that would make the trip at least 100 miles shorter.

March 11, 1942

Chao and Lena, with their new travel companions, find the trail that leads to Goalundo and leave the tracks.

The trail they were following was a good one, more like a road in most places. Small farms were located along both sides of the road. The farmers used the road to carry their produce to Goalundo in one direction or back to the railroad tracks in the other direction. The boys, who had stopped alongside the road to rest, could see five people working in the field next to the road: a man, a woman, an older man, a young boy, and a young girl. By all appearances, it was the farmer and his family who lived in the nearby house.

Chao had just killed and cleaned his last two snakes. Meanwhile, the other two boys had made a fire. Chao shared his snake meat with Lena and the other two boys, and the boys added rice to the meal. After lunch, as Chao was putting out the fire, he watched as one of the farm workers, the man, began to approach. As the farmer got closer, he waved and asked, "Do you boys want a job planting corn?"

"We'll plant corn if you pay us 3 rupees a day," one of the boys said.

"Too much," the farmer replied.

The two boys then stood up to continue their journey to Goalundo, but Chao lingered behind. The boys looked back to see if Chao was coming, but Chao signaled them to go ahead without him. Seeing that, the farmer took an interest in Chao.

"How long will planting last," Chao asked? And negotiations began.

"About three weeks if you help," the farmer answered, "But I can't pay much."

"If you provide food and a place to stay for my dog and me and give me 10 pounds of rice when I leave, I'll work for you for free until the planting is done," Chao said.

When the farmer responded with, "I won't feed a dog," Chao shook his head and lifted the handle of his cart. Seeing that Chao was about to leave, the farmer countered with,

"I'll feed your dog, but only 5 pounds of rice."

"10 pounds of corn," Chao said.

The farmer shook his head, "5 pounds of corn, I'll need the corn for planting."

If this was true, Chao knew that the farmer would have countered with rice, so Chao countered with 8 pounds of corn, and the farmer agreed. Chao had just arranged for food and shelter for Lena and himself for three weeks. It would have been a good deal even without the corn, Chao thought, and he started work immediately.

March 20, 1942

Chao and Lena got along well with the family, and the two children loved Lena. After dinner, Chao asked Sanjay Darsha, the farmer, if he would help him teach Lena the commands, WATCH, ATTACK, and GUARD. Sanjay didn't like that idea at all, so Chao decided that a demonstration was in order. He called Lena over, grabbed her neck, and shook her, signaling that play time was beginning. Chao then held out his arm and growled. Growling in response, Lena grabbed his arm, and the mock battle began. The family was startled.

After a few minutes, Chao said, "ENOUGH," and Lena released his arm. "SIT," Chao said, and Lena sat beside him. Chao scratched Lena behind her ear for a moment before he showed Sanjay his arm. There wasn't a mark on it.

"That's how we play," Chao said. "We were just pretending."

Leah, the farmer's daughter, started giggling, and then the whole family was laughing. Pretty soon Leah asked if she could try. Chao saw the doubt in Sanjay's face and said,

"Maybe we should let your father try first."

Leah wasn't happy with that, but her father seemed more receptive to the idea. Besides, it would be hard for him to refuse now that his daughter had already volunteered. Chao continued,

"Lena won't hurt you because she knows that we are friends. And she knows that you are only playing. The harder you shake your arm, the harder she will pull. If you shake your arm too hard, she might bruise you with her teeth. To be safe, we can tie a towel around your arm. Not only will it protect your arm, but it will give Lena something to grab onto. That way, if you want to shake your arm harder, she'll only have the towel in her mouth."

Turning to Suhani, the farmer's wife, Chao said,

"It might tear your towel."

Chao could tell that Suhani didn't care if the towel ripped. Instead, her expression indicated that she was looking forward to the coming show.

Although Sanjay was still a little hesitant at first, when he realized that it was the towel that Lena had in her mouth, he started to enjoy the game. He began to shake the towel harder and harder, then he said,

"Don't worry, Lena might bruise me with her teeth, but she won't bite me."

Sanjay had the whole room laughing now. He was getting into the mock battle when it suddenly ended. Lena had ripped the towel off Sanjay's arm. With everyone still laughing, Sanjay proudly showed off his uninjured arm. Then everyone wanted to play. And they learned that Lena only pulled as hard as her playmate. The kids couldn't pull as hard, so Lena didn't either.

After everyone had a chance to play 'mock battle' with Lena, and while everyone was in a good mood, Chao decided this would be a good time to start with the ATTACK command. Chao needed other people to teach Lena this command effectively. Chao spread the family around the room, each one with a towel around their arm.

"I hope Suhani doesn't run out of towels," Chao thought.

Lena, with the leash around her neck, stood at Chao's side. Chao, facing Sanjay and growling, said, "ATTACK" as he charged Sanjay using Lena's leash to bring her with him. When they reached Sanjay, as instructed, he extended his toweled arm. Lena took it, and the 'mock battle' began. After about 10 seconds of 'mock battle,' Chao shouted, "ENOUGH," pulled Lena away, and returned to his original position. Before Chao had repeated this procedure with each family member, Lena was releasing the arm when Chao gave the ENOUGH command without a tug on the leash.

Now Chao removed Lena's leash and gave the ATTACK command; but this time he only charged halfway, leaving Lena to complete the charge on her own. And she did. Back in their original position, Chao yelled "ENOUGH," and Lena returned to sit at his side. Although Chao knew that Lena understood the ATTACK and ENOUGH commands, each family member had to have their turn; and Chao knew that repetition would help to solidify the commands in Lena's memory. But Chao no longer pretended to be charging with Lena.

Chao knew that the children's bedtime was approaching, so he asked Sanjay if they could play one more game with Lena. Everyone was having so much fun. Sanjay readily agreed.

"This game is called WATCH," Chao said; then he gave Leah a towel. "Wave it at Lena and move around the room, sometimes fast and sometimes slow." Chao had Lena on a very short lead and said, "WATCH."

As Leah moved, Chao turned his body so that he was always facing Leah, and Lena's short lead forced her to do the same. And the waving towel helped to keep Lena's attention.

Leah's brother, Avi, was the next family member to help teach Lena the WATCH command. By the time the rest of the family members took their turn, Lena no longer needed her lead.

Next, Chao gave the towel to Leah again, and said,

"STAY," as he moved away from Lena.

"WATCH," Chao said, and Lena watched, following Leah's movements where ever she went.

Sanjay's family was still having fun, but when Chao told them that it was Lena's bedtime, they knew what he really meant.

"Can we play again tomorrow," Avi asked?

"I have one more game left," Chao said, "It's called WATCH/ATTACK. Try to figure out how it works, and we can play it tomorrow."

Even though Chao was pleased with Lena's ability to learn everything so quickly, something about the day was bothering him. It took him a while to figure it out, but he finally realized that his contact with the children had caused him to miss his sister.

March 21, 1942

When the children saw Chao watching them play ATTACK with Lena, they ended the game and ran to him.

"We know how WATCH/ATTACK works. Can we play it now," Leah asked?

"After dinner," Chao answered, "And if you both go help your mother with dinner, maybe I'll be able to think of another game, too."

And off they both ran into the kitchen.

While waiting for dinner, Chao Lin, Sanjay and his father, Ajeet, sat on the porch listening to the sounds in the kitchen.

"How did you get the children to help their mother in the kitchen," Sanjay asked?

"I told them that I might be able to think of a new game for Lena," Chao answered.

"By the sounds coming from the kitchen, I'm not sure if the children are helping or just getting in the way," Ajeet said, and everyone laughed.

"You are a good worker, Chao Lin," Sanjay said, "And the children like you and Lena. But you seemed moody today. Is something bothering you, Chao Lin?"

"Yes," said Chao Lin. "Being with your family has helped me to deal with the loss of my family. But hearing your children laugh reminds me of my sister."

"What happened to your sister," Ajeet asked?

"When my parents were killed by the Japanese, my sister disappeared with my cousin," Chao answered.

"Dinner is ready," coming from the kitchen, ended the conversation on the porch.

Seeing the children's excitement during dinner couldn't help but perk Chao up, but it got the children in trouble with their mother.

"People in India are starving, and you are not eating your dinner," Suhani said.

That settled the children down, and they returned their attention to their meal. Knowing the truth in her words, the men became pensive as well. Not much more was said during dinner. When dinner was over, and Chao said,

"Let's play games," the mood brightened immediately. "Who knows how to teach Lena WATCH/ATTACK?"

"I do, I do," Leah said.

"Tell us," Chao said.

"When Lena is WATCHING, tell her to ATTACK," Leah explained.

"You're right," Chao said. "Leah, will you and your brother help me?"

"Yes," both children shouted, as they jumped out of their seats.

Chao gave Leah and Avi a towel, helped them wrap it around their arms, and then separated them. Indicating, Leah, Chao gave Lena the WATCH command. Like a professional dog trainer, Leah moved around the room with Lena watching her. When Chao gave the ATTACK command, Leah was ready. She took a step toward Lena, and with her arm held out as a target, Leah growled. Lena knew what that meant. She had Leah's arm in her mouth and was playing 'mock battle' in the blink of an eye. Chao was smiling when he gave Lena the ENOUGH command. "I didn't tell her to growl," Chao thought, then he said,

"Nicely done, Leah. Avi, now it's your turn. And don't forget to take a step toward Lena and growl." As he said that, he saw Leah smile. And Chao knew that Leah knew that he had noticed and approved of the additions she had made to her training instructions.

Avi's turn produced the same results. Chao gave the WATCH/ATTACK commands twice more, and both times Lena executed them perfectly. Then, with Lena watching Suhani, instead of giving the ATTACK command, Chao gave the HEEL command, and Lena moved right to Chao's side and sat down, no longer watching Suhani. Now, after Chao gave the WATCH command, he would sometimes follow it with the ATTACK command and sometimes not. Chao wanted Lena to understand that she must be prepared for the ATTACK command when the WATCH command was given, but also to understand that the WATCH command would not always be followed by ATTACK.

Then Chao asked if anyone wanted to play one more new game before bedtime. It was a silly question. "Yeses," came from the entire family.

"The new game is called GUARD," Chao said. "Lena and I will stand in the middle of the room. One of you will walk slowly toward us; and when you reach the edge of the table, you will raise your arms like a bear, growl, and take one quick step toward us. When we growl back, lower your arms and move back quickly."

Chao gave the GUARD command, and the game began. "This is a good family of bears," Chao thought to himself. After the 4th approach, Chao stopped growling, and Lena took care of that duty on her own.

"Now approach as regular people," Chao said. "And no growling."

"Shouldn't we growl as real people a few times, first," Leah asked?

"I think you're right, Leah. We'll have the first three people be growly people. Then everyone can be regular people."

Chao growled at the growly people with Lena, and then he growled with her at the first three regular people. After that, Lena again took over the growling duty on her own.

Chao then placed the burlap bag that contained his gear, next to Lena. He gave her the STAY command, then the GUARD command, and moved away. He had Suhani approach as a regular person, but Lena didn't growl. When Suhani backed away, Chao asked, "Where is Leah the bear?"

Leah looked at Chao with an expression that seemed to say, "I could have told you that," then she approached Lena as Leah, the bear. And Lena growled. After several more growling bears, Chao tried growing people and then regular people. Lena growled at them all. The lesson was over.

March 25, 1942

Every night after dinner, but before bedtime, the children played WATCH, ATTACK, GUARD games with Lena. On March 25, 1942, sometime before midnight, the silence of the house was broken by Lena's growls. Everyone in the house was awake instantly. All Chao could see in the darkness was the shape of 3 intruders, and one was struggling with Lena. Just as Chao jumped to his feet, he was knocked back down. As soon as he hit the floor, he pulled his derringer from its holster, and, as the intruder grabbed him by the neck, Chao shot him in the chest. Chao could hear cries coming from the man who was struggling with Lena, along with sounds of a struggle from the other side of the house, as well. Then Chao heard a loud metallic sound, almost like another gunshot, more growls mixed with sounds of pain, then silence. With shaking hands, the farmer was finally able to light a lantern.

In the lantern light, the three intruders could be seen lying on the floor, two dead and one dying. The man Chao had shot was dead. The man Lena attacked was also dead. His knife was on the floor where he dropped it when Lena grabbed his arm. The farmer's wife was standing over the dead man holding the iron skillet she had used to hit him in the head. When he fell, Lena had released his arm and grabbed him by the neck. And that, Chao knew, was a result of instinct, not training. The third man was making gurgling sounds as bubbles of blood were flowing from his mouth. While Sanjay was struggling with the third intruder, his father, who had been a Gurkha in a unit of the British Army, pushed a kukri through his ribs and into his lungs. Although Ajeet was now too old to be a soldier, his Gurkha training was not forgotten. In a few seconds the third intruder, choking on his own blood, fell silent.

Suhani sat on the floor with one of her children under each arm. Chao sat on the floor with his arm around Lena, checking to make sure she was unharmed. It was Ajeet who broke the trance when he nudged his son, and the two of them began to drag the dead men, one at a time, out of the house. No one spoke. Everyone seemed to be processing what had just happened. Suhani was the first one to break the spell of silence as she spoke to her children, "Go thank Lena for saving our lives."

Then Lena had three pairs of arms around her. Suhani started to clean up the blood in the house. As Sanjay got up to help his wife, he spoke so that everyone could hear,

"Those were the same men that have robbed other farms in the area. And they are the ones who killed our neighbor's son."

Then, because it was clear that no one would be going back to sleep any time soon, Sanjay said,

"No work tomorrow."

Michigan, March 27, 1942

Isiac becomes the father of a healthy baby boy. Jayme is born.

Georgia, March 28, 1942

Basic training is completed.

March 29, 1942

Sergeant Hanley stuck his head into the barracks and yelled,

"Heimlich, Kalway, in the captain's office, now!"

Isiac and Fritz entered the captain's office and saluted the lieutenant on duty, Lieutenant Willis.

"The Captain sent for us, sir," Isiac said.

"Go right in," Lieutenant Willis said, "Captain Russel is expecting you."

"This way soldiers," Captain Russel called out through the doorway, "Come right in and have a seat."

"Yes sir," Isiac and Fritz both said as they entered the office, saluted, and sat down, as ordered.

"I have you both scheduled for two months of MP training at Fort Leonard Wood in Missouri," Captain Russel began. "Colonel Rodgers' engineers will also be training there. After training, you'll be assigned to Colonel Rodgers and perform Military Police duties for the Colonel and his engineers. I've scheduled your training to begin on April 29. Until that time, you will be helping Sergeant Hanley train the next group of new recruits. Any questions?"

"No sir," Isiac and Fritz responded.

"Kalway," the captain said, "I've been informed that you are a new father."

"Yes sir," Isiac said.

"First child?"

"Yes, sir."

"Boy or girl?"

"A boy, sir. His name is Jayme. I named him after my younger brother, Jay."

"Congratulations, Kalway," Captain Russel said. "I've been told that you two have been doing things together since you were kids." Turning toward Fritz, Captain Russel continued, "Now you can add having babies to the list. Congratulations, Heimlich, I was informed less than an hour ago, that your wife just gave birth to a healthy baby boy. I also understand that you have decided to call him, Allen."

"Yes sir," Fritz replied.

Captain Russel pulled three cigars out of his desk, "Cuban," he said and handed one to each man. Isiac and Fritz were all smiles. The Captain was also enjoying this, but he wasn't done yet. There was more news to come.

"I hear you both grew up in Michigan." Captain Russel said. "Tell me a little bit about your families."

They smoked and talked for a few minutes. But Captain Russel didn't want to delay the rest of the news.

"When you leave, you can take the cigars with you, but keep them in your pocket until you reach the barracks." The Captain was silent for a moment, and he had an ever so slight smile on his face when he began to deliver the rest of his news.

"On the way out, you can pick up your new uniforms from Lieutenant Willis. Your corporal stripes have already been sewn on. Lieutenant Willis will also explain the travel arrangements he made for you. You are both on Leave as of now. Go and see your wives and new babies. Be back in 5 days. Don't be late. Dismissed."

Michigan, March 30, 1942

Nedra's father, Frank, brought his daughter and new grandson home from the hospital. It was late morning. Frank scheduled a 'meet the baby' get together for 5 PM that same day. In the meantime, Frank made sure only the immediate family was there. He wanted Nedra to have plenty of time to rest. Nedra's mother, Agnes, was in the living room with Hannah, Lauretta, and Jay. After 30 minutes of visiting, Frank led Nedra and Jayme to a back bedroom where she could feed the baby and rest or nap if she wanted. Frank then returned to the front room and visited with the rest of the family.

Jay was quiet but fidgety. That's because he knew something that none of the others knew or suspected. Yesterday, Jay had received a call from his brother. Bud was coming home on Leave. A knock on the door interrupted the conversation.

"I'll get that," Frank said, annoyed.

"Someone is in big trouble," Agnes said, softly.

"Frank told everyone, and he made it very clear: no one arrives before 5 PM, and no one stays later than 7 PM."

When Frank opened the door, his frown turned into a smile.

"It's Bud," he shouted.

Pandemonium broke out. Everyone was talking at once. If Nedra was sleeping before, she surely wasn't now. The first thing Bud did was bend over and give his mother a kiss. After hugs and kisses all around, Frank said,

"That's enough. This way Bud," and he took Bud to meet his wife and new baby.

At the same time, a similar greeting was taking place at Wyandotte Hospital as Fritz was introduced to his new baby, Allen.

March 31, 1942

Isiac woke up in his own bed. He could smell bacon cooking. His mother was making breakfast. He greeted his mother with a kiss and then sat down at the kitchen table. It wasn't long before the smell of bacon also had his brother and sister out of bed. In Hanna's small kitchen, there was only room for three chairs at the table. Hannah always seated her children first. She always waited until one of them finished eating and left the table before she would sit down to eat.

When Jay had finished, and his mother sat down, Bud said,

"Hey Jay, let's go say hello to Mr. Konno before we go see Nedra and Jayme."

Sudden silence.

"Bud," Jay said, "They took Mr. Konno away and put him in a camp."

"Who took him away," Bud asked, his agitation showing.

"The government," Jay answered.

"Why," Bud asked, "Mr. Konno is a citizen of the United States, just like us. He was born in California."

"Because of the war with Japan," Jay said.

"Mom was born in Germany. We're at war with Germany, and they didn't take her away," Isiac countered.

"Because he looks different," Lauretta said.

Isiac, always calm, was not familiar with the emotion of anger, but he knew that he needed an outlet.

"I'm going to walk over and see Nedra and Jayme. Come over whenever you are ready."

For Isiac, the 2-block walk had changed his focus from Mr. Konno to Peg. He had taken this walk with her so many times. And when he arrived at Frank's house, with Nedra and Jayme awake, his focus changed again. Hannah, Lauretta, and Jay arrived only a few minutes later, but, by then, Jayme had already finished his breakfast and was asleep in Nedra's arms. Being with his family helped Bud deal with all the changes that had taken place in his life in such a short time.

Two hours later, loud cries came from the back of the house.

"Jayme doesn't waste any time letting everyone know when he's awake," Bud said. Then he asked Nedra, "Are you ready to go out with the baby yet? We could go to Stoney Point and introduce Jayme to his Great Grandmother and Great Grandfather Yeager."

Nedra shook her head, no, "But you should go," she said

"I don't know," Isiac said, reluctant to leave his wife and baby.

"The baby and I will be here when you get back," Nedra said, trying to make the decision easier for Bud.

"Why don't we all go," Lauretta said.

"Jay," Bud said, making his decision, "Run over to Pam's and see if Fritz is there. Ask him if he wants to go to Stoney Point to see his Mom and Dad."

Ten minutes later, Fritz walks in with Jay and says,

"Let's go; I'll drive."

And just that quickly, they were on their way to Stoney Point, with Fritz driving, Isiac in the passenger seat, and Hannah in back with Jay and Lauretta. One big family. As they approached the Estral Beach turn-off, Fritz slowed down.

"What are you doing," Bud asked, "We're going to Stoney Point, not Estral Beach."

"I know it's crowded in here, but we're going to pick up one more passenger," Fritz answered.

When they got to the 'Hotel,' they all piled out of the car, but Hanna used her arms to hold Jay and Lauretta back, motioning for Bud and Fritz to go in first. Fritz opened the door and went in first. The bar had about 20 people in it, and with a quick glance, Fritz could recognize over half of them. Bud, following Fritz into the bar, immediately knew that something wasn't right. It was too quiet for the number of people in the bar. Then Leo Chavare, sitting at the bar, yelled,

"Hey Deke, your two boys are back from the Army."

Fritz had called ahead, and that was the signal. The kitchen door opened, and, like a shot, Peg was all over Bud. Then they were both on the floor. Suddenly, the bar wasn't so silent. Cheers erupted. Hearing the cheering from outside, Hannah, Lauretta, and Jay came in and joined the party. When Deke handed each of 'his boys' a beer, Fritz said,

"I think Stoney Point can wait for a while."

Fritz spoke loud enough, but Bud didn't hear him. His concentration was totally on his dog. Then, to everyone's surprise, Hannah, who didn't drink, said,

"Deke, I'll have a glass of wine, please."

Bud didn't hear that either.

Three hours later, our happy group continued on their journey to Stoney Point. Everyone was in the same position, except Peg. She was on the floor in the front seat sitting between Bud's legs.

It was well after dark by the time they got back to Lincoln Park. Everyone was ready for bed except for Bud and Peg. They went for a walk around the neighborhood like they had so many times before.

April 1, 1942

With Agnes watching the baby, Bud and Nedra went out for a hamburger and a root beer. Peg refused to be left behind, and she was in the back seat. Everything was as it should be.

Later that afternoon, everything changed. Their Leave was over. They were heading to the train station preparing to return to their base in Georgia. Jay was driving Bud's Plymouth with his brother in the back seat. Bud had Nedra on one side and Peg on the other. Pam and Fritz were in the back seat of Fritz's Ford, with Pam's father driving.

At the train station, it was a difficult parting. Everyone had teary eyes. Like everyone else, Peg knew something bad was happening, and when Bud got out and left her in the car, she howled. Turning to Nedra, Jay said, "Peg never howls." Then, neither one of them could speak.

Georgia, April 2, 1942

Bud and Fritz returned to their base in Georgia just before midnight, both with mixed feelings.

India, April 4, 1942

No work today. The planting was completed. Chao and Sanjay sat outside on the ground, leaning against the house; and with pride, Sanjay gazed at his recently planted fields. Speaking to Chao, he said,

"Thank you for everything." Chao nodded, and Sanjay continued. "And thank you for being a better trader than me."

"My father was a trader," Chao said, not understanding what Sanjay meant until Sanjay continued, "You convinced me to feed your dog, and she saved our lives. Maybe I should get a dog."

"You saw how I trained Lena, and Leah would make a good trainer," Chao replied.

"But I'd never find a dog as good as Lena," Sanjay said.

Chao agreed but didn't respond. With no work, today, the children were outside playing with Lena. Avi came around the corner of the house to where Chao and his father were sitting and spoke, "Father, the fish peddler is coming."

They all moved to the front of the house. As they watched the fish peddler approach, Sanjay informed his family that Chao was leaving in the morning. Their disappointment was expressed by their groans. Then, so that the fish peddler didn't have to pull his cart all the way to the house, Sanjay and Chao met him on the road.

"Buy or trade," the fish peddler asked?

"Trade," Sanjay answered.

Always alert for the possibility of learning new trading tactics, Chao listened carefully as the two men bargained. When the bargaining was complete, Sanjay and Avi began carrying the agreed upon amount of fish to the house. Speaking to them as they moved away, the fish peddler said, "I'll be back tomorrow morning to start my return trip."

Over his shoulder, Sanjay said, "Your vegetables will be ready." Then Sanjay stopped and turned back to the fish peddler. "Our friend Chao is leaving tomorrow morning. He and his dog would be good travel companions."

"Travel companions are always welcome," the fish peddler said.

Chao nodded in agreement. Now, more than ever, he knew the truth of those words.

April 5, 1942

The fish peddler arrived early. "My name is Meeta Sandar," he said, introducing himself to Chao.

"My name is Chao Lin," Chao responded.

With the introductions completed, Chao, Sanjay, and his children helped Meeta Sandar load the vegetables into his cart: squash, turnips, parsnips, and beets. Squash lasted longer without refrigeration than other vegetables, and so did root crops. And refrigeration was a rare thing in India, especially in rural areas. At this time of year, these vegetables were all that was left from last fall's harvest.

After the cart was loaded and farewells were completed, Sanjay handed Chao his 8-pound bag of corn.

"If you help me pull my cart, you can throw all your things in, as well," Meeta Sandar said.

That's exactly what Chao did. What Chao didn't know is that Sanjay had already asked Meeta if Chao could load his things into his cart because Sanjay knew that Chao's new load would be too heavy for him to carry. With the cart now loaded, and with Chao and Meeta ready to leave, Sanjay said,

"Wait a minute." Then he went back into the house. When Sanjay came out of the house, he was struggling to carry a bag of beets in one hand and a bag of parsnips in the other.

"For my friend, Chao," he said, as he put the two large bags into the cart.

Leah, waving as the cart pulled away, turned to her mother and asked, "When I grow up, can I marry a China boy with a dog?"

April 6, 1942

Meeta noticed that even though it was heavily loaded, pulling the cart was much easier with Chao's help. But lightly loaded travelers were still able to move more quickly and often passed them by. Chao was aware that four men, walking behind them, were matching their pace. When the last travelers that had passed Chao and Meeta disappeared, the four men increased their pace. Their intent was obvious. They intended to reach the fish peddler's cart when no other travelers were around.

Chao spoke to Meeta, "We are going to have company, soon."

Without turning around, Meeta said, "I noticed them. I'll be ready."

"Wait until I get my walking stick free before you pull out your machete," Chao whispered.

Finally, in a friendly tone and with a wave, one of the men said,

"We can see that you are struggling to pull your cart. If we take a few things off the back, it will make your journey much easier."

With each of the four men now holding a knife at their sides, Chao and Meeta let the cart come to a stop. Using his body to shield his machete from the approaching men, Chao used it to cut the two pieces of twine that held his walking stick to the cart. Then, Chao and Meeta turned and faced the four men that were now only 20 feet from the cart. The would-be thieves stopped suddenly. What they thought would be easy prey had just shown its teeth, literally. Instead of two helpless fish peddlers, they faced the teeth of a growling dog, a man holding a machete, and another man holding a machete and a spear.

"Watch," Chao said, indicating the man directly in front of Lena. Then to the men, he said, "This cart isn't too heavy, but when the two of you that we don't kill are pulling it, we can just ride in the back and enjoy the rest of our journey."

Then Meeta added, "If you don't want to come back as a grasshopper in your next life, turn around and go back where you came from. If we ever see you on this road again, we won't give you that choice."

"Sanjay was right," Meeta said as they continued their journey. "You and Lena are good travel companions."

Sometimes they traveled in silence, and sometimes they talked. After explaining his business to Chao, Meeta ended his dialogue with,

"This is my longest route, but it is also the most profitable because I sell some of my fish and trade the rest for vegetables. I then sell half of the vegetables and use the rest to feed my family."

When Chao told Meeta that he was going to be a trader someday, Meeta said,

"Why not today? If you buy some wheels when we get back to town, I'll help you build a cart. You already have beets and parsnips that you can sell."

That gave Chao something to think about.

April 8, 1942

It only took Chao and Meeta one day to build his cart. They talked together while they worked, and Meeta gave Chao more details about his business. Meeta, during their conversations, mentioned that he planned to make one more trip to the farming area where he and Chao had met, but they needed to leave before the monsoons made the roads impassable. That gave Chao an idea. Chao was excited about visiting Sanjay and his family, and his idea started to turn into a plan. But he didn't have much time. He needed to start preparing for his planned surprise immediately.

With his cart completed, Chao began accompanying Meeta on his local deliveries. Chao felt that he again negotiated an excellent deal. One that was beneficial to both him and Meeta. It was similar to the one he made with Sanjay. In exchange for food and a place to stay for Lena and him, Chao would give Meeta half of the profits that he made from the merchandise that he carried in his cart. A business partnership of sorts was formed.

Burma, April 14, 1942

Before WW2, the United States was the only major power that did not have an organized intelligence agency. William Donovan was named coordinator of information for the armed forces in Burma. With a few hundred men and some local Burmese tribesmen, he formed Detachment 101. Detachment 101 operated behind enemy lines and was tasked with gathering intelligence, using guerilla tactics to harass the Japanese, identifying targets for allied bombers, and rescuing downed pilots.

Georgia, April 24, 1942

Sergeant Hanley and Corporal Heimlich were talking as the new recruits entered the rifle range.

"Corporal," the sergeant said, "The Army cannot function without discipline, rules, and procedures. As a drill sergeant, I know that more than anyone. And I also know that flexibility is sometimes called for. But it can never come from a drill sergeant."

"Yes, Sergeant Hanley," Fritz agreed.

Sergeant Hanley continued, "Lieutenant Samuels will be monitoring the rifle tests today. He decides who passes and who will have to repeat basic training. Lewis is one of the best men in this new group of recruits, but I have some concerns about his rifle scores."

"I don't think you have to worry about Lewis," Fritz said. "Lewis is an excellent shot."

"I know that Corporal, but Lewis broke his glasses yesterday," Sergeant Hanley said.

"When will he get new glasses, Sergeant," Fritz asked?

"Not soon enough," Sergeant Hanley answered. "Testing starts in a few minutes. If you think you could help Lewis, I'd like you to conduct Lewis' test today."

"I'm sure I can help, Sergeant," Fritz said. "But I think it would be best if you conducted his test. Besides, you might need to ask the Lieutenant some questions while Lewis is taking his test. Or you and the Lieutenant might just find something interesting to talk about. And Sergeant Hanley, if you don't have anything else for me to do while Lewis is taking his test, I'd like to ask your permission to get a little extra rifle practice, myself. Do you think it would bother Lewis if I practiced 3 or 4 stalls away?"

"It wouldn't bother Lewis at all, Corporal Heimlich," Sergeant Hanley answered, with a smile. "Permission granted."

20 minutes later, Sergeant Hanley walked over to Lewis and said, "You shoot after Conrad."

"But Sergeant Hanley, I can't even see the target," Lewis responded.

"Do you believe in God," Sergeant Hanley asked Lewis?

"Yes, Sergeant," Lewis answered, looking puzzled.

"I know you can't see the target, Lewis. But can you see the ridge behind it," Sergeant Hanley asked?

"Yes, Sergeant," Lewis answered.

"Good, aim for that," Sergeant Hanley said. "I don't want any stray bullets landing anywhere near your target. And remember, sometimes miracles happen, and problems end up solving themselves. One more thing, Lewis. Corporal Heimlich will be practicing nearby. And he hopes that his shooting doesn't distract you during your test."

"It won't bother me at all," Lewis said, as understanding finally dawned on him.

"Let's get started then," Sergeant Hanley said.

Fritz got some extra practice on the rifle range, and Lewis passed his rifle test.

India, April 29, 1942

It was almost dark when Meeta and Chao arrived at Sanjay's farm. Leah was outside, and when she saw that Chao was with the fish peddler, she ran to the carts. She was giving Chao a big hug when she saw another dog sitting next to Lena.

"You got another dog," Leah exclaimed. "Now Lena will have someone to play with."

"It's not my dog," Chao said, extricating himself from Leah's hug.

"Is it his dog," Leah asked, looking at Meeta?

"No," Chao said.

"Whose dog is it," Leah asked, looking puzzled?

"It's your dog," Chao said.

Leah's squeal of joy got the attention of her family, and they were all looking at her and wondering what was going on.

"Her name is Piper," Chao said. "Call her."

After a couple of minutes, Chao interrupted the barking and giggling of the two new playmates.

"Don't you think you should heel Piper over to meet your family," Chao asked?

"HEEL," Leah said, and she walked back to her family with Piper heeling on one side and Lena heeling on the other. When she stopped in front of her family, both dogs immediately sat beside her. Leah knew what to do next,

"OK," she said, releasing the dogs, and chaos resulted.

When things calmed down a little, Sanjay and Meeta began their trading. Beets and Parsnips had gotten soft, so Meeta traded his fish for squash, turnips, and corn. With trading completed, Chao and Meeta were invited to join the family for dinner and to spend the night. By watching the children playing with both dogs, it was obvious to everyone that bedtime would be delayed. And things got exciting when the children learned that they could play GUARD with both dogs. Lena and Piper would sit, one on each side of whatever was put in front of them, and growl at anyone who approached, except Chao.

The children each gave Chao a hug as they got ready for bed, and when Leah was hugging Chao, he whispered in her ear.

"You have to teach Piper not to growl at you when you are playing GUARD. Then, you must teach her never to growl at you except during play. Say NO loudly and sternly if she does. Can you do that?"

Leah was smiling when she shook her head, YES, and Chao believed her.

Burma, April 29, 1942

The Japanese capture Lashio in northern Burma. This cut off the Burma Road as a supply line from India to the troops stationed in China. Resupply now had to be by cargo planes flying 'over the hump.'

Missouri, April 29, 1942

Fritz and Isiac are finally sent to Fort Leonard Wood in Missouri for Military Police training.

Burma, May 1942

The Allies retreat from Burma. A new Burmese government and the New Burmese National Army are formed. The Japanese strictly control both.

India, May 1, 1942

Chao and Meeta were back in Goalundo before dark on May 1. As much as Chao had wanted to stay longer, Chao and Meeta needed to avoid being trapped on the road when the monsoons, which were expected to arrive within days, would make the roads impassable.

Washington D.C. June 13, 1942

On June 13, 1942, by executive order, President Roosevelt replaced the recently created "Coordinator of Information" with the "Office of Strategic Services," with William Donovan as the director. The OSS intelligence agency operated behind enemy lines. They engaged in propaganda, subversion, spying, and sabotage. The OSS also encouraged local people to engage in guerilla operations, act as guides, and conduct sabotage.

In China, the OSS trained Chiang-Kai-Shek's Kuomintang (Nationalist) Army, and Mao's (Communist) Red Army. During training of the Chinese troops, the OSS also began collecting information necessary for post-war planning. During WW2, the OSS personnel expanded to over 24,000 people.

Missouri, June 30, 1942

Isiac and Fritz complete Military Police training.

Oswego, New York, July 6, 1942

Colonel Rodgers' Engineers are sent to Oswego, New York. There, his MPs are used to guard German POWs while his engineers construct temporary housing for the prisoners.

California, July 23, 1942

Colonel Rodgers takes his Engineers to California to construct more POW housing. Isiac and Fritz, along with most of Colonel Rodgers' MPs, remain in New York to guard the POWs.

New York, July 24, 1942

Before this time, Colonel Rodgers' MPs had very little trouble with their German POWs. Most of the POWs seemed happy to be out of the war. On July 24, that abruptly changed. Three POWs were found dead in their barracks. Isiac and Fritz, speaking German, began to interrogate the prisoners. It seems like two factions had developed in the POW camp: the aggressive, angry, hard-core Nazis, and the Germans that were happy that the war was over for them and were trying to make the best of their situation by being more cooperative with their captors.

Although he couldn't find out exactly who killed the three German prisoners, Isiac was developing a feel for which POWs were in each group. The three murdered

German prisoners were seen by the Nazis to be too cooperative with the American MPs. The two factions were becoming more and more polarized. The Nazis seemed to hate everyone, even each other at times. And the other POWs hated the Nazis for killing three of their own soldiers. Some of the POWs were beginning to inform on the Nazis. More trouble was brewing.

July 25, 1942

Lieutenant Carter was in charge of Isiac's platoon. He didn't speak any German, so he relied heavily on Corporals Kalway and Heimlich. Now that they had a good idea of who was in each group, they discussed separating the two groups of POWs.

"Lieutenant," Isiac said, "I think it is imperative that we separate the two groups. But, before we do, I'd like to try to find several POWs who would be willing to pretend allegiance to the Nazis and act as informants. There is enough hate on each side that it might just work. And it would make our jobs easier in the long run. In fact, there's enough hate that I think I could find some volunteers even without offering them any special privileges. The trick will be to find someone who the Nazis will accept as a true believer."

"If I can find more than one volunteer, their identities and existence need to be kept a secret from each other. That way, if one of them turns out to be a Nazi, it won't compromise the other informants. And each informant needs to believe that he is the only informant. It might also be a good idea to keep the informant's identity secret from the other MPs so that they don't unintentionally give the informant special treatment. That might arouse suspicion and alert the Nazis."

"I like that idea," Lieutenant Carter said, "Anything else?"

"Yes," Isiac said. "As soon as we act on any information that we receive, for his protection, the informant needs to be immediately removed from the Nazi Group."

Was Isiac becoming a spy master?

"As soon as you can find your informants, we will do the split and separate the two groups," Lieutenant Carter said. The meeting was over.

July 31, 1942

The German POWs are split into two groups.

India, July 31, 1942

Since arriving in Goalundo in April, Chao's transport and trading activities had earned him 30 pounds. That was quite an accomplishment, and it was made possible because of the previous agreement he had made with Meeta for free room and board. Chao entered the telegraph office and sent two telegrams. One was sent to his bank in Calcutta depositing 10 pounds in his personal account and 10 pounds in the HSC Trading Company account. The other was sent to Mr. James, telling him that he was safe and earning money as a trader.

New York, August 9, 1942

Isiac's plan paid off big time on August 9 when he received information that the Nazis were planning an escape attempt tomorrow night at 11 PM. Isiac also learned that the two leaders of the plan were the same ones who murdered the 3 German POWs. Isiac certainly was no lawyer, but he hoped that his information would be enough to bring those two murderous scoundrels to justice.

August 10, 1942

The escape tunnel was short. It was less than 6 feet long, with a depth of only 5 feet, and a diameter of three feet. It opened up just outside the barracks wall. A piece of plywood had been removed from the floor under one of the bunks, and it was used to prop up the last 8 inches of soil on the outside of the barrack's wall; this kept the tunnel exit from collapsing before they were ready to escape. A tunnel collapse would have ended their escape even before it began. A section of springs was removed from one of the bunks and placed over the inside entrance of the tunnel. Then clothing was put over the springs to act as camouflage. Unless you crawled under the bunk, you'd just see clothes scattered on the floor around the bed.

The plan was for two men to push on the board to remove the last 8 inches of soil from the tunnel exit. If that didn't work, they would remove the board and dig out the remaining dirt to clear the exit. Either way, it should only take a minute or two. Then eight men would move quietly through the tunnel and to the outside fence. Using tools made from dismantled bunks, they planned to have four holes dug under the fence in less than 5 minutes. In another 5 minutes, they planned to have all their men under the fence and into the woods. Not much of a plan after that, just separate and run.

Lieutenant Carter decided he wanted to catch the POWs during the escape attempt instead of preventing it by filling the tunnel. Plans were made.

The Germans must have been anxious because they popped the tunnel open 10 minutes early. As planned, eight men hurried to the fence; but before they could start digging, it suddenly looked like daylight. In addition to the lights surrounding the camp, the engineers had strung up spotlights at the edge of the woods. Like ghosts, 20 MPs stepped out of the woods. All of them had their rifles pointed at the German

POWs. At the same time, from the inside of the fence, 10 MPs approached from each side. They also had their rifles pointed at the prisoners that were attempting to escape.

Only eight prisoners were outside the barracks. With ten more MPs surrounding the barracks, the rest of the POWs were kept inside. And, as planned, several shots were fired into the ground. That insured that Isiac had their full attention when he said over the loud speaker, in German,

"You are attempting to escape. Lay face down on the ground with arms and legs spread, or you will be shot."

Then, again, as planned, a single shot was fired. As tough as the Nazis thought they were, none hesitated. All 8 of them were sprawled out spread-eagled on the ground.

August 20, 1942

After learning who the trouble-makers were, splitting the POWs into two separate groups, using informants to foil an escape attempt, and learning the identity of the two murderers, Corporal Kalway and Corporal Heimlich are both promoted to Sergeant.

August 27, 1942

Colonel Rodgers returns from California to New York.

August 31, 1942

A call came into the Army base camp. There was a rowdy bunch of soldiers at the Oswego Tavern, which, conveniently for the soldiers, was only two blocks away. The message was relayed to the MPs, and Sergeant Kalway and Sergeant Heimlich were sent to quiet the disturbance. When they entered the tavern, it didn't take Isiac and Fritz long to see who was causing the ruckus. Colonel Rodgers and 2 of his Lieutenants were attempting to invade the entire bar and capture all the women for the soldiers.

No way the locals were going to tolerate that. At this point, it only amounted to yelling back and forth, but Isiac could see that the situation could explode any second. Approaching the three officers, Isiac spoke to the Colonel.

"Sir," Isiac said, "For your own protection, I'd like to escort you out of the bar before there is any real trouble."

"I don't need any protection," Colonel Rodgers said. "If there is any trouble, I can handle it myself. Do you know who I am, Sergeant?"

"Yes Sir," Isiac said. "You are my commanding officer, Colonel Rodgers."

"Good," Colonel Rodgers said. "And I've heard all about how quickly you two have risen in the ranks. So, unless you both want to be busted back to corporals, leave before you two are the ones in trouble. Dismissed."

"I'm Sorry, Colonel," Isiac said, "You're drunk, and I'd prefer to escort you out of this bar rather than arrest you."

"Not a chance," Colonel Rodgers said as he and his 2 Lieutenants stood up.

"Sir," Isiac said, "I am going to escort you out of this bar. We can do it the easy way or the hard way."

Fritz could see it in Isiac's eyes. He was done playing "nice cop." Fritz shifted his position, so he was closer to the Lieutenants. He knew that the Colonel would be the instigator if any trouble started, and Isiac would handle him. He was watching the Lieutenants. And then it happened.

"You're the one who is going to get the hard way," Colonel Rodgers said as he made a quick move, taking a swing at Isiac.

The Colonel wasn't quick enough though, and he ended up on the floor, flat on his back. Obviously, the Colonel didn't know ALL about Sergeant Kalway and Sergeant Heimlich. But he was learning quickly because, when his 2 Lieutenants tried to intervene, they both ended up on the floor next to the Colonel. Somehow, with a little help from Fritz, the Lieutenants appeared to trip over each other. Still holding the Colonel by the wrist in a way that precluded any further resistance, Isiac said loudly enough so everyone in the bar could hear,

"No more trouble tonight or we'll be back. "Then, facing the Colonel and changing his grip on his wrist, Isiac said,

"Let me help you up, Sir."

Isiac and Fritz left the 2 Lieutenants on the floor and escorted Colonel Rodgers back to the brig.

September 1, 1942

Colonel Rodgers watched as Isiac walked back to his cell.

"Striking an MP while on duty. How am I going to explain that," Colonel Rodgers wondered?

"Sorry for the bruises last night, sir," Isiac said as he opened the door to the Colonel's cell.

Looking puzzled, Colonel Rodgers asked, "What are the charges, Sergeant?"

"There are no charges, Colonel," Isiac said. "You just had a little too much to drink and lost your balance. I wasn't able to catch you before you fell."

"What about my 2 Lieutenants," Colonel Rodgers asked?

"They were drunk too, sir. Sergeant Heimlich told me that, when they tried to help you regain your balance, they tripped over each other. He was sure that they could get up on their own, so he left them there. You're free to go, Colonel Rodgers," Isiac said.

"Thank you, Sergeant Kalway," the Colonel said as he left the brig still processing everything that happened.

Detroit, September 9, 1942

Nedra and Pam, carrying their babies, take the streetcar to the train station in Detroit and board the train for Oswego, New York. They are on their way to visit their husbands, Bud and Fritz.

New York, September 10, 1942

No Leaves were being granted, so Bud and Fritz couldn't meet the girls at the train station. But they left them a message that they would meet them at their hotel after they were off-duty the next morning.

September 11, 1942

The hotel was within walking distance of the base, less than a mile away. Bud and Fritz arrived at the hotel early, and after affectionate greeting all around, they took the girls and their baby boys to breakfast. Bud and Fritz were amazed at how much their boys, now 6-months old, had grown. After breakfast, each couple retired to their rooms for some much-anticipated alone time. Understandably, Bud and Fritz spent all their off-duty time with their wives and kids.

Family is everything.

September 13, 1942

Colonel Rodgers was already seated when he saw Isiac and Fritz enter the hotel dining room. The colonel stood up and said,

"Over here sergeants, join me for lunch. I'd like to meet your families, and lunch is on me."

"Are you sure," Fritz asked?

"It's an order, and I know from experience how well you two follow orders."

After introductions had been made, they talked as they ate. The colonel's off-duty personality was surprisingly pleasant compared to his on-duty persona. Shortly after lunch, Isiac and Fritz had to excuse themselves. They had to be back on duty in an hour. As they were leaving the dining room, the Colonel said, "Sergeants, I'd like to hear some more stories about you two. Do you mind if I escort your wives to dinner?"

"It's alright with me, sir," Fritz said, "But you better ask the girls."

Colonel Rodgers turned toward Nedra and Pam, and they were both shaking their heads, yes. "And very pretty heads they are, and two very lucky men those sergeants are," the Colonel thought. Then, as he left, he said out loud, "See you ladies at 5 PM."

Later that day

After they ordered, but before their food arrived, Colonel Rodgers asked the girls, "Did either of the boys tell you about our adventure together?"

"No, Colonel Rodgers," Nedra said.

"Call me Paul, please," Colonel Rodgers said. "Now that we're all friends, there is no need to be so formal. Besides, only the soldiers call me Colonel. Now I think I should share our story with you."

And that's how the girls heard about the Oswego Tavern incident.

Everyone seemed to be enjoying their dinner, and, as they ate, Colonel Rodgers asked the girls lots of questions. He learned that "Bud" was Isiac's nickname. And, by the time dinner was over, the colonel learned a whole lot more. He now knew the life stories of Isiac and Fritz, as well as the life stories of their wives.

September 15, 1942

With their babies, Nedra and Pam board the train for their trip back to Michigan.

September 16, 1942

As soon as Sergeants Heimlich and Kalway entered Lieutenant Carter's office, the Lieutenant said, "Colonel Rodgers wants the 3 of us in his office, let's go."

"Do you know why," Fritz asked.

As they headed to Colonel Rodgers office, Lieutenant Carter said, "It's about the three murdered German POWs."

"As I live and breathe," Colonel Rodgers said after the men entered his office and saluted. "If it isn't my three master spies and POW experts from Company A. Sit down men. I've been informed that according to the Articles of War Act, we have enough evidence to convict the two murderers. An appeal is automatically made; and although a conviction is almost guaranteed, because the only witness willing to testify can only supply hearsay evidence, there is a chance that the Appeal process could be a lengthy one."

"Two things bother me about that: an almost guaranteed conviction and a long, drawn-out appeal process. I don't like almost, and I don't like delays. But, if we had an eye witness to the murders who would be willing to identify the murderers, and either testify or sign a statement to that effect, I've been assured that the Appeal process would be a mere formality and proceed quickly, very quickly. I understand that, as of now, no POWs that witnessed the murder have been willing to come forward."

"Your assignment is to develop another one of your devious plans that will provide us with the witness we need, or their signed statement, identifying the murderers. You are relieved of all other duties. This is a priority. It needs to happen before the murderers are formally charged and before the appeal process begins. Any questions?"

"No sir," replies came from Lieutenant Carter, Sergeant Kalway, and Sergeant Heimlich.

"Make it happen then. I'm leaving for California tomorrow with my Engineers. Most of my MPs will remain here to guard the POWs. Captain Wilson is informed of the situation and will provide you with any assistance you need. That's all."

Lieutenant Carter and Sergeants Kalway and Heimlich didn't say anything as they left the Colonel's office, but they were all thinking. Finally, Lieutenant Carter said,

"We'll start right now. I'll inform one of the cooks to keep us supplied with food and drinks." In Lieutenant Carter's office, the planning began.

"I think signed statements would be easier than trying to coerce any of the POWs to testify," Lieutenant Carter said.

Nods of agreement from Isiac and Fritz.

"We've already tried the direct approach," Fritz said. "And that didn't work. The way it stands now, if anyone agreed to testify, they'd be dead before morning."

"Then let's change the way things stand," Isiac said.

"If you have an idea, let's hear it," Lieutenant Carter said.

"We could recombine the two groups of German POWs," Isiac said. "That would change the way things stand. Probably lead to more murders though."

"It would certainly shake things up," Fritz said.

"We can't do that," Lieutenant Carter said, "Any more murders and the Colonel might put us in front of a firing squad. We'd be in the brig for neglect of duty, for sure."

"No, we can't do that," Isiac agreed, "But the POWs don't know that."

"What are you getting at, Sergeant," the Lieutenant asked?

Isiac responded. "Just like us, the Nazis know that recombining the two groups would certainly result in more killings. But, even though their group isn't as large as the other group of Germans, the Nazis think that their superiority and toughness would insure that they would be the killers. All we have to do is convince the Nazis that, after reunification, any deaths that occurred would be, without a doubt, Nazis."

"How do we do that," Lieutenant Carter asked?

"We combine what the Nazis do know with what they don't know," Fritz said.

"Exactly," Isiac said.

"I think I understand," Lieutenant Carter said, "Since the Nazis don't know that we can't recombine them with the other German POWs, we use it as a threat. But how do we convince them that only Nazis would be killed when the groups are reunited?"

Fritz answered, "Nazis understand how to use power. That's how they gained control of Germany in the first place. All we have to do is give the power to the other German POWs."

Sharing his thoughts, Isiac said, "Maybe Colonel Rodgers will give us orders to protect anyone who signs a statement naming the murderers by keeping them separated when the groups are recombined. But, I'm sure that the Colonel would feel that, anyone who signed a statement that they had no knowledge of the murders, would have nothing to fear from the other Germans and would no longer need to be kept separated. And I think Colonel Rodgers is getting tired of the difficulties involved in keeping the two groups separated."

"I'm not sure, but I might have heard the Colonel say something to that effect," Lieutenant Carter said.

"Lieutenant," Isiac said, "Sergeant Heimlich and I are the only ones who speak German, so we would have to do all the paperwork ourselves. That would take a while and make the transfer a rather slow process. We might only be able to transfer 2 Nazis at a time."

"I'm sure we'd be able to deal with that," the Lieutenant said, smiling.

"Let's see," Fritz said, "There are over 80 German POWs in the other group. If we only transfer 2 Nazis at a time, that makes the odds over 40:1. I think the Nazis will be able to apply that concept to their understanding of power."

"They'd be sure to complain about that," Lieutenant Carter said, "But even if I agree with them, what can I do? I have my orders."

They had a plan. The rest of the day they worked out the details.

September 17, 1942

Colonel Rodgers takes his engineers to California to build more temporary housing for the POWs. Isiac and Fritz stay behind, with most of Colonel Rodgers MPs, to guard the prisoners in New York.

September 18, 1942

The German POWs received fewer rations today, a lot less. And they noticed. Now, with the German's attention, Isiac and Fritz started rumors that the Colonel wanted changes made in all the POW camps, both here and in California. The rumors spread to the other MPs and eventually to the POWs. And Isiac and Fritz made it sound like Colonel Rodgers was going to be promoted to General and put in charge of all the POW camps in America. If you are going to start a rumor, you might as well make it a good one.

Colonel Rodgers was in California building more housing for POWs. Maybe Lieutenant Carter misunderstood what Colonel Rodgers was doing in California. Either that or he was also adding to the rumor mill because he was telling his MPs that to save building costs, the Colonel wanted more POWs packed into each barracks. And supposedly, the POWs were eating too much, and more food was needed to feed our expanding army. And finally, Lieutenant Carter added a real whopper. Colonel Rodgers would be bringing a large group of Japanese POWs with him when he returned from California.

September 20, 1942

Having given the rumors time to spread, Lieutenant Carter started the next part of the plan. He had Sergeants Kalway and Heimlich choose 2 POWs from the hard-core Nazi group to be reinterrogated about the murders of the 3 German POWs. Conveniently, the interrogations took place just outside the Lieutenant's office. Although the interrogations would be entirely conducted in German, Isiac and Fritz had purposely selected POWs that could speak English. There was a good reason for this. During the interrogation, the

POWs could easily hear the gossiping soldiers working at desks that were just outside of the Lieutenant's door. Only this gossip had been prepared, in advance, by Colonel Rodgers' 3, so-called, spy masters: Lieutenant Carter, Sergeant Kalway, and Sergeant Heimlich. As the German POWs continued to insist that they knew nothing about their murdered comrades, they listened to the American banter. And what they heard confirmed the rumors that had already been circulated.

Changes were planned for the POW camps, and Colonel Rodgers would be returning from California with hundreds of Japanese POWs. One conversation, which Isiac and Fritz made sure that the Germans heard clearly, was that Colonel Rodgers didn't want to waste resources by constructing new barracks. Speculation was that he would move all the Germans into one barracks and put the, soon to be arriving Japanese, into the empty one. After the interrogations, the Germans were returned to their barracks where they informed their fellow Nazis what they heard from the poorly disciplined American soldiers.

September 21, 1942

Time to implement the final stage of the plan. Lieutenant Carter, Sergeant Kalway, and Sergeant Heimlich, along with 8, armed MPs, entered the Nazi barracks. Lieutenant Carter, with Sergeant Kalway interpreting, spoke to the Germans.

"I've been ordered to reunite you with the other German POWs. Colonel Rodgers knows that you are the group that has caused all the problems, so, to avoid future problems, he suggested that I reunite the groups gradually. My Sergeants told me that reuniting the two groups would result in more bloodshed. When I relayed that information to the Colonel, he told me to prevent bloodshed if I could, but the reunification must start by tomorrow, no matter what."

"Colonel Rodgers also told me not to waste any more time with interrogations. As ordered, I have prepared two different forms. Each form is written in both German and English. One form states that you have no knowledge of the murders. The other form leaves blank spaces where you add the names of the murderers if you witnessed the crime. If you have no knowledge of the murders and sign that form, the Colonel feels that you have nothing to fear from the other German POWs. But I was ordered to protect anyone with knowledge of the murders. Anyone who signs a statement naming the murderers will be transferred to the American jail for their own safety."

"Beginning tomorrow, I will transfer two members of your group to the other German barracks every three days. No one with knowledge of the murders will be transferred."

Anger was instantaneous among the Nazis. Just as instantaneously, the MPs had their 45's aimed at the POWs. It seemed that not all of the anger was directed toward the Americans, however. Several groups of POWs were engaged in heated discussions among themselves, arguments actually. Finally, Sergeant Kraus addressed Isiac in German, using his sergeant's voice so everyone could hear,

"The other prisoners will kill us even if we sign a paper saying we know nothing about the murders."

Isiac translated that for Lieutenant Carter and then translated his reply.

"Tell him that I agree with him, Sergeant Kalway, but those are my orders. If we do have any more murders, all I can do is investigate, just like we did with the last murders. American justice isn't as swift as they are accustomed to in Germany, but it does work."

Then Lieutenant Carter delivered his game-winning pitch,

"In fact, Colonel Rodgers told me before he left for California that the Army has enough evidence against Captain Weber and Lieutenant Wagner that they are going to face a firing squad anyway."

Now the arguments among the POWs were punctuated with punches thrown. Some of the German prisoners began to restrain the ones that were beating on each other. Sergeant Kraus again shouted over the noise of the crowd,

"Captain Weber and Lieutenant Wagner are already dead men. They got us into this mess, let them suffer the consequences. The war is over for us. Sergeant Kalway, give me a paper to sign. I saw Captain Weber and Lieutenant Wagner kill our soldiers." Then, turning to his men, Sergeant Kraus shook the paper at them and continued, "If you saw the murders, sign the papers."

Captain Weber and Lieutenant Wagner were now being restrained by their own soldiers, and even before Isiac could translate what Sergeant Kraus said, another German POW shouted,

"Captain Weber and Lieutenant Wagner don't care about us. They were willing to let us die with them. I'll sign a paper."

By the time Sergeant Kalway finished translating, two more Germans were asking for papers to sign.

"Private Woods, you and Private Lang take the two prisoners to the brig. Use your cuffs," Lieutenant Carter said.

Isiac was passing out more papers. Fritz was collecting the signed ones and returning them to Lieutenant Carter. One of the younger POWs got Isiac's attention, and Isiac motioned him forward. He spoke to Isiac in German,

"Sergeant Kalway, 4 of us didn't see the killings. We were in the latrine. What should we do?"

"Sign the paper that says that you didn't see anything," Isiac said. "I'll make sure you are protected."

"Thank you, Sergeant Kalway," the young soldier said as he returned to his three waiting comrades with Isiac's message.

October 1, 1942

Colonel Rodgers returns to New York and is ordered to transport German prisoners from New York to California. In California, he is to await further orders regarding his eventual deployment to the India, northern Burma, China Theater of operations to work on road construction. Most of the supplies for allied troops in China were delivered from India via the Burma Road. When the Japanese took control of the Burma Road, 90% of supplies being sent to China had to be flown over a section of the Himalaya Mountains that was referred to as flying "over the hump." Not only was this a logistical problem, but it also made the air transport planes vulnerable to attack by Japanese fighter planes stationed in Myitkyina, Burma. For that reason, construction of the Ledo Road was considered essential to the supply of allied troops stationed in China.

Before departure, Colonel Rodgers tells Captain Wilson to promote Sergeant Kalway to Staff Sergeant in charge of Squad 1, Team 1. Sergeant Heimlich will be in charge of Team 2. And Private Woods is to be promoted to Corporal. Then he sent for Lieutenant Carter, Sergeant Kalway, and Sergeant Heimlich.

With his three spy masters sitting in his office, Colonel Rodgers asked,

"Which one of you promoted me to General?"

"That would be me, sir," Isiac said.

"This must be something new for the army," the Colonel said, "I've never heard of a sergeant promoting a Colonel before."

That got everyone laughing.

"Good work on your last assignment, now start packing, we're heading to California."

California, October 10, 1942
Colonel Rodgers arrives in California. While his engineers work to construct more housing for the POWs, his MPs continue to guard the prisoners.

California, October 29, 1942
Colonel Rodgers receives orders: Prepare for departure to India.

India, October 29, 1942

General Stillwell orders the Ledo Road built.

Chao Lin receives a telegram from Mr. James:

"Sister safe with Lu Ming in Jinhua. All merchandise sold. Money transferred. HSC Balance 495 pounds."

China, November 1942

SOS is established in Kunming, China, the eventual destination of the supply road from India to China, and the current location of the supply depot for supplies arriving by air transport.

India, November 1, 1942

Chao had learned a lot during his stay with Meeta and his family. Meeta had helped him to refine his trading skills and had shown him some new ones. Also, when Chao realized how valuable food preservative was for a trader, Meeta taught Chao the techniques for drying, smoking, salting, and pickling food.

Chao already knew that Ledo had become a large staging area for supplies being flown over the hump to the troops in China. Now that construction of the Ledo road was imminent, he decided to go to Ledo to take advantage of the opportunities he was likely to find there.

Meeta Sandar did not think that was a good idea. Besides, Meeta had become comfortable with the relationship that had developed between him and Chao. But when Chao explained the trading opportunities that might develop with Chao in Ledo and him in Goalundo, Meeta became more interested. When Chao added his plan to book passage on a barge and to accompany a load of goods on his trip to Ledo, Meeta was all for the idea, but only if Chao promised to return to Goalundo if the situation in Ledo didn't work out as hoped. Chao agreed.

November 2, 1942

Chao and Meeta went to the docks and talked to a barge Captain that Meeta knew. Meeta introduced Chao to Captain Olson.

"Captain Olson, are you planning to make a trip to Dibrugarh," Chao asked?

"Yes," Captain Olson answered, "But not until November 8th."

"Can I buy passage for my dog and me on this barge," Chao asked?

Captain Olson looked at Lena and then said, "4 rupees."

"Agreed," Chao said.

"We leave at first light," the Captain replied.

Then Chao asked, "If Meeta and I could supply you with goods to ship to Dibrugarh, would you be willing to buy them if we offered you a fair price?"

"I would," Captain Olson answered, "But I don't have any money at the moment."

Chao was ready for that answer, in fact, that was the answer he was hoping for. Chao then asked,

"Would you be willing to ship the goods to Dibrugarh if we offered you 8% of the sale price?"

Dealing with traders was an essential part of Captain Olson's business. He knew that this was only their first offer. He liked Meeta, but business was business. Captain Olson said, "12%."

Chao countered with, "10%, and if you include free passage for me and my dog, it's a deal."

"Agreed," Captain Olson said. "Have the goods ready to be loaded in the morning on November 7th."

As Chao and Meeta left, they discussed what kind of goods they should consider for shipment to Dibrugarh. Chao wondered if this could be the beginning of a new partnership. Every trading company needs a means to transport goods. Chao in no way intended to limit himself to the use of carts as his primary mode of transportation any longer than necessary.

The HSC Trading Company no longer had any ships or warehouses. The company didn't own anything. All it had was a bank account in Calcutta with a balance of

495 pounds. But Captain Olson and his barge got Chao thinking about the possibility of new trading opportunities that he might be able to take advantage of after the war.

California, November 2, 1942
Colonel Rodgers' Engineers board ship for transport to India.

India, November 8, 1942
The 3 new partners had loaded their goods on the barge the day before, and Chao was on the barge with Lena lying beside him. They were on their way to Dibrugarh.

Pacific Ocean, November 9, 1942
The calm seas that Colonel Rodgers and his men had experienced since they left California are replaced by the gales of November.

India, November 14, 1942
Captain Olson's barge arrives in Dibrugarh.

Pacific Ocean, November 14, 1942
While most of the soldiers had been sick for the past week, Isiac and Fritz were enjoying their dinner. Earlier in the week, Alvin, the cook, had heard them telling

some of the other soldiers how good the food was and that it was the best food they have eaten since joining the Army. Since most of the soldiers were eating very little or not eating at all, there was more than enough food for Isiac and Fritz. And Alvin made sure that they got nothing but the best, and as much as they wanted. It never hurts to compliment the cook. And Isiac and Fritz both agreed that this was the best part of the Army so far, because, not only was the food so good, but also because the soldiers were too sick to cause any trouble for the MPs. That meant no duties.

India, November 15, 1942

Chao stood on the dock with Captain Olson watching the new crates of goods being loaded on the barge in preparation for his return trip to Goalundo. Captain Olson had just sold their goods for 60 pounds. They could have sold their goods for more if they sold parts of the cargo separately, but when a single buyer offered to buy all their goods for 60 pounds that made the sale easier and much quicker because he was already holding the money in his hand. After subtracting 6 pounds as his share, Captain Olsen gave Chao his share, 27 pounds.

"What are you going to do with all that money," Captain Olson asked?

"Save it in case another trading opportunity presents itself," Chao said.

"That's a lot of money to be carrying around," Captain Olson said.

Chao moved 20 feet away from Captain Olson and stopped. Still holding the money in his hand, Chao said,

"GUARD," and then to Captain Olson, "Try to take the money from my hand."

When the Captain entered the 10-foot safety zone, Lena growled with fangs showing.

"Now backup two steps," Chao said, and the growling stopped. "OK," Chao said, releasing Lena from the GUARD command. Then he and Lena walked back and stood beside the Captain.

"Do you want to sell that dog," Captain Olson asked, but he already knew the answer before Chao shook his head, no.

"Instead of me carrying the money back to Goalundo," the Captain said, "Why don't we wire the money to Meeta?"

Chao hadn't thought of that, "Good idea," he said.

"Can you take care of it," the Captain asked, as he handed Meeta's money to Chao. "I need to stay here and supervise the loading of the barge."

"I'll do it right now," Chao said, as he walked off the dock looking for a telegraph office.

Finding the telegraph office nearby, Chao wired the money to Meeta Sandar with the following message:

"Sale price 60 pounds. Leave for Ledo tomorrow."

The cost of purchasing the goods was 32 pounds. He and Meeta had each made 11 pounds. That was almost a 70% profit. Chao continued calculating as he and Lena returned to the docks.

Since Chao had been working with Meeta, he had been earning about 10 pounds a month. It took Chao and Meeta 6 days to purchase, gather, and load their goods on Captain Olson's barge. It took another six days for Chao and the cargo to move up the Brahmaputra River to Dibrugarh. In 12 days, less than half a month, Chao had earned 11 pounds. That was more than he had earned for a full month's work while he was working with Meeta. And half of that time was just a relaxing boat ride. No wonder his father had liked trading so much.

When Chao and Lena returned to the docks, they spent the rest of the day with Captain Olson. The Captain, knowing that Chao planned to leave for Ledo in the morning, suggested that Chao and Lena spend the night on the barge.

November 17, 1942

The road from Dibrugarh to Ledo ran alongside the railroad tracks. It was heavily traveled, with most of the traffic heading toward Ledo. Even with the early implications of what to expect at the end of this heavily traveled road, Chao was still unprepared for what he saw when he reached Ledo. Although Ledo could in no way compare to the size and complexity of Calcutta, there was activity everywhere. Warehouses were everywhere. And near existing warehouses, new ones were popping up like mushrooms. Some of the warehouses being built already had supplies stacked nearby, waiting for construction to be completed. Tents and what appeared to be housing units for the laborers that were flooding into Ledo were scattered everywhere. The camps for the allied troops were more organized, but they were also undergoing heavy construction in preparation for the expected arrival of more troops and supplies.

Chao's first thought was that he was looking at a newly developing mining camp that had been, somehow, removed from an American movie of the old west and placed in India. Chao soon discovered that his analogy, comparing Ledo to a wild western town from America's past, fit perfectly.

November 18, 1942

Chao had spent the night with a group of laborers who were sleeping along the outside wall of one of the older buildings, an old warehouse or an old dwelling; it was hard to tell. Chao knew the importance of finding a safe place to live, and that was his priority as he wandered around looking and listening. He also needed to learn as much as he could about the city so that he could decide on his next plan of action.

The composition of Ledo was mostly Indian, of course, but the army was here also, so there were a lot of British soldiers, as well. Some American soldiers had also arrived, and Chao learned that many more Americans would be arriving soon. There was also a considerable number of Chinese in Ledo. That didn't surprise Chao because this part of India was only a few hundred miles from China's western border, with only the northern part of Burma in between. Chao noticed that, although much of the population was organized into separate groups, of British, Americans, Indians, and Chinese, the groups didn't seem to have any trouble interacting with one another. And some groups were so heterogeneous that they defied labeling.

Chao noticed a Chinese boy leaving the British Army Camp. He was pulling a wagon that obviously contained a pile of British uniforms. The boy appeared to be a couple of years younger than Chao.

"Hello, my name is Chao. Do you work for the soldiers," Chao asked?

"My name is Ling," the boy answered, straightening his shoulders with pride. "I am the servant of a British soldier. The British like the Chinese because we make better servants than the Indians. Most Chinese servants make 3 rupees each week. I am the very best servant. I make 4 rupees each week."

"Where do you sleep, Ling," Chao asked?

"I sleep in an old tent with three other boys. We found a tent that the soldiers threw away. It had lots of holes. We fixed the holes. Now we live for free."

"Is there any extra room in your tent," Chao asked?

Ling didn't answer right away. Finally, he said, "Maybe."

Chao understood his caution with a stranger.

"Would there be room in your tent for 1 rupee per month," Chao asked?

Ling's response to this came much more quickly. "I think yes, but you couldn't tell the other boys."

Chao understood this response as well. "Do any of the servants live with the soldiers," Chao asked?

"Yes," Ling said. "Some of the soldiers like it if their servant is always there to help them. Other soldiers like it when their servant leaves for the night."

Ling told Chao how to find his tent before he left to have the soldier's uniforms cleaned.

Armed with this new information, Chao continued to wander around the city. He paid particular attention to the places where food could be purchased, and clean water could be found. He also wandered into various shops to see what could be bought and what the prices were. The end of the day found Chao standing in front of Ling's tent.

"Ling," Chao called out. When Ling came out of the tent, Chao discretely handed him a rupee.

"Do you have room for me in your tent," Chao asked?

"Yes, Chao. Come in and meet my friends," Ling said, as he led Chao and Lena into the tent.

Chao immediately removed a bag of fresh fruit and vegetables from his cart. The first thing Chao said to the boys was,

"I have extra food tonight. Will you boys share it with me?" Chao knew how to make a good first impression.

November 24, 1942

Chao had learned a lot about Ledo in less than a week. As a trader, he saw a lot of potential opportunities if he could figure out a way to take advantage of them. Since he arrived, Chao had spent at least part of each day in and around the British Camp. Although Chao could live with the boys for one rupee per month, which was slightly over 1 cent American, per day, Chao could see advantages of living on the army base. Chao had already received three offers to work as a servant for 3 rupees per week, but he turned them all down. He wanted more than just a job with servant's pay. Just as Chao was getting ready to go back to Ling's tent, he saw a British soldier intentionally approaching him. Very likely, another job offer was about to be presented.

"I'm Private Morley. I've seen you around here lately."

"My name is Chao Lin. I've been here about a week."

"Your English is very good, Chao Lin," Private Morley said, complimenting Chao Lin.

"Thank you, sir," Chao Lin said. "I'm a British Subject. I was born in Hong Kong."

"I'm not an officer. You can call me Private Morley."

Chao nodded, and Private Morley continued, "Word has it that you have already turned down two job offers to work as a servant."

"I turned down 3," Chao corrected.

"Didn't they offer you enough money, or are you looking for some other kind of job," Private Morley asked?

"A job as a servant would be fine, and the amount of pay wasn't the reason I turned down the other job offers. There were other issues that could not be resolved," Chao answered.

"What were the other issues," Private Morley asked? And the bargaining began.

"My dog must be allowed to accompany me as I work," Chao said.

"She looks like a nice dog," Private Morley said. "Is she friendly?"

Chao nodded yes, then spoke to Lena, "OK."

"You can pet her now, Private Morley." Lena licked Private Morley's hand as he reached out to pet her.

"Most servants work for 2 or 3 rupees per week. A very few of the best work for 4 rupees per week," Private Morley said.

Chao already knew that, but he remained silent and waited for Private Morley to make his offer.

"Lena can come to work with you for the first three days," Private Morley said. "But only on a trial basis. After three days, if she causes no problems and doesn't interfere with your work, she can come to work with you every day."

"Agreed," Chao said, and then waited for Private Morley to complete his offer.

"I can offer you 3 rupees per week," Private Morley said.

Now it was Chao's turn. "Agreed," Chao said. "I will accept 3 rupees per week, but I would also need you to provide food for Lena and me and a place to stay."

"I have room for both you and your dog, and I could probably scrounge up enough food to feed you, but why should I feed your dog," Private Morley asked?

This wasn't the first time that Chao was asked that question.

"As part of her payment for working for you," Chao said.

"Why would I want a dog working for me," Private Morley asked?

Chao began his explanation.

"There are a lot of people around here that have no jobs and have no money. They will steal anything if they think they can sell it to buy food. And Lena is a guard dog."

Private Morley laughed, "She doesn't look like a guard dog."

Chao took 3 rupees out of his pocket, put them in a small cloth bag, walked 20 feet away from Private Morley, and put the money on the ground.

"GUARD," he told Lena. Then he walked back to Private Morley. "I just put one week's pay on the ground," Chao told Private Morley. "I offer it to you freely if you can go and pick it up."

Private Morley was still young, or he would have known that no one, not even a young boy, offers to give away one week's pay without a catch. And as Private Morley approached the money Chao had put on the ground, Lena's growl and bared fangs stopped him in his tracks, demonstrating "the catch."

"FETCH," Chao said, and Lena picked up the bag of money and returned to Chao's side, waiting for him to take it out of her mouth. Then Chao presented Private Morley with his final offer,

"Private Morley, if you provide food and a place to stay for Lena and me, Lena and I will work for you for 1 rupee each, per week."

Private Morley was somewhat stunned, but not so much that he didn't realize that Chao had presented him with a good deal.

"Agreed," he said.

December 1, 1942

Ledo Road construction is transferred from British to American operations. Lack of infrastructure in Burma made the American Army Engineers an important part of the Burma Campaign.

December 16, 1942

Construction of the Ledo Road begins.

Isiac and Fritz Arrive in Calcutta, India

India, December 22, 1942

Colonel Rodgers and his Independent 495th Engineers Brigade arrive in Calcutta, India. The MPs were in charge of the security of both the engineers and their equipment. The MPs spent the majority of their time patrolling in jeeps.

December 25, 1942

Colonel Rodgers' Brigade was looking forward to Christmas dinner before departing for Ledo tomorrow morning. With the start of dinner just a few minutes away, Lieutenant Carter got a report from the MPs of Squad 3. They were having trouble with the locals at Supply Depot B and were calling for assistance.

"Sergeant Kalway," Lieutenant Carter called out.

"I'm afraid you're going to be late for Christmas dinner. The MPs of Squad 3 are having some trouble at Depot B. They just called and asked for help. Take your squad and solve whatever problem Squad 3 is having."

"Yes sir," Sergeant Kalway said. Isiac saw Fritz across the room and called out, "Sergeant Heimlich, have your men ready to depart from the motor pool in 5 minutes."

Isiac didn't even wait for a reply. He knew that Fritz would probably be waiting for him at the motor pool even before he could get his own team together. And just as expected, when Isiac arrived, Fritz and his team were sitting in 2 jeeps with their motors running. And two more empty jeeps were parked next to Fritz, also with their motors running, just waiting for Isiac's team to jump in.

As Isiac and Fritz approached Depot B, they could immediately see the problem. Too many supplies had arrived too fast, and with no room left in the warehouse, the newly arrived supplies were stacked up against an outside wall. The MPs of Squad 3 had formed a semi-circle around the supplies. But they were, in turn, surrounded by a very large and noisy crowd of Indian laborers hoping to snatch anything they could get. Isiac saw that, even with his squad as reinforcements, the crowd outnumbered the MPs by at least 3 to 1. But they were MPs.

"A few have sticks that I can see, but watch out for knives," Isiac said. "With gun-hands free and batons in the other hand, approach quietly from behind, and remember what I taught you. If their back is turned, pull back on their hair or collars and, at the same time, kick the back of their knee. As soon as your man hits the ground, grab the next one. If anyone turns around to face you, use your baton, stay in pairs and if things start to get out of control, move toward Sergeant Heimlich and me. We'll be in the center. If your buddy goes down, shoot his assailant in the leg, and we'll come to you."

"Busby and Linder, you each take a jeep and push into the crowd from the flanks. Gently, or not so gently, use your judgment. But do not stop. Keep moving toward Squad 3's position, one hand on the wheel and your .45 in the other hand. As soon as the crowd turns around, hit the horn and hold it down. Keep moving and try to speed up a little if you can. Everyone start on my signal."

Over 20 of the crowd were on the ground when the horns sounded on each flank. The crowd panicked, but before they could disperse, another dozen of them was on the ground; and they were trying to get up quickly to avoid being trampled by the rest of the retreating crowd. When Isiac's 1st squad reached the 3rd squad, they were still holding their semi-circle position; but now, all of them were smiling like they had just witnessed the funniest thing. But in reality, the 3rd squad knew that they had avoided what could have been a dangerous situation. Instead, many of the crowd would have bumps and bruises when they reported for work tomorrow and some might not be able to report at all.

Isiac waited until the crowd was thoroughly dispersed before he said,

"Good job, men. No one is left lying on the ground, so it looks like we didn't kill anyone."

After 15 minutes, with everything quiet, Isiac spoke again, this time to Sergeant Garcia of 3rd squad, "If you think you can handle things from here, we're late for Christmas dinner."

"I don't think we'll have any more trouble tonight," Sergeant Garcia said. "And now that the locals understand what it means when MPs give orders to disperse, I don't think that the MPs that remain here after we leave tomorrow will have any more trouble either. Thanks for your help, Sergeant Kalway, and enjoy your dinner."

When Isiac's 1st squad returned to the mess hall, Isiac immediately reported to Lieutenant Carter, "Problem solved, sir."

"Thank you, Sergeant," Lieutenant Carter said. "The good news is that dinner is still being served. The bad news is that they ran out of turkey. But there is still plenty of ham left."

"I'm sure the men will be happy with ham, sir," Isiac responded.

"Enjoy your Christmas dinner, Sergeant, and be sure to give the entire squad my compliments," Lieutenant Carter said.

Early morning, December 26, 1942

As soon as Isiac heard the barrack's door open, he was awake and on his feet. Then came Sergeant O'Malley's booming voice,

"Sergeant Kalway, get your men out of bed, now."

Isiac could see that Sergeant O'Malley's loud voice had already accomplished that. With Isiac's squad at attention, ten men in their underwear, Sergeant O'Malley looked closely at each man. "Anyone sick," he asked?

"No Sergeant," the whole squad responded.

Sergeant O'Malley continued, "You made the company news, soldiers. Everyone in the Company is talking about your little adventure yesterday. It seems like you men have become a permanent part of Company lore. I also heard that none of you complained about being late for Christmas dinner when all the turkey was gone. You can consider that a reward for a job well done. All the men who ate turkey yesterday are sick with food poisoning. And that has also become part of the story, the luck of 1st Squad. And none of you are Irish. Imagine that."

That brought smiles to everyone, including Sergeant O'Malley, as he continued to explain the situation and give them their orders.

"Departure for Ledo has been delayed indefinitely. I don't know the exact figures, but well over half of our Company is sick. Sergeant Kalway, your Squad and 3rd Squad are the only squads in the Company without illness. I want you to join Squad 3 and round up anyone else you can find from the other squads who isn't sick. Then transport anyone in the Company that is sick to the infirmary. I don't know about the other companies yet, so after you take care of all our men, report to Lieutenant Carter. He's already in the infirmary, so don't expect him to be at his best."

"Yes, Sergeant O'Malley," Isiac said, then to Fritz, he said, "Sergeant Heimlich, find Squad 3 and bring them to the Motor Pool. We'll meet you there in 10 minutes."

Early morning, December 31, 1942

Colonel Rodgers' now healthy 495th Engineers Brigade arrives in Ledo on New Year's Eve. Most of Colonel Rodgers soldiers were kept busy settling into the new camp. Lt. Colonel Bolla assembled his 712th MP Battalion shortly after arriving in Ledo, India, and addressed his MPs.

"Be ready for a busy night. It's New Year's Eve, but the men don't need a reason to celebrate. They're ready to blow off steam. Each company will be assigned to patrol a separate battalion. See your Captains for details."

With all of his MPs assembled, Captain Wilson said,

"We have been ordered to patrol and guard the 623rd Battalion. Assignments will be made in two hours. Our Company is developing a no-nonsense reputation. Continue the good work. But understand this. If any of my off-duty MPs are arrested, I will take it as a personal insult, and punishment will be severe."

"If any of the 623rd Battalion soldiers look like they might have a problem making it back to their barracks on their own, you can help them get back. If any of the soldiers look like they are about to cause trouble, I want 2 MPs to each quickly and forcefully grab an arm. When you are in control, you can explain that you are now escorting them out. Then give them a choice of their final destination: back to their barracks or the brig. Lack of cooperation automatically lands them in the brig with whatever force necessary to get them there. Any questions?"

Sergeant Heimlich had a question, "Captain Wilson, Sir, are we using the carrot and the stick approach?"

"Indeed we are, Sergeant Heimlich, but I suggest that a touch of the stick before the carrot is offered might occasionally be helpful. Use your judgment. Even if they're drunk, that should help to persuade the soldiers

171

that the decision to choose the carrot would be the wisest one. Lieutenants and Sergeants, meet me in 5. Everyone else take a break. Be back here in 2 hours. Dismissed."

After a short break, Captain Wilson addressed his four lieutenants and 15 sergeants, "I don't know how long we'll be here, but Ledo has the feel of a wild, wide-open town. The soldiers of our Brigade know that we deal with problems quickly and forcefully, but the locals might need convincing. Any suggestions?"

"We could send Sergeant Kalway and Sergeant Heimlich out with their teams to look for another riot to break up," Sergeant Garcia said. Laughter followed.

"Good idea, Sergeant Garcia, and if I was sure that they could find one before tonight, I'd do it," and Captain Wilson got even more laughs than Sergeant Garcia did.

"Sir," Isiac said, "If it can be arranged, at least for tonight, it might be a good idea to require all off-duty soldiers of the 623rd Battalion that want to leave their barracks to stay in a group and be escorted by one of our squads or teams, for their own protection of course."

"For their own protection, Sergeant Kalway?" Captain Wilson asked. "Or should I call you Sergeant Mother Goose?"

172

This time it took longer for the laughter to settle down. Finally, Isiac was able to answer, "Sir, with us, right there looking over their shoulders, the men might have a little more incentive to behave themselves." That barely brought a chuckle from the men.

"I'll go and ask Colonel Rodgers if I can relay our request to the 623rd Battalion, and I might just mention that the idea originated with Sergeant Kalway; that way, if he doesn't like the idea, I'll have a scapegoat."

Captain Wilson already knew that Colonel Rodgers had used Sergeant Kalway in the past as a "problem solver." And Captain Wilson was almost certain that mentioning that it was Sergeant Kalway's idea would ensure implementation. The men knew it too. And Captain Wilson didn't seem to mind a bit that he had to, again, wait for the laughter to subside before he could end the meeting. When it finally settled down enough for him to be heard, Captain Wilson ended the meeting with, "Sergeant O'Malley will pass out your assignments. Dismissed."

January 1, 1943

Colonel Rodgers met with all his Lt. Colonels to get status reports from his Headquarters Company and 5 Battalions. After listening to all their reports, Colonel Rodgers addressed Colonel Green, "I heard that your battalion was the only one that didn't have anyone arrested last night. Congratulations."

"Thank you, Colonel Rodgers," Colonel Green said, "But Captain Wilson deserves the credit."

As he looked at Captain Wilson, Colonel Rodgers asked Colonel Green, "Why is that," but Colonel Rodgers already knew the answer.

Answering Colonel Rodger's question, Colonel Green said, "Captain Wilson suggested that all off-duty soldiers be required to be accompanied by his MPs if they wanted to leave the barracks. I just gave the order."

"Take note, Colonel Bolla," Colonel Rodgers said, not letting Colonel Bolla know that Captain Wilson had already given him that information without running it through the regular chain of command.

"Yes sir," Colonel Bolla said, "All 4 Companies will be following the same procedure as of right now."

"And sir," Colonel Green added, "Captain Wilson got the idea from one of his sergeants; the same one that prevented a potential riot in Calcutta, Sergeant Kalway."

Still playing along, Colonel Rodgers said, "That doesn't surprise me Colonel Green, but thank you for the information. Sergeant Kalway and I have already become acquainted." Then to himself, he thought, "In the Army, less than a year and Sergeant Kalway is already making his mark. I wonder what a little more experience will bring?" He would soon find out.

Wrapping up his meeting, Colonel Rodgers continued,

"We've been ordered by General Stillwell to begin working on his road tomorrow. Headquarters will have the schedules for work details by sunrise tomorrow. Be there with your troops and the transport needed to move them to their designated work sites. Dismissed."

January 3, 1943

Ledo had become a huge staging area for the supplies that were being flown "over the hump" to China. Because of the lack of infrastructure, Colonel Rodgers Engineers, in addition to road work, were put to work repairing old storage structures and building new ones. The standard of living in Ledo was so poor that the American and British soldiers lived like kings compared to the local population. Many of the allied soldiers stationed there could afford to hire servants, and they did.

Isiac and Fritz saw that most of the British soldiers had servants. Since most of the Indians spoke English, some better than the soldiers they served, communication was not a problem. They also learned that some of the men preferred to hire Chinese. Although communication was sometimes a bit of a problem, the quality of service that the soldiers received from the Chinese was, for the most part, excellent.

January 5, 1943

Sergeant First Class O'Malley, after giving instructions to his sergeants, spoke to Isiac and Fritz.

"I heard you two boys have already had trouble with the servant you hired yesterday."

"He's no longer with us," Fritz said. "Too much stuff seemed to turn up missing. We were told that it must have been misplaced. But after we told him that we were MPs and explained some of our policing powers, most of the stuff miraculously reappeared. After that, he seemed more than willing to seek employment elsewhere."

"Some of the British troops are being reassigned next week," Sergeant O'Malley said. "If you can wait that long, a lot of current servants are going to be looking for a job. The transferring British troops would probably be glad to give you a recommendation. I've heard that some of the British get very attached to their servants. I'll bet they would be happy to know that their servants had another job waiting after they transfer out."

"Thanks, Sergeant O'Malley," Isiac said. "We've lived our whole lives without a servant. We're not even sure we want one. Waiting won't be a problem. And it might be good PR to associate a little more with our British allies."

January 8, 1943

Isiac and Fritz were out hunting for British soldiers tonight. No, they hadn't changed sides in the war; they were out looking for a dependable servant. If anyone ever told Isiac that someday he would have a servant, he would have thought that to be about as likely as a Great Lakes boy moving his family to the desert. In other words, impossible. The second British soldier they talked to, ended their search. He was being transferred in 3 days, and his servant was the best they could find, even if they searched all of India.

"I don't consider him to be my servant at all," the British soldier said, "He's more of an assistant."

"I like the way you put that," Isiac said. "The concept of hiring a servant didn't sit well with me. Hiring an assistant, on the other hand, would be much easier for me to deal with."

"Much easier to explain to your mother, too," Fritz said, and he was only partially kidding.

"What's his name," Isiac asked?

"His name is Chao Lin," the young soldier answered. "He's an orphaned Chinese boy just 14 years old. Both his parents were killed on the first day of the war when the Japanese bombed Shanghai. He says that he is a

British Subject, and I believe him. In addition to Chinese, Chao also speaks fluent Hindi and perfect English."

When Fritz saw the look in Isiac's eyes, he knew exactly what Isiac was thinking. Isiac had grown up without a father, and now Chao Lin would have to grow up without a father or a mother.

Finally, Isiac asked, "What's the going pay rate?"

"Chao Lin doesn't go by the going pay rate," the British soldier said. "But don't worry; he'll negotiate a deal you won't have any trouble agreeing to unless you don't like dogs. If you try to separate him from his dog that will be a deal-breaker."

Fritz told the soldier where Chao Lin could find them. And then Fritz thought to himself, as they walked away,

"An orphan boy and a dog. This ought to be interesting."

Isiac was thinking the same thing.

January 12, 1943

Chao Lin started work yesterday, and Isiac and Fritz already knew they had a gem. Chao confirmed what his former employer had told them; but seeing how much Isiac and Fritz liked both him and Lena, Chao went into more detail.

"I was born in Hong Kong, and I am a British Subject."

"That's certainly starting at the beginning of the story," Fritz interrupted, and everyone laughed.

Then Chao continued, "I am 14 years old. My father was a Merchant Seaman. My father and his partner started with a small boat and formed a trading company in Hong Kong. They eventually expanded to 3 ships and opened warehouses in Hong Kong, Shanghai, and Calcutta. When my family moved to Calcutta, my Uncle remained in Hong Kong to handle business there. I already spoke English and Chinese when I came to Calcutta, and I quickly learned Hindi. I attended a British school until I was 13 years old."

Fritz thought to himself, "Isiac has to be picking up on the similarities between him and Chao: both without a father, both forced to quit school, and both speaking multiple languages. Isiac got his dog at 12. Chao got his dog at 13." As usual, Fritz was right. Fritz then refocused on Chao's story.

"My father and mother were killed in Shanghai on the first day of the war when his ship was sunk, and our warehouse was destroyed. My sister escaped into the countryside with my cousin, Lu Ming. When Hong Kong was invaded, our ship and warehouse were confiscated by the Japanese. When Calcutta was bombed, our 3rd ship was sunk. That left us with only one warehouse full of goods and no ships to move them. Then Shawn McGregor was called back to active duty in the British Navy. We had no choice but to sell everything."

"That's quite a story," Isiac said. "Someone could write a book about your life, Chao. Is anyone getting hungry? I'm going to make a quick trip to the kitchen and see if I can grab something to eat. Then you can continue your story. I'll be back in a few minutes."

"Thanks, Isiac," Chao said, "How did you know I was getting hungry?"

"I was your age once, and I was always hungry. And call me Bud."

Isiac went to find them some food, and as soon as he was out of hearing range, Fritz spoke to Chao.

"Only Isiac's family and his closest friends call him Bud."

"I guess that means he likes me," Chao said.

"More than that," Fritz said, "Isiac sees himself when he looks at you." To clarify that, Fritz gave Chao a brief summary of Isiac's life.

"Isiac's father deserted his family when Isiac was only five years old, so he knows what it's like to grow up without a father. And just like you, Isiac also got his dog, Peg, when he was young, only 12 years old. When we got drafted into the Army, Peg was already ten years old. He had to leave her with friends, knowing that she would probably die before he could return home and that he would probably never see her again. I think that was the hardest day of his life. And Isiac sees the love between you and Lena."

Chao didn't say a word, but he shook his head signifying that he understood. Fritz could see the effect his story had on Chao, but like Chao, Fritz remained silent.

Chao finally spoke, "Why don't you call Isiac, Bud?"

"That's a good question, Chao," Fritz said. "We've been friends since we were kids, and I just always called him Isiac."

When Isiac returned with 6 Spam sandwiches and six bottles of Pepsi, he noticed the solemn silence between Chao and Fritz. They had obviously had some conversation while he was gone that affected their attitudes. The sight of Spam sandwiches didn't do much, but the sight of the Pepsi bottles broke the silence and lightened the mood.

"How did you get the Pepsi, Isiac," Fritz asked?

"You know me, Fritz," Isiac said, "I'm always nice to the cooks. And I knew you liked Pepsi better than Coke."

"I do, Isiac, but it's too bad we don't have Alvin here to turn this spam into a gourmet meal," Fritz said, "because no matter how nice you are to the cooks, we'll never find another one as good as Alvin."

"That's so true, Fritz," Isiac said, then turning toward Chao, Isiac asked,

"Are you ready to continue your story, Chao?"

With his mouth still full, Chao could only nod. Then, as the three of them ate their Spam sandwiches and drank their Pepsi, Chao continued his story.

"As part of the sales agreement, I was allowed to continue living in the warehouse so I could continue to go to school. After the bombing of Calcutta, crime increased, and new gangs began to form. When a Chinese gang tried to recruit me, they made it clear that saying NO was not an option. So, I decided that, as they say in your western movies, 'it was time to get out of town.' I followed the railroad tracks that lead north and met a young Indian boy. His parents told him that if he didn't sell his dog or trade her for food, they were going to eat her. That's how I got Lena."

"Lena and I found an isolated place in the hills and spent a month there, just the two of us. That's how we became so close. When we left the hills, Lena and I spent some time with a farmer and his family, before we traveled to Goalundo with a fish peddler. I stayed with him and his family, and we became good friends. Lena and I accompanied him on his trading routes, and, like my father, I became a trader. Then I left Goalundo for Ledo, and here I am." Then, with a bow, Chao said, "The end."

"If you ever decide that trading is not for you, you'd make a good story teller," Fritz said.

Later that afternoon, Isiac and the other sergeants of 2nd Platoon received a notice to report to Lieutenant Carter.

"New orders sergeants," Lieutenant Carter said. "We're going to China tomorrow. We will be providing escort for the supplies being sent to Kunming. Get your men ready. We are leaving tomorrow at 0800 hours."

"Are you coming with us, Lieutenant," Sergeant O'Malley asked?

"That I am," the Lieutenant answered. "There are five transports leaving in the morning. I will travel with Squad 1. You will be traveling with Squad 2. Dismissed."

As Isiac and Fritz left the meeting, Isiac said,

"Now that we're going to be world travelers let's see if we can get a map from the engineers that shows India, Burma, and China."

"Not a bad idea," Fritz said. "A map might come in handy somewhere down the road, no pun intended."

The engineers had lots of maps, but none that they were eager to give away. So Isiac asked,

"Do you mind if I make copies?"

The engineers didn't have a problem with that, so Isiac made two hand drawn copies of India, northern Burma, and China, one for him and one for Fritz. Even though the copies were made on paper that was small enough to fit in their wallets when folded, they were also detailed enough to show the major cities and rivers in the area.

Isiac's Map

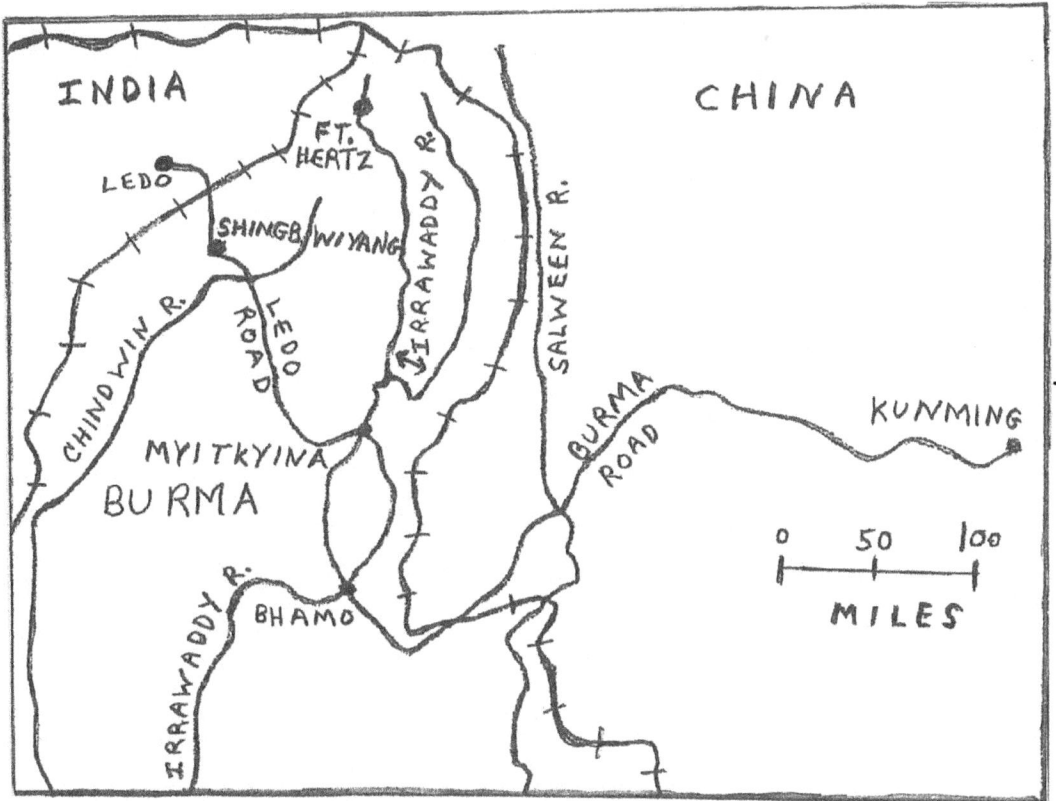

Burma, January 19, 1943

Lieutenant Carter was flying in a C-47 with 1st Squad. This was their 4th flight over the hump. They were returning to the Tinsukia airstrip after delivering a load of supplies to Kunming, China. Two American fighters were escorting the five C-47's. The soldiers had to raise their voices to be heard over the engine noise as they joked with one another.

"This sure beats walking," Private Lang said.

"How about boat rides," Isiac asked, knowing full well that Private Lang didn't handle the crossing well.

"I don't think I ever want to see the ocean again," Private Lang said, and everybody laughed.

The laughing stopped abruptly as the sound of machine guns could be heard over the engine noise. Lieutenant Carter and his men could feel the impact of the 50-caliber rounds slamming into the transport. The pilot was killed on the first pass of the Japanese fighters. The co-pilot instantly took control of the plane and rolled it down and to the left, trying to avoid the 2nd Japanese fighter. The two Japanese fighters were hiding in the clouds before they dropped down on the transports.

The two American fighters made tight circles as they attempted to intercept the Japanese fighters before they could make another pass at the transports. The lead American fighter caught one of the Japanese planes before it could complete its turn back toward the transports. That Japanese fighter erupted in a ball of flames. However, the American fighter pilot, while concentrating on his first target, lost track of the other Japanese plane. As the other Japanese fighter attacked unseen from above, Isiac could see the American plane take a hit, but within seconds, a parachute opened as the American pilot was able to eject.

Then Isiac saw something that made his blood turn cold; the Japanese fighter changed course and turned back to zero in on the helpless American pilot as he slowly floated to the ground. That deliberate heinous act cost the Japanese pilot his life because his deviation in course allowed the other American pilot to catch him from behind. Then the 2nd Japanese fighter burst into flames. The American fighter circled his descending fellow pilot before returning to the transports.

With the aerial show over, Isiac looked around the plane. The flight engineer was sprawled out on the floor, and Isiac thought that he might have fallen when the pilot rolled the plane. Then he saw the blood. Two men dead from machine gun fire. The plane shuddered as the co-pilot tried to pull it out of its roll. The co-pilot finally leveled off, but when he tried to climb, the vibrations increased.

"I can't climb, but I'll try to keep us up long enough to find a place to land," the co-pilot's voice came over the intercom.

Isiac could hear the strain in the co-pilot's voice. When he went to investigate, Isiac saw blood on the co-pilot's left leg. The bullet that killed the pilot must have ricocheted down and into the co-pilot's leg.

"Medic," Isiac yelled, "Up front now! Help the co-pilot!" Isiac immediately applied pressure to Lieutenant

Peer's leg and held it until Corporal Graham, the medic, arrived.

"Who else can fly this plane," Isiac asked, as Corporal Graham took over.

"I've had three lessons," Sergeant Crane, the navigator said, "But I haven't done a landing yet."

"Don't worry about that," Isiac said. "We're not landing; we're crashing. Now help me move the pilot, and you take his seat."

"How far are we from Fort Hertz," Isiac asked? "There is an emergency landing strip there."

"Over 150 miles," Sergeant Crane said.

"We'll never make it that far," Lieutenant Peer said, as Corporal Graham tried to stop the bleeding. "I'll never make it that far."

Isiac could see that Lieutenant Peer was starting to get drowsy like he might pass out any second.

"Just relax, Lieutenant," Isiac said. "Your Navigator is getting his pilot's license today. You can give him instructions as long as you can stay awake. I can see that the morphine is taking effect."

"It is, Sergeant," Lieutenant Peer spoke slowly, "Doesn't hurt so much, but my eyelids are getting heavy."

"The bullet went straight through without hitting an artery or a bone, and that's good," Corporal Graham said. "But it made a big hole, and that's bad. And the bleeding has stopped which is good."

"Good or bad, Corporal, you can't seem to make up your mind," Lieutenant Peer said in a slightly slurred speech.

"It's good, Lieutenant Peer," Corporal Graham said. "You're not going to die."

Turning slightly, without moving his injured leg, Lieutenant Peer said,

"Sergeant Crane, I've just been informed that I'm not going to die from this gunshot, so try not to kill me with your landing. You should be seeing the east branch of the Irrawaddy River any minute now. About 40 miles past that is the west branch. Turn right and follow the river north. Look for a flat shallow spot wide enough to land on. Be sure to stay in the middle, and don't put down the landing gear. You're going to make a belly landing. Just before impact, pull the nose up and cut the power completely. That should make the tail of the plane hit the ground first, so you don't somersault. If you have enough altitude when you see the east branch, you can try for the west branch. That will lead you directly to Fort Hertz. I'll try to stay awake long enough to help you decide."

But Isiac could see that the lieutenant was struggling to keep his eyes open. Less than a minute later, Sergeant Crane said, "I can see the river, sir."

189

Lieutenant Peer looked at the altimeter with heavy eyes, then said, "Try for the west branch, Sergeant. You're on your own now." And Lieutenant Peer closed his eyes and drifted off to sleep.

Isiac looked at the speedometer and calculated that they were traveling over 2 miles per minute. Returning to Lieutenant Carter, Isiac said,

"If we can stay up that long, we should make it to the river in less than 20 minutes."

The plane seemed to stress the "if" in Isiac's last statement as it shuddered again.

"You did the calculations, Sergeant?"

"Yes, Lieutenant," Isiac answered.

"Can you calculate our chances of surviving a landing in the river," Lieutenant Carter asked?

"No sir," Isiac answered.

Eighteen minutes later, Sergeant Crane's voice was heard over the intercom.

"West Branch of the river straight ahead."

"I know he didn't have a very long nap, but see if you can wake up Lieutenant Peer," Isiac told Corporal Graham.

Surprisingly, Lieutenant Peer opened his eyes.

"Have a nice nap," Isiac asked?

"How long was I asleep," Lieutenant Peer asked?

"About 20 minutes," Isiac answered.

"Pain's bearable, where are we," the co-pilot asked?

"Starting our approach to the river," Isiac said, "Think you can take over?"

"Please do." Sergeant Crane pleaded.

"I don't understand how it happened, but my concentration is better, and I think I can keep my eyes open long enough to land," Lieutenant Peer said.

"Corporal Graham gave you an IV while you were sleeping," Isiac said.

"That helped counteract some of the effects of your blood loss," Corporal Graham explained. "Plus, your body is adjusting to the morphine."

"I guess that explains it then," Lieutenant Peer said. "You better go strap in. I'll take over, Sergeant Crane."

"Thank the Lord," Sergeant Crane said.

"Good idea, Sergeant, we could sure use the power of prayer right about now," Lieutenant Peer said, as he approached the river.

Isiac could see the plane arcing toward the river below. Even with the plane threatening to shake into pieces, Lieutenant Peer was able to control the decent. And that didn't take long because they weren't very high, to begin with. The river began to appear larger as they flew closer. Then Isiac lost sight of it as Lieutenant Peer pulled the nose up and cut the power.

Everyone was thrown forward in their straps when the tail of the plane made contact with the water, and the plane slowed abruptly. They received another jolt when the belly of the aircraft began scrapping the gravel of the river bottom. The speed of the plane was rapidly decreasing, and it was still traveling in a relatively straight line. This gave hope that they just might survive this landing. After several more seconds of deceleration, however, the plane made an abrupt turn to the left and began to slide sideways. That sudden change in speed and direction shook the men like rag dolls. Then all motion stopped.

The initial silence, which only lasted a second or two, was replaced by cheers as the soldiers realized that they had survived the crash. But some groans could be heard, as well.

"Corporal Graham," Lieutenant Carter shouted, "Are you OK?"

"Yes sir," came Corporal Graham's response.

"Check the men for injuries, and give me a report," Lieutenant Carter said, in obvious pain.

Some of the soldiers just sat there for a moment while others were removing their straps.

"Sergeant Heimlich, are you OK," Isiac asked?

"I'm OK," Fritz answered.

"See if you can help me unstrap," Isiac said with a slight strain in his voice.

"I've seen you look better," Fritz said.

"Good thing I'm left-handed," Isiac said, cradling his right arm as Fritz removed his straps.

The medic stopped and checked on Isiac. It only took one look to see that Isiac had a broken arm.

"I'll be right back," Corporal Graham said as he headed back to Lieutenant Carter to give his report.

"One dead, sir," Corporal Graham said. "Private Balog broke his neck. Sergeant Kalway has a broken arm, and, as I'm sure you know, you have a broken leg. Everyone else was shaken up pretty good, lots of bruises. But they should be OK. They just won't feel OK for a while."

"Sergeant Heimlich," Isiac said, "Set up a perimeter around the plane. Then find a defendable position close to the plane to use as a temporary camp. Then get everyone off the plane. Have everyone carry as many useful items from the plane, as possible, and take them to the camp. Do it quickly. You never know when company might arrive."

"On it," Fritz said.

"One more thing," Isiac added, using a hunting term they used to locate downed ducks. "Did you mark the American fighter pilot?"

"I did," Fritz said.

"Can you find him," Isiac asked?

"Yes," Fritz answered.

"Then, when the camp is secure," Isiac said, "See if you can retrieve that pilot."

"You didn't say fetch," Fritz said with a smirk.

"Fetch," Isiac said, trying to smile through the pain, "Then meet me at Fort Hertz. I'm going to follow the river and lead the men to the Fort. With both of the Lieutenants unable to walk, you might beat us there."

To Corporal Graham, Isiac said, "You're in charge of getting the Lieutenants to the camp. And Corporal, get them ready to travel."

"What about you, Sergeant," Corporal Graham asked? "I need to take care of your arm."

"I need to check on a few things first; then I'll be along."

With the three remaining men of his team guarding the camp, Isiac returned to the plane with Sergeant Crane and Sergeant Heimlich. Strapped to the wall of the plane were a 6-man inflatable raft, a dolly, and a four-wheeled platform that looked like a cart with the sides removed. It had been used to unload the cargo they had delivered to Kunming.

To Sergeant Crane Isiac said, "See if you can get that dolly and cart back to camp." Then, looking at the inflatable, Isiac said to Fritz, "There's your ride across the river."

Before returning to camp, Isiac shouted "Good hunting" and watched until Fritz and his team crossed the river and disappeared into the woods.

Back at camp, Isiac saw that Corporal Graham had another IV in Lieutenant Peer. The Lieutenant didn't look like he was in too much pain, so he probably got another shot of morphine, as well.

"I'm going to set the Lieutenant's leg, Sergeant Kalway." Corporal Graham said. "Can you get two of your men to hold him down? It's going to hurt. And Sergeant, you're next."

"I'll be right back," Isiac said.

But he didn't come right back. When Isiac found Private Lang and Private Linder, he sent them back to help Corporal Graham set Lieutenant Carter's leg. Then, with his good arm, Isiac pulled out his .45 and remained to help Corporal Woods guard the camp.

It didn't take long for Corporal Graham to set Lieutenant Carter's leg.

"It's a clean break." Corporal Graham told Lieutenant Carter. "It should heal nicely."

Lieutenant Carter had to remove the piece of wood from his mouth before he could answer.

"Thanks, Corporal," he said.

"We have to return to guard duty, Corporal Graham," Private Lang said.

"When you get there, send the Sergeant back," Corporal Graham said. "And tell him it's his turn."

When Isiac returned, Corporal Graham was putting a splint on Lieutenant Carter's leg. Isiac heard the corporal tell Lieutenant Carter,

"You're a lucky man Lieutenant. In training, I specialized in setting broken bones. And I can make a splint as good as any cast. And it won't itch as much. And if it does itch, you'll be able to scratch it easily."

When Corporal Graham was finished with the Lieutenant, he started to work on Sergeant Kalway.

"This goes in your mouth, so you don't bite your tongue off," the medic said to Isiac as he handed him a piece of wood. "Your arm is fractured, but I don't think it's a massive fracture because your arm isn't swollen very much. I should be able to line up the edges of the fracture easy enough and pull them together. Easy enough for me I mean. Not so easy for you, though. It's going to hurt more than enough to get your attention. I can tell you that because I'll have to palpate your arm to make sure that the bones are lined up properly."

And the Corporal was right. As the Corporal had Isiac's arm splinted and was about to give Isiac a shot of morphine, Isiac said, "Not so fast, I can't afford to go to sleep just now. I have too many things to do."

"How about just enough to take the edge off," Corporal Graham asked?

"That will work," Isiac said.

Isiac had no choice. He had to call his men in from guard duty. In case there were any Japanese in the area that had seen their plane crash, Isiac had to buy some time. He told his men to make a clear trail in the opposite direction of Fort Hertz.

"When you are about 100 yards from the plane, move straight away from the river," Isiac said. "Use your knives to clear a trail that the Japanese can easily find. It doesn't have to be very long. Head for the nearest open area. That will make them search for the trail. It won't fool them very long, but it will buy us some time. Then return to the river and walk in the water until you return to the plane. You need to do this in less than an hour, so get started."

Watching Privates Lang and Linder follow Corporal Woods down the shoreline, Isiac reached into his pocket. He could feel the dog tags that he had removed from the three dead soldiers on his last trip to the plane. Isiac did not have time to dwell on that. He walked away from the river until he was above the high-water mark. He needed to find a place to bury their dead, and if he wanted to avoid burying any more of his men, he needed to do it in a hurry. He was looking for a place that was close to the plane with ground soft enough to dig. This was a rocky area, so that presented a problem. The only ground soft enough to dig was along the river. Any graves dug there would be flooded every spring.

Realizing that his current line of thinking wouldn't provide a solution, Isiac changed his line of thought. He was no longer looking for soft ground. Isiac remembered that some American Indians buried their dead under rock cairns. With soft-ground no longer a necessity, Isiac moved toward the rocky cliffs. There, he found a spot where two large boulders leaned against the rocky cliff side forming a narrow chute that was too steep to climb. Isiac then hurried back to camp.

"Sergeant Crane, Corporal Graham, take the dolly back to the plane," Isiac said. "You're on burial detail."

Isiac showed them where to take the bodies. They could only fit one body on the dolly, so they had to make three trips. While Sergeant Crane was returning to the plane for the last body, Isiac showed Corporal Graham how to put a slip knot around the bodies and then attach another rope that would, when pulled, release the slip knot and return both ropes to be used again. By the time Sergeant Crane returned with the last body, one of the bodies had already been lowered into the chute. When all three bodies were at the bottom of the chute, Isiac had the men use sand and the little bit of soil found nearby to completely cover the bodies. Then they threw small rocks on top of the sand, and larger rocks on top of the smaller rocks. This took longer than Isiac wanted, but he didn't want to mangle the bodies by simply throwing them into the hole and then bombing them with large rocks.

By the time they were done, Lang, Linder, and Woods were back from making the false trail. After

Corporal Graham had finished a short prayer, Isiac addressed the men,

"Remember this spot. Then, whoever survives this war, can relocate these men so they can be returned home to be buried with honor."

A little over 3 hours of daylight remained, and Isiac didn't want to waste any of it. By the time Isiac and the men got back to camp, Isiac already had a plan.

"Time to leave," Isiac said. "We need to be farther from the plane before we camp for the night. Corporal Woods, find a high spot on that cliff so you can see if any unwanted visitors are coming. Wait until dark and then follow us up the river, walking in the water for 20 minutes, so you don't leave any tracks. After that, take the easiest route possible. We will have someone waiting for you by the river to lead you to the new camp."

"Private Lang and Linder, find a piece of wood and attach it to the handle of the cart, so there is enough room for three people to push. Sergeant Crane and Corporal Graham, load the gear onto the cart and tie it down securely. Don't forget to leave room for the lieutenants. Try to arrange the gear so that the lieutenants have something to lean against so they can sit up. And use some rope to make hand-holds, so they have something to hold on to. Get a move on. I want to be out of here in 10 minutes."

They were ready to leave in 12 minutes, and Isiac was pleased with that. The men were busting Butt. Isiac gave final instructions.

"Corporal Graham, you follow the cart and use your boots to erase any wheel marks that can be seen. And keep an eye on the lieutenants. Everybody else push the cart. Try to use the river to hide the cart tracks as much as possible. But after 20 minutes, leave the river and take the easiest route you can find. If any Japanese are following, they will find our tracks eventually anyway. We are just trying to slow them down. And remember to look behind you once in a while. I'm going to scout ahead for a place to spend the night."

"See you at our new camp," was the last thing Isiac said as he hurried up the river.

It was almost dark when Isiac found a place to spend the night. A group of large rocks formed a ring, of sorts, that had only two ways in or out. And the rocks, although high enough to provide a place to hide, were low enough to look or shoot over if need be. It was close enough to the river to be reached easily, but far enough away so that it couldn't be seen from the river. Isiac knew it would be safer farther from the river, but that would make tomorrow's trip that much longer. Besides, Isiac didn't plan for his men to still be in the camp when morning came.

When Isiac returned to the river, it was dark. The moon hadn't risen yet, so the stars provided the only light. To make it easier to find his way back to the rock shelter, Isiac used his boot to make a mark on the trail that followed the river. Backtracking down the river, Isiac found his men and led them to the new camp. He then returned to the river to wait for Corporal Woods.

Using his flashlight and looking at his hand-drawn map, Isiac estimated that they were 60 to 80 miles from Fort Hertz, as the crow flies. But they were not crows. Depending on the terrain between here and the fort, actual travel distance could be double that. Traveling would be slow with the two injured lieutenants, maybe only one mile per hour. With only about 10 hours of daylight at this time of year, they might only be able to travel 10 miles a day. They could go for several hours during the night, but traveling at night would be even slower than traveling during the day. With all these estimates and guesses, Isiac figured they could be anywhere between 6 and 12 days from Fort Hertz.

Seeing Corporal Woods moving along the river, Isiac moved to a spot where he could easily be seen and gave a whistle. All of Isiac's men could recognize Isiac's whistle. When Corporal Wood's hand signal indicated that he had spotted his Sergeant, Isiac stepped back into the shadows and waited for Corporal Woods' arrival.

"No Japs spotted," Corporal Woods reported as soon as he reached Isiac.

"Good," Isiac said, "That should give us at least a 2-hour lead if they find the plane tonight." Then leading Corporal Woods back to their rock shelter, Isiac said, "Get some sleep. We'll be making an early start tomorrow."

January 20, 1943

Sergeant Heimlich had his men up and moving at 4 AM. Although they traveled for 2 hours after dark yesterday, their late start only allowed them to cover 12 miles. They needed to do better today. And they did. When they stopped 2 hours after dark, Fritz spoke to his men.

"We covered another 25 miles today. That's twice as much as yesterday, and I'm pleased with our progress, but we're going to see if we can improve on that tomorrow. We're not on a pleasure hike enjoying the scenery in some National Park, we're on a mission. We don't know what the pilot's situation is. We need to find him as soon as possible. Tomorrow we travel from midnight to 8PM. You'll have to survive on 4 hours of sleep. Pleasant dreams."

Without complaint, the men settled down to sleep.

Even before the sky began to lighten, Isiac started to get the men ready to move.

"Make sure you have easy access to some food and water; we eat as we walk," Isiac said. "Corporal Woods," Isiac called.

"Yes Sergeant," Corporal Woods responded.

"Travel with us until we can find a good spot for you to watch our back trail," Isiac continued. "Watch for 4 hours. Then follow our tracks until you catch up. We won't be trying to hide our tracks today. You'll be able to travel a lot faster than us. You should be able to catch us about 2 hours after you leave your observation point. If you spot any Japanese, don't wait. Head back immediately."

"Yes, Sergeant Kalway," Corporal Woods said.

After about an hour and a half of travel time, they reached a point where the west side of the valley began to pinch in toward the river. Just north of the narrowest part of the valley, a small tributary entered the main river. Both the Irrawaddy and its tributary had to flow around a small tree-covered hill before they could join downstream of the hill. On the other side of the hill, the valley began to widen again. A high spot at a choke point in the valley. Perfect. When Isiac looked at Corporal Woods, he could see that Corporal Woods had seen the spot, as well, and was already moving in that direction. A nod from Isiac indicated that he agreed with Corporal Woods' choice.

It was almost 11 AM when Isiac saw Corporal Woods returning from his observation post. He was earlier than expected and moving quickly. Isiac knew that meant that Corporal Woods' report would not be a good one.

"The Japs are following our trail," Corporal Woods said, even before he reached Isiac. "I was able to stay long enough to see their entire patrol, and it's a big one. I counted twice, 31 Japs. They only had one scout about 20 yards in front and no rear guard. They seemed pretty confident, not very cautious. And they were moving pretty fast."

"They're hunting us," Isiac said, "And they think we'll be easy prey. Well, they're making a big mistake. I've been a hunter my entire life, and I don't intent to be anybody's prey."

Everyone was listening as Corporal Woods gave his report. They also heard Sergeant Kalway's reply and continued to listen as Isiac spoke to Lieutenant Carter.

"Permission to become the hunter, sir?"

"Permission granted, Sergeant Kalway," Lieutenant Carter answered. "Sergeant Kalway is now in command. Everyone will follow his orders. There's no way two crippled lieutenants are going to get in his way."

"Sergeant Crane and Corporal Graham, continue to move the Lieutenants up the river for at least an hour.

Then find a defendable position," Sergeant Kalway said. "Then keep watch for our return so you can lead us to your position. We'll probably be moving pretty fast. Privates Lang and Linder, get the dolly and load it with rocks, so the wheel marks are clearly visible. Then load the cooking utensils and any other non-essential gear on the dolly and follow Corporal Woods and me."

Isiac and Corporal Woods walked in the soft ground along the river. When Isiac turned around, he could see that Privates Lang and Linder had wasted no time. They were already following with the dolly.

"Do you think the Japanese are good enough to follow our trail," Isiac asked Corporal Woods?

"I'm sure they are, but something tells me that they would be better off if they couldn't," Corporal Woods answered.

"Smart man, Corporal," Isiac said. "The hunters have now become the hunted."

Isiac found a shallow spot in the river and waited for Lang and Linder to bring the dolly. When the dolly arrived, Isiac told the men to unload the rocks and use them to prop it up on its side so that part of the dolly was visible above the water.

"Now scatter the gear, so it looks like the dolly tipped over," Isiac said. "But leave some of the gear on the dolly so it will be easy for the Japanese to help themselves to our abandoned equipment."

Turning toward Corporal Woods, Isiac handed him some fishing line.

"Tie the fishing line to part of the dolly that is underwater. Then give me the other end," Isiac said. "Time to get out of the water, Corporal."

After the men had moved away, Isiac tied the other end of the fishing line to a softball-sized rock. The rock that the dolly was leaning against had a u-shaped grove that extended from the top of the rock into the water. Isiac ran the fishing line under water to the groove on the stone, pulling it tight. He then pulled the pin on one of his grenades and carefully placed it in the groove of the rock so that it was just above the surface of the water. He then placed the rock, with the string attached, on top of the grenade to hold the handle in place and to make the grenade invisible. Isiac then returned to shore, joined his team, and explained:

"If someone moves the dolly or kicks the fishing line, the rock will be pulled off the grenade...BOOM. We will be hiding just inside the tree line. Our targets will be anyone foolish enough to be out in the open when the grenade explodes. Keep firing as long as you have good targets. If they don't examine the dolly and there is no explosion, my shot will be the signal to start shooting. If the Japanese move toward your position as a group, retreat immediately and return to Lieutenant

Carter's position. And don't wait for me. I'll still be out hunting. Don't expect me back before dark."

When Isiac spotted the approaching Japanese, Corporal Woods' description proved to be accurate: only one scout 20 yards ahead and no attempt at concealment. It was going to be like hunting early season redheads that have never been shot at before. Take advantage of the situation while you can because, like redheads, Isiac expected the Japanese to wise up quickly. But, unlike redheads, the Japanese could shoot back.

The Japanese scout spotted the dolly, and shortly after that, found where the tracks of the dolly and four men entered the river. The scout returned to the main body of Japanese, and Isiac could see him explaining what he had found to another soldier, probably an officer or a sergeant. Isiac now had his first target marked.

As the scout returned to his position at the front of the column, two men from the main group moved up the river bank until they reached the spot where the dolly had entered the river. The two Japanese soldiers then entered the river and moved toward the dolly. While Isiac waited for the soldiers to reach the dolly, he began searching for his second target. He found it when he saw a soldier leading five men toward a small stand of trees that was close to the Japanese position on the beach.

Isiac was behind a large rock surrounded by thick bushes. He was only 30 yards from the trees that appeared to be the destination of the small group of Japanese moving away from the beach. Isiac had already cleared three shooting lanes through the bushes by removing three 6-inch circles of branches and leaves. One shooting lane lined up with his first target, and another lined up with the men approaching the trees. The third shooting lane lined up with the main group of Japanese on the beach. Isiac could hold the forearm of his rifle with his splinted arm, but he didn't want any pain from his splinted arm to distract his shooting, so he rolled up his jacket and placed it under his rifle barrel, just like shooting from a sandbag.

As soon as Isiac saw one of the soldiers getting close to the dolly, he sighted in on his first target, waiting for the boom. The explosion of the grenade was immediately followed by the POP of 4 rifles. With his first target down, Isiac moved to his second target and found him just before he reached the trees. POP, the second target was down. The 4 Japanese that were following Isiac's second target were in the trees before he could fire another shot. Half of the remaining soldiers charged the position of Isiac's men, and the other half hit the ground along the river bank, trying to find any cover they could among the rocks.

Isiac sighted in on a soldier who was trying to hide behind a rock that was too small to conceal him, POP, third target down. Glancing quickly at the Japanese that were charging his men, Isiac found the soldier at the rear of the charge, usually the safest place to be, in his sights. But not today. POP, target number 4 was down.

When the charging Japanese reached the position of Isiac's three men, his men were gone. After taking one shot each at the charging Japanese, they had disappeared, as ordered. By the time the remaining Japanese had zeroed in on Isiac's position and began to return fire, Isiac, like his men, had already disappeared into the trees.

Again, like his men, Isiac moved directly away from the river. But, unlike his men, after about 50 yards, instead of turning right and moving back up river toward Lieutenant Carter's position, Isiac turned left and moved toward the enemy's rear. As Isiac was moving quietly toward the enemy's rear, he heard a single shot. He guessed that one of his men was trying to discourage the Japanese from pursuing them up the river. And Isiac would later find out that his guess was correct. Corporal Woods shot the leader of the charging Japanese, and that halted the Japanese up-river advance.

After flanking the Japanese, Isiac approached from the rear. He found a group of 6 Japanese in a thick stand of trees with a hill to their backs. The Japanese had plenty of cover and probably believed they had chosen a good defensive position. But Isiac would have never chosen such a spot. An advancing enemy would have just as much cover as the defenders. And the Japanese had no clear sight lines in any direction. And Isiac wasn't going to advance; he was going to snipe.

Isiac remembered his back-up plans for back-up plans that he developed during his bootlegging days. Before settling into a shooting position, Isiac located a position that he could retreat to if the Japanese pursued him after he took his shot. Isiac didn't think the Japanese would pursue him in this thick cover, but he certainly didn't want to be DEAD wrong. Besides, Isiac couldn't snipe moving targets in heavy cover; so, any sign of Japanese pursuit was Isiac's signal for immediate retreat. Even if the Japanese didn't pursue, Isiac planned to move. But then his move would be a lateral one, instead of a retreat, so he could set up another shooting position.

Isiac wanted to get in close, but he continued to turn around, not checking to see if any Japanese were behind him; but making sure that his line of retreat could not be seen from the enemy camp. Sixty yards from the camp, Isiac found a good sight line. There was some movement in the camp, so Isiac waited to see if anyone would enter his sight line. After almost twenty minutes of waiting, Isiac decided he needed to find a target first and then search for a sight line. He had to move a little closer to do that, and he didn't want to get too much closer.

Finally, Isiac found a target, but couldn't find a sight line. He tried another target, the same result. Isiac knew that the 3rd target was the one. He had a clear sight line on a soldier's head and chest. His line of retreat, however, wasn't perfect, so Isiac moved so that his target was right on the edge of his sight line. Now he could still make the shot, and his line of retreat was secure.

Return gunfire followed Isaac's shot, but he was already behind two large trees. As he moved away, Isiac was careful to keep those trees between him and the Japanese soldiers. Fifth target eliminated. After moving more than 100 yards from his last position, Isiac found a slight depression in the forest floor and stopped. Listening for sounds of pursuit, Isiac heard none. He then used that depression to begin his lateral movement. The depression, which was about three feet lower than the surrounding area, allowed Isiac to move rapidly and still stay out of sight. Isiac then moved another 60 yards and stopped. Still no sounds of pursuit.

Following the same procedure as last time, Isiac first located a position to retreat to, if pursued. And Isiac felt that he would be pursued this time. The Japanese couldn't allow him to keep picking them off one man at a time.

He had a good retreat position this time. It was located on the crest of a small hill that was about 12 feet higher than the forest floor. Not only could Isiac use this hill as a retreat position, but he could also use it as a shooting position if he was pursued. And it would be easy for Isiac to disappear into the trees behind the hill.

When Isiac returned to his shooting position, he could only locate 3 Japanese. The other two were either well-hidden, or they were out looking for him. Before taking his shot, Isiac waited to see if he could locate the missing Japanese. Everything was quiet for over 10 minutes. Then, birds startled into flight on Isiac's right, helped Isiac locate one man who was between him and his last shooting position. Isiac guessed that the other missing soldier had been sent to the other side of his previous shooting position. Isiac hoped so because that would remove him as an immediate threat.

Now Isiac had a decision to make; go after the soldier that was hunting him, retreat, or take his shot and retreat with one or two Japanese soldiers pursuing him. Isiac was sure that he could find the soldier on his right that was hunting him, but he couldn't be sure that he would be able to find a clear shot, and he would lose his line of retreat. Isiac chose to take the clear shot at their camp and retreat option, even though he knew that he would be located and pursued. Actually, Isiac hoped that would be the case.

Isiac's line of escape would lead him away from both the Japanese camp and from the soldier on his right who was hunting him. The trees, brush, and undergrowth, between Isiac and the soldier on his right, were extremely thick, almost impenetrable. Isiac's line of retreat, on the other hand, was clear enough that he could run to his retreat position, and find another shooting position. That might give Isiac the possibility of further reducing the number of Japanese that were pursuing him and his unit.

Once his decision was made, Isiac returned his attention to the sight line to the camp that he had previously established. The soldiers that remained in the camp were now extremely cautious and well hidden. The only shot available was a quartering shot to a spot just below his target's right knee. Isiac might not have a better shot if he waited for the rest of the day, and there wasn't much day left. A sound to his right also made it clear that time was running out.

Isiac, knowing that his target would most certainly move when he felt the impact of the bullet in his leg, planned to be ready to take a second shot if any part of his target remained in his sight line. Three seconds was all he was allowing himself to reacquire his target and fire a second shot. Besides, a second shot wasn't an absolute necessity because a man wounded in the leg would no longer be able to participate if the Japanese continued their pursuit. Continuing to plan ahead, Isiac decided to wait for several seconds after he made his shot so he could listen for any movement from the Japanese soldier on his right. A moving soldier was not a sighting soldier.

After Isiac's first shot, the wounded soldier rolled to his left, and Isiac's second shot caught him in his left side, just beneath his armpit. Isiac didn't have to wait; he immediately heard movement on his right. That was his signal to move quickly to his next ambush position. And he did. Watching from the side of the hill, Isiac wondered if the Japanese hunter would continue his pursuit or return to the two soldiers that remained at the base of the hill. Because returning to join his fellow soldiers would just make him another target, Isiac guessed that the Japanese hunter would continue his hunt.

Because the cover surrounding Isiac's ambush point was sparse, target acquisition would most likely be by sight, not sound. But Isiac listened anyway as he watched and waited. Over 20 minutes had passed before Isiac saw movement. As hoped, the Japanese soldier was following the trail Isiac had left. Isiac had purposely turned toward the hill 30 yards before he reached his shooting position. This put the trail through the only area that had plenty of cover between it and the hill ahead. Hopefully, this would suggest a safe approach. But Isiac wasn't ahead. He was off to the side, and, from his angle, Isiac had a clear sight line along the trail. The fact that his pursuer was moving cautiously and slowly, only made Isiac's shot through his left side that much easier.

After his shot, Isiac quickly moved away from the river. When he reached another hill with a good view in all directions, Isiac stopped to rest and to reassess the situation. Unless they had reestablished contact with each other, there were now three separate groups of Japanese soldiers:3 in the woods that he had just left, 4 in the group that headed for the trees after the initial attack plus those who took cover on the beach, and an unknown number in the group that had charged his men.

Their surprise attack had seriously damaged the Japanese patrol. Isiac tried to calculate how many of the Japanese were left to pursue him and his men. Isiac had killed two men on the beach, one man from the group trying to reach the safety of the trees, and one man from the group that had charged his men. Then he killed three men from the group he had just left. That was 7. The grenade killed two more. That was 9.

His men had killed at least three men in the initial Attack, and at least 2 of the charging Japanese before they retreated. That was at least five more dead and maybe more. That made a total of at least 14 dead. That left the Japanese with, at most, 17 men. But with these Japanese soldiers between him and the rest of his men, Isiac needed to head back to rejoin his unit, and maybe do a little more hunting on the way.

Now that the adrenaline in his system was decreasing, Isiac was aware of the pain in his arm. But it was bearable.

Isiac moved north for over 3 miles before he returned to the river. He wanted to make sure that he moved past Lieutenant Carter's position. That way Isiac could approach his men from the up-river direction, which was the opposite direction from which he expected the Japanese to approach. Isiac knew that Lieutenant Carter could only move a mile or a little more in the hour he had given them to find a good defensive position. That meant that since the battle began, Isiac was always close enough to hear any shots fired from Lieutenant Carter's new position. And he hadn't. That meant that neither Woods, Linder, and Lang, nor Lieutenant Carter had been engaged. Hopefully, Woods, Linder, and Lang had rejoined Lieutenant Carter, and all were safe.

Shortly before sunset, sooner than expected, Isiac found the new camp. And as hoped, all his men were safe.

January 21, 1943

Isiac's men got 5 hours of sleep before Isiac woke them up shortly after midnight. The Japanese were too close to delay their departure any longer. They set out with Corporal Woods in the lead and Lang as rear guard. Isiac and Private Linder remained at the camp to delay the Japanese when they arrived. They waited until 10 AM. No Japanese. With his men now at least 10 miles ahead of the Japanese, Isiac and Private Linder hurried to catch up. And it was a good thing they hurried because his men traveled farther than expected. They covered over 15 miles that day, and Isiac and Private Linder didn't catch up until after 5 PM.

January 22, 1943

With the same plan as yesterday, Isiac got the men up and moving by 3 AM, but he and Private Linder only waited until sunrise to see if they were being followed. They traveled another 12 miles that day. Still no Japanese.

January 23, 1943

Plans changed today. Something didn't feel right.

Isiac and Private Linder left at 2 AM and backtracked to look for the Japanese. They needed to find out if the Japanese were still following them, and if so, why they hadn't caught up by now. After the beating they gave the Japanese, Isiac found it hard to believe that the Japanese would just give up the chase. Before leaving, Isiac gave orders to the rest of the group. Leave for Fort Hertz at 4 AM.

At 6 AM, Isiac and Private Linder found their first sign of the Japanese. The Japanese were no longer following them. They didn't need to. The Japanese knew exactly where they were going, to Fort Hertz.

"The Japanese are trying to flank us," Isiac said. "They will try to set up an ambush of their own. We need to reach our men before they walk into a Japanese trap. We need to hustle, Private Linder, let's go."

Reversing direction, Isiac and Private Linder started jogging back up the river. Isiac could feel the pain in his arm with every step.

Just before 1 PM, they caught up with Private Lang who was at the rear-guard position. Out of breath, Isiac said,

"Private Lang, run to the main group and tell them to stop and wait for us. And tell them to be alert. Then leave all your gear except your rifle, and run to Corporal Woods and bring him back. The Japanese have flanked us and are now in front of us, probably setting up an ambush of their own."

By the time Private Lang and Corporal Woods returned, Isiac had already explained the new situation to the men.

"Corporal Woods, are there any good ambush spots ahead," Isiac asked?

"A cliff runs close to the river less than half a mile from here," Corporal Woods said.

"Show me," Isiac said. And then turning to the rest of the group, "Catch up to us, on the double."

In less than 5 minutes, Corporal Woods and Isiac arrived at the cliff.

"We are going to set up our own ambush here and wait," Isiac said. "When we don't walk into their trap, they'll have to come back and look for us."

The cliff was about 80 yards from the river. Between the cliff and the river was a small, rocky channel that ran parallel to the river. The channel was lined on both sides by thick trees and brush. The channel was dry now but obviously filled up every year during the rainy season. There was a ledge that ran across the cliff that was about 30 feet wide and equally as long. Directly beneath the ledge were large sections of rock that had fallen from the cliff side to form the ledge. The rest of the ground between the ledge and the small dry river channel was rocky but free of vegetation. Two large boulders that appeared to be the ancient remains of another smaller cliff, laid along the small channel almost directly in front of the ledge.

After Isiac surveyed the landscape and with his plan forming, he asked Corporal Woods, "Can you get to the top of the cliff?"

"Yes," Corporal Woods answered.

"Good," Isiac said. "That will be your position for the ambush. Right now, go up river and find a good observation point, so the Japanese don't surprise us before we set up our ambush."

When the others arrived, Isiac explained his plan to Lieutenant Carter and began to set his plan into motion.

"We are going to pull the cart between the gap in those two boulders and drag it up to that shelf," Isiac said, pointing toward the shelf. "Drop off Lieutenant Carter and Lieutenant Peer, with all our gear, behind the boulders at the base of the cliff. Corporal Graham, your position will be with the cart on the ledge. You are my decoy. I want you to make sure that the Japanese see you. Act like a Jack-in-the-box, so it appears that more than one man is with the cart. But corporal, don't get shot."

"I wouldn't think of it, Sergeant," Corporal Graham said.

Handing his last grenade to Sergeant Crane, Isiac continued,

"Sergeant Crane, find a place for the Lieutenants to hide behind the rocks, and then, in front of the rocks, find a place to conceal your three grenades. Try to place them 10 to 15 feet apart. None of the grenades can be more than 30 feet from the lieutenants. And Sergeant, don't pull the pins. I'll be back in a few minutes."

Isiac then moved from the boulders that were at the base of the ledge, to the boulders that were along the small dry channel about 30 yards from the cliff. From there, Isiac could easily see the back end of the cart that wasn't, by design, completely concealed.

"Give me your rifle and grenades," Isiac told Private Linder when he found the place he wanted. "This is your hidey-hole. Climb in and make sure you're in a comfortable position because you might be there for a long time."

Linder climbed down into a cavity in the rocks. "I could go to sleep in here," he said.

"Do you snore, Private," Isiac asked?

"I don't know, Sergeant, why," Linder asked.

Isiac made it simple, "If the Japanese hear you snoring, you're a dead man."

Private Linder's response was also simple,

"Understood, Sergeant."

Isiac gave Private Linder the end of some fishing line with instructions,

"Attach this securely to something that you won't bump by accident. But make sure that you can pull on it if the need arises; that would be if you're discovered by the Japanese, or if I give the order, PULL. Private Lang and I will be on the other side of these rocks. And, Private Linder, there will be two grenades with the pins pulled on the other end of your fishing line. Be careful not to touch this line, but when you do, give it a hard tug."

"Understood, Sergeant," Private Linder said again.

Isiac took his end of the fishing line and ran it up the trunk of a tree.

"Time to climb," Isiac told Private Lang after he handed him the end of the fishing line and Private Linder's two grenades. "Stand on that lowest branch and tie your fishing line to the end of that small branch above you. Then find two places, about 10 feet apart, where you can safely balance your grenades."

"Done, Sergeant," Lang said.

"Now see if you can shake the branch lightly without the grenades falling," Isiac instructed.

When Private Lang shook the branch slightly, one of the grenades fell, and the other one remained balanced on the branch.

"Come down and find another spot for this one," Isiac said, as he handed the grenade back to Private Lang along with a roll of black electrical tape. "But it still needs to be on the same branch."

Private Lang climbed back up and repositioned the second grenade. This time, after a light shake, both grenades remained in place.

"Now run a piece of electrical tape over the top of each grenade," Isiac said, "So that about half an inch of tape makes contact with the branch on each side of the grenade. This will add a little stability. But, electrical tape isn't very sticky, so it shouldn't keep the grenades from falling when Private Linder pulls on the branch."

While Lang was taping the grenades, Isiac took the end of the fishing line that was attached to the tree branch and tied it to the loop that he had previously tied at the end of Private Linder's line.

"Get out of the tree, Private Lang," Isiac said.

After Lang had moved away from the tree, Isiac spoke to Private Linder,

"Grenades are not live, Private Linder. Time for a test. PULL."

Both grenades fell from the tree.

"You can relax for a little while now, Private Linder," Isiac said. "Test worked perfectly, and no Japanese in sight."

Speaking to Private Lang, Isiac said,

"Now it's time to see how well you've learned your new lessons. It's time to place the grenades in the tree with the pins pulled. No second chance on this part. Maybe you should use a little extra tape on the end of each grenade, but only a little. Use your judgment."

"Thanks, Sergeant Kalway, but if I used my judgment, I wouldn't be in this tree with live grenades."

"You're right, Private Lang," Isiac said. "And it would probably be best to wait until you are out of the tree before expressing gratitude."

When Lang was safely out of the tree, Isiac again spoke to Private Linder,

"Private Linder, you are now live. If you pull your string, you will hear a big BOOM."

"OK, Sergeant," Linder said.

"Time to take a walk," Isiac said to Private Lang. Go get Corporal Woods' 2 grenades and bring them back."

"I'd be happy to, Sergeant. Anything that keeps me out of that tree is a blessing," Lang said.

"I thought you'd be pleased to be given another assignment," Isiac said. "And tell Corporal Woods to wait 15 minutes, and then return and take a position on top of the cliff. His orders are to shoot at any target that presents itself. When you get back, find a place in that bush for Corporal Woods' 2 grenades."

Looking at the bush that Isiac indicated, Private Lang said,

"At least I don't have to climb the bush, that's a little better, but not much." Private Lang then started off to find Corporal Woods.

While Lang was gone, Isiac checked on the position and condition of the Lieutenants and their grenades.

"Can you maintain your current position for hours, if need be," Isiac asked?

Isiac got an affirmative answer from both lieutenants. Isiac then moved some rocks and brush to better conceal the lieutenants. Each lieutenant was given a length of fishing line. Then they were given the same speech that he had given Private Linder. With the other end of Lieutenant Peer's fishing line, Isiac returned to the grenade nearest to Lieutenant Peer. Isiac tied the fishing line to a small rock and placed the grenade on top of the small rock. Then a larger rock was placed on top of the grenade. The large rock would be used to hold the handle of the grenade in place when the pin was pulled.

"Lieutenant Peer, PULL," Isiac said.

When Lieutenant Peer pulled his line, his grenade rolled down the crevice it was placed in.

"Lieutenant Peer," Isiac said, "The next time you pull your string you are going to hear a big BOOM."

Isiac then proceeded to reposition the grenade and the two rocks, only this time Lieutenant Peer's grenade had its pin pulled. Isiac then tied a loop at the end of

Lieutenant Carter's fishing line. With a piece of line running to the two remaining grenades, Isiac tied each line to the loop in Lieutenant Carter's line. Adjusting the last two grenades and the rocks used to sandwich them, Isiac was ready to conduct Lieutenant Carter's test. To make sure that no mistakes were made, Isiac walked back to Lieutenant Peer.

"I'm going to test Lieutenant Carter's line now," Isiac said, "I'd like you to put your hands in your pockets, sir. If you pull your line when I yell PULL for Lieutenant Carter, I'm a dead man."

"Understood, Sergeant Kalway," Lieutenant Peer said, and Isiac smiled when the Lieutenant actually did put his hands in his pockets.

Lieutenant Carter's test also worked perfectly, and Isiac replaced the grenades in their proper position with the pins pulled. This part of the trap was now armed.

"Lieutenant Carter, sir, can I have your two grenades," Isiac asked?

"They are all yours, Sergeant," Lieutenant Carter said, "I can't throw them from in here anyway."

Walking over to Sergeant Crane, Isiac gave him one of Lieutenant Carter's grenades, and said,

"Take this and find a place to hide along the cliff face. I'm sure the Japanese will approach the ledge along the cliff face from both directions."

"I saved one for you, Corporal," Isiac said, "Come down and get it. If you have to throw this grenade, make sure that you don't throw it anywhere near the Lieutenants."

Isiac didn't wait for Corporal Graham to climb down, he just placed the grenade on the ground where the corporal could see it. He was in a hurry. He needed to find a place for himself and Private Lang to hide. As Isiac walked past Private Linder, he asked,

"Are you OK in there, Private Linder?"

"I'm OK, Sergeant," Linder answered.

Isiac moved to the brushy area on the other side of the little dry channel that was directly behind Private Linder's position, and he began to search for a hiding place. He found it in a cavity that water had created under a boulder on the down river side of the dry river channel. Their position would be perfectly concealed from the expected down river advance of the Japanese. Isiac moved some rocks and brush to further conceal their position. By the time Isiac had created a shooting position on each side of their hide, he saw Lang returning with Corporal Woods' grenades. And Lang was running.

"Sergeant," Private Lang said as he stopped in front of Isiac, almost out of breath, "Corporal Woods didn't wait 15 minutes before leaving his observation post. He started running about 5 minutes after I left. He must have spotted the Japanese."

"I believe you're right," Isiac said. "And that doesn't give us much time. Let's get those last two grenades placed."

Isiac reached out, and Private Lang gave him one of Corporal Words' grenades.

"No test for these 2," Isiac said, "We need to do it right the first time."

When Isiac and Private Lang were finished, Private Linder had two separate lines with two grenades attached to the end of each line, all with their pins pulled. Just in time, too, because Corporal Woods had just come into view. Corporal Woods raised his hand three times, showing all five fingers…. 15 Japanese. Then he tapped the watch on his wrist and repeated the gesture…. 15 minutes away.

"Did you give Corporal Woods his orders," Isiac asked?

"Yes Sergeant," Private Lang answered. "Shoot any targets that become available. And I told him twice."

"Good work, Private Lang," Isiac said. Then he gave Private Linder his final orders.

"Private Linder, no matter what happens, do not come out of your hidey-hole unless I call you. Even if you hear the other grenades go off or shots being fired, do not pull your lines unless I yell PULL. We are going to try to capture some of these Japanese."

"Understood Sergeant Kalway," Private Linder said.

Speaking to Private Lang, Isiac said, "Now it's time for us to get into our blind."

"Just like hunting ducks, right Sergeant," Private Lang Joked.

"Not exactly," Isiac said. "These ducks can shoot back."

"If we capture some Japanese," Private Lang continued to joke, "This could be a joint lesson. How to hunt ducks and how to trap ducks."

"Let's hope so," Isiac said, sincerely, as he continued to prepare for contingencies. "If the Japanese enter our trap, we give them only one chance to surrender. If only one or two Japanese turn around still holding their rifles, you shoot the one on the right; and I'll shoot the one on the left. If that doesn't convince them to surrender, duck back behind our rock because I'm going to yell PULL."

"Crystal clear, Sergeant," Private Lang said indicating that he understood the plan.

Everyone had their orders, now came the waiting. And they didn't have to wait long. In less than 20 minutes, a single Japanese soldier carefully approached the two large boulders that were directly in front of Isiac and Private Lang. The Japanese scout noticed, as hoped, the cart tracks that lead from the two large boulders to the ledge in the cliff face. Also, as hoped, the scout was using the two large boulders, as what he thought would be a safe vantage point, to surveil the ledge and the surrounding area. Although the Japanese were now much more cautious, they still didn't realize that appearances were often misleading.

The Japanese scout quickly spotted the cart that was only partially concealed on the ledge. Then movement caught his eye. Corporal Graham was playing Jack-in-the-box. The Japanese scout waited and watched for another 10 minutes before he left to deliver his report.

The same soldier returned a few minutes later with five more soldiers. It was clear that a Japanese sergeant was in charge. Isiac listened as the sergeant made plans and gave orders.

"There are at least 2 or 3 men with the cart on that ledge," the Japanese Sergeant said. (Corporal Graham was a good Jack-in-the-box). "They think they are safe on that ledge, but this time they made a mistake. They trapped themselves on that ledge. There is no way they can climb the cliff face, and we're going to put some men in those boulders at the base of the cliff, so they won't be able to climb down either. Then we wait until dark, move to the ledge, and no more Americans."

The Japanese Sergeant then sent one man in each direction down the dry river channel with orders to approach the ledge along the base of the cliff. He sent a third man back to his main group to move six men into the boulders at the base of the cliff and to send the rest of his men to his position.

There were now seven soldiers behind the large boulders along the dry river channel. Two more men, one on each side of the cliff face, moved toward the ledge from opposite directions. The other six soldiers were carefully approaching the rocks at the base of the ledge. When they were a little over half way to the ledge, a shot rang out. One of them wasn't careful enough, and Corporal Woods made his shot. The remaining five men ran to the safety of the rocks as fast as they could.

Like any good soldier, the Japanese Sergeant didn't like to lose any of his men; but he used the idea, that the trap was now closed around the Americans, to console himself for the loss of another one of his soldiers. In war, each soldier needs to deal with death as best he can.

"That shot came from the top of the cliff," Isiac heard the Japanese Sergeant say. "They have 2 or 3 men at the cart and one or more men on top of the cliff. We've seen six sets of tracks, so that leaves 2 or 3 men unaccounted for. Be careful. Now we wait until nightfall."

Isiac had counted 15 Japanese, but Private Woods had reduced that to 14. Isiac now waited for Sergeant

Crane and Corporal Woods to spot the 2 Japanese that were moving along the cliff face, and he also waited for his 2 Lieutenants to blow their grenades. Isiac didn't know which would come first. A shot from Sergeant Crane answered that question. Although Isiac couldn't see the results of Sergeant Crane's shot, the fact that there was only one shot suggested that there were now only 13 Japanese left. Just as Isiac was doing the math, the lieutenants blew their grenades, and the numbers changed again.

Reacting to the exploding grenades, the Japanese dove for cover. Peering carefully over the top of the boulders, they could see the bodies of their comrades scattered across the ground.

In Japanese, Isiac spoke. "There are grenades in the trees above your head, Sergeant. Drop your..."

At the sound of Isiac's voice, two of the Japanese soldiers tried to turn around quickly with their rifles and find a target. The distinctive sound of two 45's dropped the two Japanese even before they could complete their turns.

"No more fooling around, Sergeant," Isiac said. "Drop your guns and surrender, or I'll blow you all up." The tone in Isiac's voice made it clear to the Japanese Sergeant that death was imminent.

"Drop your rifles, men," the Japanese Sergeant said.

"On your bellies, arms and legs spread," came Isiac's next order. "Sergeant, you and your men are not safe there. The grenades could fall from the trees at any moment. Have two of your men crawl to the center of the dry river channel."

The Japanese Sergeant spoke, and two of his men started crawling. Isiac then continued with his instructions.

"When they reach the center of the dry river channel, I'm going to throw them handcuffs. Each soldier puts one of the cuffs on his right arm. If the cuffs aren't tight when I check them, I'll make sure that they are tight."

When the first two soldiers were handcuffed, Isiac said,

"Send the next two." And the procedure was repeated. "Now you can walk over Sergeant," Isiac continued, "with your hands on your head. Then sit down next to your men, but not too close, and take the laces out of your boots. Then get on your knees and put one hand behind your back and one hand on your stomach. If you make any attempt to struggle, I will shoot you in the head. Do you understand, Sergeant?"

A nod from the Sergeant indicated that he did. Then Isiac motioned to Private Lang, and without incident, Private Lang used the boot laces to tie one hand in front of the Japanese Sergeant and one hand behind his back.

"Sergeant Crane, if your man is eliminated call out," Isiac shouted.

"Eliminated," came the reply.

"Corporal Woods, status report," Isiac yelled again.

"One man located at the base of the cliff, easy shot," Corporal Woods yelled back.

"Hold that thought, Corporal," Isiac yelled. Then to his Japanese counterpart, Isiac said, "Sergeant, my man just said 'target located, easy shot.' "You have a chance to save one more of your men. Call for him to surrender and walk toward you with his hands on his head."

The Japanese Sergeant wasted no time in relaying the message to his last armed soldier, and what Isiac thought was the last living Japanese soldier. The soldier then walked into the open with his hands on his head. But then, from the rocks at the base of the ledge, Isiac heard in Japanese,

"Isuzu is wounded." Looking toward the sound of the voice, Isiac saw a Japanese soldier sitting on the ground with his hands on his head.

"Keep your hands on your head and walk toward us," Isiac told the sitting Japanese soldier in Japanese.

When the soldier got to his feet, Isiac shouted,

"Corporal Graham, this new walker is your responsibility."

"In my sights," Corporal Graham yelled back.

"Sergeant Crane, check out the other soldiers by the rocks," Isiac said, making sure that they had total control of the situation.

"Three dead one wounded," came Sergeant Crane's reply.

"Disarm and secure the injured soldier, Sergeant Crane," Isiac ordered. Then speaking to the Japanese Sergeant, Isiac said,

"I could have killed you and all of your men, but I allowed you to surrender. That proves that I have honor. Do you have honor?"

"I have honor," the Japanese Sergeant said.

"Do you have any more men in the area," Isiac asked?

"No," was the answer Isiac received.

Pointing his .45 at the Japanese sergeant and quoting what Mr. Konno had taught him, Isiac said,

"Once trust is lost, honor is lost, and it can never be regained."

"I understand," the Japanese Sergeant said, surprised by Isiac's understanding of Japanese culture. "I have no more men."

When the two approaching Japanese reached the other prisoners, Private Lang used their boot laces to secure them just like he had done with their sergeant. As soon as the last two prisoners were secured, Isiac said,

"Corporal Graham, check on the wounded man. Do what you can, then give me a report."

To Private Linder, Isiac said, "Can you get out of your hidey-hole without help and without tripping your grenades?"

"No problem, Sergeant," Linder responded.

"Good," Isiac said, and then gave Private Linder further orders. "When you get out, go help Sergeant Crane get the Lieutenants out of their holes. Then help the Sergeant get the cart off the ledge and reload it."

After Isiac and Private Lang had used rope to further secure the prisoners, they rejoined the rest of their men. While Sergeant Crane and Private Linder were reloading the cart, Corporal Graham gave Isiac his report,

"The prisoner lost a thumb and took a hard blow to the head with bleeding from the ears. Broken eardrums and concussion for sure, but you can never tell with head injuries.

Isiac had just demonstrated his ability to use deception and make quick decisions, two more traits essential to "The Making of a Spy."

East of Isiac's position, near the Burma/Chinese border.

January 23, 1943

True to his word, Fritz had marked the pilot's position well. At noon, Private Howard spotted the parachute from his point position. When they reached the parachute, however, the pilot was gone. But they did find eight sets of tracks leading away from the chute. They followed the trail until they reached the crest of a hill. From there, they could see a village nestled in the hollow between two hills.

"A Kachin village," Fritz said. "That should be good for us because they hate the Japanese, but be careful and be polite."

As they neared the village, they called out, "Americans," every minute or so.

Before they were within half a mile of the village, a dozen Kachins appeared from both sides of the trail, as well as from ahead and behind.

"Easy men," Fritz said, and then he repeated, "Americans."

Of course, the Kachins knew they were Americans, but what else could Fritz say, "How's hunting or shoot any Japanese today?" That did sound pretty good, but he doubted that any of the Kachins spoke English. He was wrong.

"We found your pilot," one of the Kachins said in English with a noticeable British accent. "Follow us."

Fritz and his team followed the Kachins to their village and found the pilot resting in the shade with three giggling Kachin women.

"We came to rescue you, Lieutenant, but it looks like someone else beat us to it."

"Yes, they did Sergeant, and they are a lot better looking than you guys."

"Be careful Lieutenant, or you might end up married to one of those beauties," Fritz said.

Amin Shan, the Kachin who spoke English, must have translated Fritz's remarks because the 3 Kachin women were now laughing and blushing at the same time. The Kachins seemed like happy people. Wasting no time, Fritz took out the map Isiac had given him, showed it to Amin Shan, and asked,

"Which is the best way to Fort Hertz?"

Amin Shan took Fritz's pencil and made a mark at the exact location of his village. Not only could he speak English, but he could also read a map. From the 'x' representing his village, Amin Shan drew another line, north, along the river, and placed another 'x.'

"My father's village," Amin Shan said. From there he drew a line due west to Fort Hertz, and continued, "Good trails all the way. Seven days' travel, no Japanese."

That left Fritz with only one question,

"How can we thank you?"

Without hesitation, Amin Shan said, "Your .45 with extra ammunition."

Also, without hesitation, Fritz handed him his .45 with two extra clips and 12 more shells.

"Very good present," Amin Shan said.

"Very good friend," Fritz responded before he turned to his men. "We have half a day left, and we are burning daylight. We don't want the Lieutenant's friends to continue to worry about him. Saddle up."

India, January 26, 1943

The Ledo Road reaches Mile Post 34.5 which was called "Hellgate." From there, the road began its ascent into the Patkai Mountain Range.

Burma, January 30, 1943

Fort Hertz was spotted as Isiac's group, following a well-used trail, topped a small rise. Just in case there were any Japanese scouts watching Fort Hertz, Isiac had Private Linder and Corporal Woods on point with Lang as rear guard.

"Sergeant Crane," Isiac said, "Go tell Private Linder to leave his point position and proceed to the Fort. He is to tell them that we are coming in with four injured men. Corporal Woods will continue on point. Although they haven't given us any trouble, you will return to help guard the prisoners."

When Private Linder arrived at the Fort with Isiac's message, he immediately became the center of attention. Shortly after that, Isiac arrived, and his group received a hero's welcome. The first thing Isiac did was to find an officer and ask if they had received any word from Sergeant Heimlich and his team. Receiving a negative response, Isiac gave the officer a brief report. The British officer only asked Isiac one question,

"Sergeant Kalway, did any of the Japanese get away?"

"No sir," Isiac answered.

When Isiac was leaving the room, the British officer was left shaking his head in disbelief. When all the prisoners had been secured and the injured attended to, Isiac and his men became the guests of honor at a celebratory luncheon that had quickly been thrown together. The luncheon had barely begun when cheering could be heard.

"Hold on everyone," A British Sergeant said, interrupting the luncheon. "We have more guests joining us for lunch." And standing next to him was Private Busby.

Isiac and his men were on their feet instantly and surrounded Private Busby. They were greeting him and asking him questions faster than he could answer.

"Everyone is fine," Private Busby announced, "Including the pilot."

Ten minutes later, cheering erupted again when Sergeant Heimlich entered the room with the rest of his men. The luncheon was temporarily suspended, but these men were all hungry after their 300-mile trip, and the luncheon soon resumed, although much louder than when it had started.

That afternoon, Lieutenant Carter and his men, Including Lieutenant Peer, Sergeant Crane, and Corporal Graham, along with the newest member of the group, Lieutenant Brody, the fighter pilot, were flown back to India.

India, January 31, 1943

By 8 AM, Lieutenant Carter and Sergeant Kalway each had a new cast. X-rays confirmed that their bones were set perfectly and healing nicely. After being discharged from the hospital, they were being driven back to join their unit.

"Lieutenant," Isiac said, "When we get back, I'm going to try to get my hands on a bottle of booze for Corporal Graham to show him my appreciation."

"Make that two bottles, Sergeant," Lieutenant Carter said, "I'm in."

When Isiac and Lieutenant Carter got back to camp, Sergeant Heimlich and Chao Lin were outside waiting for them. It was easy to tell that Fritz was holding something behind his back.

"Sergeant Kalway," Fritz addressed Isiac, "Yesterday you said you were looking for a bottle of whiskey. Will this do?"

From behind his back, Fritz handed Isiac a bottle of Southern Comfort.

Now the Lieutenant joined the conversation. "Think you could find another bottle of that, Sergeant Heimlich?"

"Just a minute, sir," Fritz said as he went back inside and returned with another bottle.

"Where did you find that Sergeant Heimlich," Lieutenant Carter asked?

"Under Sergeant Kalway's bed," Fritz answered.

"How much do I owe you, Sergeant," Lieutenant Carter asked?

Pointing to Chao Lin, Sergeant Heimlich said, "Ask him, Lieutenant. Chao Lin is the trader in this outfit. If you need anything, all you have to do is ask Chao Lin. If it's anywhere around, he can find it.

"I'll remember that," the Lieutenant said.

Then, after Lieutenant Carter and Chao Lin completed their transaction, the Lieutenant and Isiac set off to find Corporal Graham and deliver their gifts.

Isiac and Fritz Become Spies

February 1, 1943

Major James Ruben, escorted by two military police sergeants, entered the 495th Brigade Headquarters and walked directly to intelligence officer, Wayne Goodman.

"Your orders, Captain. Open in private," Major Ruben said as he handed Captain Goodman a thick sealed cardboard package with nothing written on it except, Captain Wayne Goodman, 495th Engineers Brigade.

Without saying another word, the Major and his two MPs turned and left headquarters, leaving a surprised Captain holding a mysterious package. Wasting no time, Captain Goodman entered his office and locked his door. Even though Captain Goodman was an experienced intelligence officer, he had never received information in this manner before. Opening the package, the captain found a fist-sized box, a folded sheet of paper with his name on it, and another plain, sealed envelope with no writing.

Captain Goodman unfolded the paper that had his name on it and read his orders:

"Captain Goodman, you are now a member of the OSS under my command. You are to deliver the enclosed box and sealed envelope to Colonel Rodgers immediately and stay with him while he opens both the box and the sealed envelope. Remain with him until he finishes reading the contents of the letter. You are expected to offer all necessary assistance to Colonel Rodgers in the completion of his duties."

"As of now, all correspondence between us is top secret. The identity of all personnel involved is to be recorded, but kept secret, for my eyes only. Give this note to Colonel Rodgers and have him read it before you give him the box and sealed envelope. Then destroy this note."

The note was signed, "Major General Donovan"

"Corporal Anderson, come with me," Captain Goodman said, as they left headquarters. "We're going for a ride."

"Yes sir," the corporal answered. "Where to?"

"Find Colonel Rodgers," was all Captain Goodman said.

They found Colonel Rodgers watching a couple of his engineers trying to give instructions to some newly arrived laborers, none of whom spoke English.

"Sorry to interrupt you, Colonel Rodgers," Captain Goodman said. "I would like to request a private meeting with you in your office."

"It must be urgent if you had to come all the way out here to find me," Colonel Rodgers responded.

"I believe it is, sir," Captain Goodman replied.

"Is that your jeep," Colonel Rodgers asked?

"Yes sir," Captain Goodman answered.

"Then, let's get back to Headquarters and find out what is so urgent, Captain," the Colonel said as they walked back to the jeep.

"Back to Headquarters, Corporal Anderson," Captain Goodman said as the two officers got in the jeep.

When Captain Goodman and Colonel Rodgers returned to headquarters, Captain Goodman asked,

"Colonel, can I meet you in your office in 2 minutes? I need to retrieve some items from my office."

"I can hardly wait," Colonel Rodgers said, with a slight smile.

Captain Goodman returned in less than two minutes. "Can we lock the door, Colonel," Captain Goodman asked?

The Colonel nodded his assent. After locking the Colonel's door, Captain Goodman walked to the Colonel's desk. Captain Goodman, handing the note that he had already read to the Colonel, waited, as ordered, for the Colonel to read the note.

"Have a seat, Captain," Colonel Rodgers said as he unfolded the note and began reading. When he finished reading the note, the Colonel reached into his desk and withdrew a pack of matches. The Colonel then slid the matches and the note across his desk to Captain Goodman. Captain Goodman lit a match, held the note over the Colonel's wastebasket, and touched the match to the note, destroying it, as ordered.

Captain Goodman then handed Colonel Rodgers the envelope and the box. Colonel Rodgers opened the envelope and began reading:

"Colonel Rodgers, you are now a member of the OSS under my command. Your orders will come directly from me and can only be countermanded by me or the President of the United States. You are to develop a unit of OSS operatives that report only to you. The identity of these operatives, and all activities of these operatives are to be considered TOP SECRET."

"Create an independent company of MPs to use as a cover for OSS operatives. This company will be independent in name only and will secretly continue to be under your command. All members are required to take an oath of secrecy, violation of which is to be dealt with immediately by you as deemed necessary, not to exclude court martial or immediate execution as a spy without trial. This has all been authorized by the President of the United States."

"You have the authority to do whatever necessary to support your newly created unit. Use the enclosed stamp from the Joint Chiefs of Staff to make promotions and transfers, to requisition equipment and supplies, and to issue orders. Two transport planes will be made available for the exclusive use of your newly created Military Police Company. I expect your new OSS unit to be fully operational by February 8, 1943. All operatives will continue to be paid according to their rank, plus, they will receive an additional under the table payment of $40 per month. All future orders will be relayed to you from me by way of Captain Goodman."

This note also ended with the signature, "Major General Donovan"

The long silence that followed was finally interrupted when Colonel Rodgers handed his instructions to Captain Goodman and said,

"I think you better read these instructions, as well, Captain."

More silence followed as Captain Goodman read the instructions that had been given to Colonel Rodgers. When Colonel Rodgers saw that the Captain was done reading, he opened the box, and both men looked at the official stamp of the Joint Chiefs of Staff of the United States Armed Forces. After exchanging glances that indicated both the Colonel and the Captain were aware of the immense responsibility that had been placed on their shoulders, Colonel Rodgers took the papers from Captain Goodman, and along with the stamp, locked them in his safe.

"It seems like the criticism that the United States lacks an organized central intelligence system is being addressed," Colonel Rodgers said.

"It certainly looks that way, Colonel," Captain Goodman said.

Colonel Rodgers continued, "Captain, you and I have a lot of planning to do and only a short time to do it. Feel free to offer ideas and suggestions. In fact, I expect you to do so, even if your opinions differ from mine. Do you understand, Captain?"

"Yes sir," Captain Goodman said, shaking his head 'yes' for emphasis.

"Any suggestions for the name of our new unit," the Colonel asked? "We can't just call it the 1st US Spy Unit."

Colonel Rodgers watched Captain Goodman, and when he saw the Captain's eyebrows, that were lowered in concentration, rise again, he said, "It looks like you have an idea, Captain."

"I do, Colonel," the Captain responded. "We could call our new unit the First Independent Military Police Special Assignment Company."

With a smile, Colonel Rodgers said, "Perfect, that's our new name. We now have to choose the personnel. And I already have a good idea. 712th Battalion, A Company, 2nd Platoon."

"Isn't that the same platoon that survived the plane crash, rescued an American pilot, and captured a group of Japanese," Captain Goodman asked?

"The very same, Captain," Colonel Rodgers said. "And I know both Sergeant Kalway and Sergeant Heimlich personally."

"How did you meet them," the Captain asked?

"I guess you could say I got acquainted with them in the brig," Colonel Rodgers answered.

"I don't understand, Colonel," Captain Goodman exclaimed. "Are you sure it is wise to select trouble-makers to be part of our new intelligence company?"

"No, you don't understand, Captain," the Colonel said and started to laugh. "Let me explain. I was the trouble-maker."

Now the Captain began to laugh, as well, as the Colonel began to tell him a story.

"Sergeants Kalway and Heimlich grew up in Michigan along the shores of Lake Erie. When they weren't fishing in Lake Erie, they were hunting in the surrounding marshes and woods. Even as children, they were recognized as excellent marsh men and woodsmen; and their shooting skills were recognized by the local hunters in the area."

"When Sergeant Kalway was 5 years old, his father deserted his family. By the time he was 6 years old, Sergeant Kalway was fishing and hunting small game to help feed his family. When Sergeant Kalway was 14 years old, he quit school and got a full-time job to support his family. But the Sergeant is a voracious reader, so his learning never stopped. It's hard to believe how smart he is."

"How did you learn all that," Captain Goodman asked?

"I learned that in New York from their wives," the Colonel said. "And their wives are both stunners; I can tell you that."

Then the Colonel returned to his story.

"In New York, I was in a bar just off base with two of my Lieutenants. We were really plastered. I was apparently trying to invade and capture the bar for the exclusive use of my men. The locals were pretty steamed about that, and someone called the MPs just before all Hell broke loose. They immediately recognized that I was the instigator of the brewing storm, and, without hesitation, approached me and offered to escort me out of the bar, 'for my own protection,' they said."

"But you are a lot bigger than either one of the sergeants," the Captain said.

"That's what I thought too, and when I made it clear that I was their Colonel, and I wasn't going anywhere with them," Sergeant Kalway calmly stated, "You are leaving with us, Colonel. You can do it the easy way or the hard way." I took that as a challenge, but nobody told me that Sergeant Kalway holds the highest black belt possible in Judo, so when I stood up and tried to throw a punch at the Sergeant, I found myself on the floor."

"Then, with me on the floor and two MPs standing beside me, back to back, Sergeant Kalway yelled, 'There will be no more disturbances here tonight. If there is anyone who doesn't understand that, step forward, and we'll explain it.' Everyone understood because the bar quieted immediately."

"What happened to your two Lieutenants, Colonel," Captain Goodman asked?

"My Lieutenants were also both on the floor,"

Colonel Rodgers answered, "And when Sergeant Kalway was politely helping me up, I heard Sergeant Heimlich say to Sergeant Kalway, 'Sorry, Sergeant, but it seems like the two lieutenants tripped over each other.' At that point, I had sobered up enough to realize that 'the easy way' was going to be the best option, and without further trouble from me, they escorted me to the brig."

"In the morning, I knew I was in trouble. Attempting to strike an MP is not a trivial matter. At that point, my future looked pretty dim: jail time, court-martial, or demotion to Major, if I was lucky. Then Sergeant Kalway walked up to my cell and apologized for any scrapes or bruises. Not wasting any time, I immediately asked Sergeant Kalway, 'what are the charges?' When Sergeant Kalway told me that there were no charges, I was too stunned to reply. Then he opened my cell and wished me a good day."

"That's quite a story, Colonel," Captain Goodman said. "My concerns have been totally erased. Sergeant Heimlich and Sergeant Kalway will be perfect for our new unit."

"No more time for stories today, Captain," Colonel Rodgers said. "Go find Sergeant O'Malley. I'm promoting him to Master Sergeant and transferring him to Headquarters. We'll use him as our go between, so we can avoid unwanted suspicion that more frequent meetings between us might create. And on your way, think up some kind of ceremonial oath of secrecy. Make it short, but give it some teeth."

"Yes sir," Captain Goodman said. Then he left the Colonel's office to carry out his orders.

After a few minutes of writing, Colonel Rodgers had his next set of orders ready. He found Captain Malone, the personnel officer, with a cup of coffee in his hand, and said,

"In my office, Captain Malone, and you can bring your coffee."

"Yes sir," Captain Malone said, as he followed Colonel Rodgers into his office.

"I want you to deliver Lt. Colonel Bolla his new orders," Colonel Rodgers said and handed Captain Malone those orders. "But, before you give the Colonel his orders, explain to him that you have specific orders from me to deliver the orders only, and are not authorized to make comments or answer questions. Then give Colonel Bolla these verbal orders: The 2nd platoon of Company A is being removed from your command. It will become the First Independent Military Police Special Assignment Company. Transfer one squad from Companies B, C, and D to Company A."

"When you finish the verbal orders, hand him his written orders and return to Headquarters. I'll have more work for you to do soon."

When Captain Goodman returned with Sergeant O'Malley, Colonel Rodgers wasted no time and immediately began his explanation,

"Sergeant O'Malley, you have been chosen for special duty. You will be required to swear an oath of secrecy. Violation of that oath could result in court-martial or death. Do you understand, Sergeant?"

"Yes sir," Sergeant O'Malley answered.

"Are you prepared to take the oath, Sergeant," the Colonel asked?

Again, Sergeant O'Malley answered, "Yes, Sir."

Colonel Rodgers then proceeded to administer the oath,

"Sergeant O'Malley, do you swear to keep secret all activities and information that you are involved in or have knowledge of from this moment on?"

"Yes, sir." Sergeant O'Malley said for the 3rd time.

"You are now part of OSS," Colonel Rodgers said. "You are now promoted to Master Sergeant and transferred to Headquarters. You will perform all duties that are required of you at Headquarters. That will be your cover, but orders from me and Captain

Goodman will be your top priority and will be carried out promptly and discretely."

Sergeant O'Malley expanded his vocabulary this time. Instead of, "Yes sir," he said,

"Understood, Colonel."

"Welcome to the team, Master Sergeant O'Malley," Colonel Rodgers said. "Now go find Lieutenant Carter, Sergeant Heimlich, Sergeant Kalway, and Corporal Woods; and bring them here."

Colonel Rodgers had Carter, Kalway, Heimlich, and Woods take the oath of secrecy and welcomed them to the OSS. ISIAC WAS NOW A SPY!

"Lieutenant Carter, you have been promoted to Captain. Your platoon has been converted into the First Independent Military Police Special Assignment Company with you in command. Sergeant Kalway, you have been promoted to Sergeant First Class and will serve as Captain Carter's Company Sergeant. Sergeant Heimlich, you have been promoted to Staff Sergeant. You will be in charge of Squad 1, and leader of team 2. Corporal Woods, you have been promoted to Sergeant and will replace Sergeant Kalway as the leader of Team 1."

"Officially, the duties of your new company will be internal investigation, security, training, and search and rescue. In reality, although you probably will be performing all of the duties just mentioned, your orders will come directly from me or Captain Goodman. Your main mission will be to establish an intelligence network in India, Burma, and China. More specific missions will follow. Captain Goodman will now explain your immediate duties."

"Two transports have been assigned for the exclusive use of your new Company," Captain Goodman began. "Captain Carter, with the help of Sergeants O'Malley, Kalway, Heimlich, and Woods, you will examine and evaluate all the men from your former Platoon. Remove any that you consider unfit or unlikely to be able to perform the new duties expected of them. You can replace them with anyone from the 495th Brigade under the rank of Captain."

"Start with Squad 1. All Privates in Squad 1 are promoted to Corporals. When Squad 1's adjustments are completed, bring them all here to be sworn in. Then you can start work on Squad 2. We need personnel selection completed in 2 days. Get started men. Dismissed."

"Sergeant Woods and Sergeant Heimlich," Captain Carter said. "Go get your teams and meet me and Sergeant Kalway behind Headquarters. Move!"

Captain Carter and Sergeant Kalway went directly to Captain Malone's office.

"Captain Malone, we need all the personnel records of the 712th Brigade," Captain Carter said.

"Colonel Rodgers told me to expect changes," Captain Malone said. "This looks like the beginning."

"It is, Captain Malone," Captain Carter said. "And before the day is over, you'll be receiving multiple transfer requests from me."

Sitting on the benches behind Headquarters, Captain Carter and Sergeant Kalway started with Squad 1, as ordered.

"Sergeant Heimlich's team is intact," Captain Carter said. "But your old team needs 2 replacements. Anyone from the 712th Battalion come to mind as a possible replacement?"

"I think Private Mason from B Company would be a good candidate," Isiac said. "He was a school teacher and is several years older than most of the other MPs in his Platoon. He seems like a pretty smart guy, but I was more impressed by his common sense. And he's an excellent shot. If we are going to need snipers, he'd be a good choice."

"Consider it done," Captain Carter said. "Anyone else, Sergeant?"

"Not right off hand," Isiac answered.

"Well, keep thinking," the Captain said.

Just then Sergeant Heimlich and Sergeant Woods arrived with Squad 1.

"Salute your new Captain," Fritz told his men.

After returning the salute, Captain Carter said,

"Men, you have all been promoted to Corporals. We are all being transferred to a newly formed Company. Team 2 will remain intact, but we need 2 new men to fill the vacancies in Sergeant Woods' team. Sergeant Kalway and I have chosen Private Mason from B Company, but we need to find another MP to complete Sergeant Woods' team. Keep in mind that our new Company will be involved in top secret missions, and you will all be required to take an oath of secrecy. That automatically eliminates anyone with a big mouth."

"I currently have the records for 712th Battalion, but we can choose anyone from the 495th Brigade. We are pressed for time, so I am asking for suggestions."

The men talked it over for a few minutes before Sergeant Woods spoke, "Corporal Lang went to school with Private White from Company B. They played football together."

"Would you trust him with your life, Corporal Lang," Captain Carter asked?

"Yes sir," Corporal Lang answered.

"Sergeant Woods, you and Corporal Lang go to Captain Malone's office and give him this note,"

Captain Carter said. "And tell him we need the transfers immediately. Captain Malone knows that we are in a hurry. He'll arrange for the transfers to be delivered, but you don't have to wait. Go get Privates Mason and White and bring them back to Headquarters, immediately. If anyone questions you, tell them you are MPs on duty, and anyone who interferes with your duties will be arrested. The rest of the squad will be waiting. Now Move."

With all ten members of Squad 1 crowded into Colonel Rodgers' office, he said,

"Private Mason and Private White, you have both been promoted to corporals. Meet your new Squad."

After Squad 1 was sworn in, the colonel spoke to Captain Carter,

"Good work, Captain, now go fill out the rest of your new Company. Dismissed, men."

All the other squads had full teams, but Captain Carter, with input from Sergeants O'Malley, Kalway, Heimlich, and Woods, replaced one sergeant and three privates with men they felt would be better suited to fulfill the duties that would be required by their new Company. When all squads had been sworn in as OSS operatives, Captain Carter addressed the Colonel,

"Sir, we are ready to start working on supplies, but, not knowing exactly what kind of missions we will be involved in, provides a bit of a problem."

"That problem is easily solved, Captain Carter," Colonel Rodgers said with a chuckle, "Just choose supplies you might need if you didn't know what your future missions might be."

Also, with a chuckle, Captain Carter said, "Understood, Colonel." The Colonel had just given them permission to gather any supplies they need and any supplies that they might need. In other words, nothing was off limits.

"Colonel Rodgers," Isiac said, "We would like permission to choose our own flight crews and have them assigned to our Company."

"Permission granted," Colonel Rodgers said, "And tell Lieutenant Peer that he is promoted to Captain and will be in charge of both flight crews. And when he is not busy with his flight crews, he will assist Captain Carter with Company management. And I suppose you'd like Sergeant Crane, as well?"

"Yes, sir," Isiac and Captain Carter answered, simultaneously.

"Permission granted, Captain," Colonel Rodgers said again. "And tell Sergeant Crane that he has been promoted to Staff Sergeant."

"Thank you, sir," Captain Carter said.

"Anything else, Captain," Colonel Rodgers asked?

"Yes sir, we'd like Corporal Graham and 4 additional medical personnel assigned to our Company," Captain Carter said.

"Good idea, Captain Carter," Colonel Rodgers said. "Tell Corporal Graham he is promoted to Sergeant. He will be in charge of the Company's medical team. And tell Sergeant Graham that there are no restrictions on his team selection. Just have him give Captain Malone the list, and Captain Malone will take care of all necessary paperwork. Now, what about you, Sergeant Kalway, do you have any more requests?"

"Yes sir, I'd like to order 50 scoped rifles and 50 High Standard .22's with silencers."

"That might come in handy," Colonel Rodgers said. "And now that all of our plane crash survivors are reunited, all with promotions, we have another matter that needs to be dealt with. I want the rumor that your company is locating and removing incompetent officers to become fact. One of my Lieutenants needs to be removed. He and some of his men have been mistreating some of our Negro soldiers, and they are the best workers I have. I want to put an end to that before it becomes more serious. And I know that

Sergeant Kalway and Sergeant Heimlich know how to deal with an unruly officer."

Captain Carter listened and watched as Colonel Rodgers and his 2 Sergeants exchanged glances and laughter. Captain Carter realized that he was out of the loop on this one.

"Captain Carter," Colonel Rodgers said, "I want this arrest to be made at the construction site to guarantee a large audience. I might even happen to be around to view the show myself. And make no mistake, I do want you to put on a good show. Use your entire Company. And Captain Carter, I have no doubt that you and your 2 Michigan Sergeants will come up with a good plan. I want all the officers in the Brigade to understand what happens if anyone interferes with your Company. Now go and prepare for tomorrow's show."

"What was that about you and Sergeant Heimlich arresting officers," Captain Carter asked?

"Can't tell you, sir. Top secret," Isiac replied.

Even though Captain Carter had to laugh at Sergeant Kalway's reply, he was impressed with his Sergeant's discretion.

February 2, 1943

Captain Carter knew the easiest way to arrest Lieutenant Bellows would be to do it before he joined his Platoon, but Colonel Rodgers wanted a show. And Captain Carter knew that this show would, not only remove an incompetent officer, but would also demonstrate that interference with his newly created Company would not be tolerated.

Before daylight, Captain Carter accompanied Squads 4 and 5 to a position past the current construction site. Squads 2 and 3 were hidden, one on each side of the road. Squad 1, accompanied by Sergeant Kalway marched down the road with their batons drawn. Sergeant Woods stopped directly in front of Lieutenant Bellows and in a loud voice said, "Lieutenant Bellows, you are under arrest for conduct unbecoming an officer. Mistreating some soldiers while showing favoritism to others is not allowable."

Lieutenant Bellows wasn't smart enough to allow Sergeant Woods to escort him back to headquarters and deal with the problem there. Instead, just as expected, and hoped for, he showed his cockiness and involved his whole Platoon when he said,

"There must be some mistake, Sergeant." Then to his men, Lieutenant Bellows asked, "Men, have I mistreated anyone?"

"No," came from over a dozen of his soldiers.

"See, Sergeant," Lieutenant Bellows said with a smirk, and continued with his cocky attitude, "You made a

264

mistake, now leave us alone so we can get back to work."

"Sir, you are under arrest," Sergeant Woods said.

With his handcuffs, Sergeant Woods reached for Lieutenant Bellows' wrist. As Lieutenant Bellows slapped Sergeant Woods' hand away, Sergeant Woods, using a move Sergeant Kalway had taught him, had Lieutenant Bellows on his knees. As Sergeant Woods attempted to cuff him, Lieutenant Bellows struggled and called out,

"Sergeant Keller, Help."

Sergeant Keller and 2 of his men rushed forward to rescue their Lieutenant from Sergeant Woods' control. Seeing that, Corporal Linder immediately grabbed Lieutenant Bellows' other arm and helped Sergeant Woods cuff him. At the same time, Isiac, Fritz, and Corporal Lang moved between Sergeant Woods and the 3 charging soldiers. Using their batons, Isiac, Fritz, and Corporal Lang put down the charging soldiers. Lieutenant Bellows had just escalated his charges to attempting to incite mutiny.

As Squad 1 tightened the circle around their prisoners, Isiac, Fritz, and Corporal Lang took several steps toward the agitated soldiers and Isiac shouted, "Sergeants, control your men or your whole Platoon will be joining Lieutenant Bellows and his 3 pals in the Brig for the rest of the war."

Isiac could see that the sergeants were having trouble getting their men to stand down. It was the perfect time to implement the rest of the plan. Isiac blew his whistle. Forty more MPs appeared out of the morning mist. The shock of being completely surrounded by MPs, all with their .45's drawn, had the intended effect. These MPs meant business. To further emphasize that, Captain Carter, limping on his cast but without crutches, moved in front of his two Squads and spoke.

"Ranking sergeant, step forward. I will not repeat myself."

"Master Sergeant Reese, sir," the Master Sergeant said, as he stepped forward, approached the Captain, and saluted.

"Sergeant Reese, you are now in command of this Platoon until your new Lieutenant arrives. And you are responsible for its actions. You are to return to base and assemble your entire Platoon, no exceptions. A squad of my MPs will accompany you and be there to offer assistance if needed. You are to make sure that every man in your Platoon understands the seriousness of what just happened and what I am about to say."

Now speaking to the entire Platoon, Captain Carter said,

"You are soldiers, not hooligans. We are at war, not on a picnic. Any action interpreted as mutiny or deemed an attempt to incite mutiny is likely to result in a death sentence."

In seconds, the grumbling stopped, replaced by silence.

Speaking again to Sergeant Reese, Captain Carter continued with his orders,

"Sergeant Reese, if any of your men give any indication of dissention, hand them over to my MPs, immediately. This is an order, not a request."

"You will resume work tomorrow morning with your new Lieutenant. Your full support is expected during this change of command. Once a week, for the rest of the month, you will deliver a report to Captain Malone concerning the behavior and morale of your Platoon. If you feel that any further charges or changes need to be made, you will discuss them with Captain Malone. Do you understand your orders, Sergeant Reese?"

"Yes sir, Captain Carter," Sergeant Reese said.

"Good," Captain Carter said, "This has been a Military Police action and is part of an ongoing Military Police investigation. If anyone tries to change or countermand my orders, it will be considered as interfering in a Military Police matter. If that happens, report to me or to Captain Malone, immediately, and appropriate measures will be taken. Dismissed, Sergeant."

Later that day, to further emphasize that their Company was different from all other Companies, Captain Carter and Captain Peer decided that eating with the enlisted men of their Company would become standard procedure. And that's what they did.

During lunch, Corporal Lang handed Captain Carter a note that had been handed to him by Sergeant O'Malley. All it said was, "Headquarters, 1300."

Sergeant O'Malley was waiting for him when Captain Carter entered headquarters.

"Follow me, sir," Sergeant O'Malley said, as he led the Captain to Colonel Rodgers' office. The door was open.

"Come in, Captain Carter, and close the door," Colonel Rodgers said.

Captain Carter relaxed when he saw the big smile on the Colonel's face, in fact, the Colonel was almost laughing. That was a good sign because Captain Carter knew that a review of his performance was forthcoming. It appeared that Colonel Rodgers was having trouble getting started. Finally, still shaking his head and smiling, Colonel Rodgers began.

"Captain Carter, I asked you to put on a show, and you did. I watched discretely, but I was close enough to hear your speech and watch Squad 1 make the arrest. Your speech even scared me, and I'm your boss."

Now both men were laughing, but Colonel Rodgers finally continued,

"I've already had a visit from 2 Colonels and a Captain trying to find out what's going on, and what I'm going to do about my 'out of control' MPs. First, I told them that your Company is no longer under my Command. Then, I told them that I witnessed the arrest, and I didn't intend to do anything about it. I also told them that whoever created your new Company certainly has more authority than I feel comfortable dealing with, and that I intended to do my job, and that did not include interfering with a military police action. I suggested that they do the same. I am holding a meeting tonight with all my colonels to explain that, if any other officers in their Battalions are potential troublemakers, I expect them to handle the problem before the MPs become aware of it and to bring it to my attention immediately. Not only did your show discourage any future interference with your Company, but it is also going to improve the accountability of my officers. Good job Captain."

"Sergeant Kalway, have our flight crew and medical team been established," Captain Carter asked?

"Yes sir," Isiac answered.

"Can you think of anyone else we should add to our Company," Captain Carter asked?

"Yes sir, but he's not a soldier," Isiac said.

"The Colonel made it clear that we could use civilians as needed," the Captain said, "Who is he?"

"Chao Lin," was Isiac's response.

"I remember Chao Lin," Captain Carter said. "He's skilled in procurement. Does he have any other skills?"

"He's teaching Sergeant Heimlich and me to speak Chinese," Isiac said. "He also speaks English, as you know, and excellent Hindi."

"We'll need an interpreter," the Captain said, "Anything else I should know?"

"He has a trained guard dog," Isiac continued, "And that could be very advantageous to us in certain situations. But they come as a package deal, Captain. Chao Lin could never be persuaded to leave his dog."

Captain Carter was pensive for a moment, and then he said, "A guard dog is a good idea, and there are no regulations that I know of that prohibit civilians from having dogs. Have him sworn in. He'll start at Private's pay, plus receive the $40 per month expense account.

That's the new name I'm using for our 'off the books' payments."

China, February 8, 1943

Captain Carter's 2 transport planes were carrying his new Company and their equipment to Kunming, China as part of a group of 10 transports. They were being escorted by 2 American Fighters. As they approached the Irrawaddy River, Captain Carter was watching Squad 1. He saw no overt signs of nervousness, but he knew the men of Squad 1 were aware that they were approaching their crash site. Captain Carter's thoughts of the plane crash were interrupted by Captain Peer when he came on the intercom.

"Attention, Squad 1, anyone interested in fighting the Japanese in this area must use their parachutes. I am not going to crash this plane just so you can play with the Japanese in these mountains."

A professional comedian could work his whole life and never experience the laughter created by Captain Peer's remarks. No one jumped out of the plane, and in good spirits, they landed safely in Kunming.

"Sergeant Kalway," Captain Carter said as he and Captain Peer exited the plane, "Keep everyone on board until you see me leave our other transport."

A corporal approached the two Captains and saluted.

"I have a jeep for your use Captain Carter," the corporal said. "And I've been ordered to show you around the base. Your Company has been assigned to a separate area of the base with your own barracks, warehouses, and offices. And all the services of the base are available for your use."

"Thank you, Corporal," Captain Carter said. "Captain Peer and I would appreciate a tour of the base. If you can wait a few minutes, Corporal, we need to address our men before they leave the planes."

"I'll be waiting, Captain Carter," the Corporal said.

As the two Captains limped toward their second plane, Captain Carter spoke to Captain Peer, "Your idea to keep the men on the plane for a few minutes appears to be working as planned. We already have an audience. And I'd bet that some of them are wondering why our men are still on the planes."

"I think you could change Some to Most," Captain Peer said, chuckling.

As soon as both Captains boarded their second transport, Captain Carter addressed the men.

"Men, I want everyone to be pleasant and helpful unless the situation dictates otherwise. Remember, you are more than just MPs. Abuse of power will not be tolerated. Likewise, refusal to use your authority, when necessary, will not be tolerated. Use good judgment. I don't think that we'll have any trouble here after the show we put on in India. It appears that our reputation reached this base before we did. But I have a card for each of you to carry that clearly states that anyone who interferes with you while you are carrying out your duty will be subject to immediate arrest. This is your big stick. And it bears the stamp of the Joint Chiefs of Staff. And you can consider yourselves to always be on duty. If you are in a position to help someone outside our Company, you may do so, but only if you first make it clear that you are offering assistance only and are not subject to anyone's orders but mine. And listen carefully. This speech is to be memorized and used to avoid using your card."

"I have orders to arrest anyone who interferes with me while carrying out my duties. Now in unison repeat your new speech."

After everyone on the plane repeated their new speech, Captain Carter continued,

"And remember to add, sir, to your speech if you are addressing an officer. If anyone attempts to give you orders or attempts to change your orders, this is the second line of your speech. 'I am not allowed to accept orders from anyone who is not my superior in my Company.' If that doesn't work, out comes the card; and your pleasant attitude is replaced with your 'I am in charge and arrest is imminent' attitude. Any time your card is used, notify me or Captain Peer. Then it will be time for us to put on another show."

"Can we arrest Generals, Captain?" came from an MP in the back of the plane.

"Only if you include me in on the fun," Captain Carter said, laughing along with his men. "But I wouldn't try to arrest Major General Donovan, he's our boss." More laughter.

Captain Carter expected the playful response from his men because he had already given the same speech when he passed out cards to the men on Captain Peer's plane before it landed. When Sergeant Kalway saw his two Captains leave the other plane, as ordered, he led his men off the plane so that the departure from the two planes was simultaneous.

Before leaving on his tour of the base, Captain Carter gave instructions to his sergeants to delay unloading their supplies until he was shown their warehouse and returned with jeeps and trucks from the motor pool. As it turned out, they didn't need to visit the motor pool. In addition to a barracks, warehouse, and office building, their Command Center had its own motor pool with 20 jeeps and 2 trucks.

"Corporal, can you arrange to have these 2 trucks and a couple of jeeps delivered to our planes so my men can unload," Captain Carter asked?

"Yes sir," the Corporal answered. "And I can provide some men to help you unload."

"Thank you, Corporal. And who is your commanding officer," Captain Carter asked?

"Lieutenant Banks, sir," the Corporal answered.

"Tell Lieutenant Banks that he has my gratitude," Captain Carter said, using a little carrot. He was sure that the officers of the base already knew that he carried a big stick.

The unloading was accomplished without incident; and with all his men back at their new Command Center, this is how Captain Carter informed his men that they were on 48 hours Leave:

"Men, you are now ordered to become familiar with the base and the surrounding area. Jeeps are available. For the next 48 hours, returning to our Command Center is optional, not mandatory."

February 9, 1943

When Captain Carter and Captain Peer entered base headquarters, the noise level dropped.

"It looks like our reputation is firmly established," Captain Peer whispered to Captain Carter.

In a return whisper, Captain Carter said, "We can thank the Colonel for that," being careful not to mention the Colonel's name.

"Can I help you, Captains," a Master Sergeant asked?

"We were hoping that you could arrange for us to meet with Colonel Hardy at his earliest convenience," Captain Peer said.

"The Colonel is in his office," the Master Sergeant said. "If you give me a moment, I'll inform him, sir."

"Thank you, Sergeant," Captain Carter said. "Is there somewhere I can sit while we wait? This leg has been giving me some trouble today."

"Use my chair, Captain. It's the most comfortable chair on the base," the Master Sergeant bragged.

"Thank you, Sergeant."

The Master Sergeant knocked and entered Colonel Hardy's office. Captain Carter had less than a minute to test the Sergeant's chair before the Sergeant returned and said, "Colonel Hardy will see you now, Captains."

"Sergeant, I only had a moment to test your chair, but if you ever decide to sell it, I'd be interested," Captain Carter said, as he stood up and walked toward Colonel Hardy's office.

As soon as they entered the Colonel's office, Colonel Hardy immediately offered each crippled Captain a chair.

"Thank you, Colonel Hardy," Captain Carter said, as he sat down. "We've been ordered to assist you in the training of the new Chinese recruits and to provide additional security for the base."

"We can certainly use the help," Colonel Hardy said. "And I've been ordered to make available to you all the services provided by the base, and to supply you with whatever equipment you might need."

"Thank you, Colonel," Captain Carter said. "I'd like your advice about setting up a system for basic training, sir."

Without delay, the Colonel replied, "Set up 2 separate facilities. The Nationalists and the Communists don't play well together."

"Thank you for the advice, Colonel. We intend to set up additional patrols, to conduct reconnaissance missions, and to set up observation posts in some of the outlying areas. We could use 2 additional trucks and 5 more jeeps whenever they become available."

"They'll be available when the next shipment of supplies arrives," Colonel Hardy said.

"Thank you, sir. We'll be sure to mention the excellent cooperation we've received from everyone at your base in our next report," Captain Carter said, offering another carrot. "We have a lot of work to do, Colonel, may we be dismissed?"

"Dismissed, gentlemen," the Colonel said, obviously pleased with his first meeting with the two Captains of this newly created Independent MP Company.

February 10, 1943

Captain Carter was in his office with his 11sergeants.

"Time to go to work, men," Captain Carter said as he opened the meeting. "We start training 100 Chinese troops the day after tomorrow. We are going to split them into 2 groups of 50. Squads 2 and 3 will be responsible for training the first group, and Squads 4 and 5 will be responsible for the second group. We are going to run a 10-week program."

"We were advised to keep the Communists and Nationalist troops separated, so keep that in mind, Sergeants. Train the troops well, but remember that our primary mission here is to establish an intelligence network, so watch for opportunities to establish special relationships whenever possible. Some of the supplies that we brought here are for you to use as gifts to help establish new relationships. They are clearly marked. Don't limit yourself to the Chinese trainees. Chinese that work on the base or in surrounding areas are also potential candidates."

"Officially, we are looking for eyes and ears to help us secure this area. Use that as your cover for establishing our intelligence network. Anyone you think might be suitable for long-term undercover work should be referred to Sergeant Kalway. Any questions?"

"It might be useful to put Chao Lin in one of the groups of trainees, Captain," Isiac said.

"I like that idea, Sergeant, but do you think you can separate him from his dog long enough for training," Captain Carter asked?

The men's laughter temporarily interrupted the meeting and delayed Isiac's response.

"Chao and Lena are quite popular with the men, sir, as you can see, but I think we can make some arrangements for Lena while Chao Lin is involved in training."

"Make it happen then, Sergeant," Captain Carter said, and then continued, "Squads 2 through 5 will set up a patrol schedule for the base, just to make sure that the officers don't forget that we have eyes and ears of our own. Squad 1 will start patrolling around the base using base security as their cover for widening our intelligence network." With, "That's all men," Captain Carter ended the meeting.

February 12, 1943

Basic training begins for the Chinese troops in Kunming. Chao Lin participates in the training program.

February 15, 1943

This was the fourth day of basic training and Isiac wanted to see how much progress was being made. From the observations that he had made at the Nationalist's training camp, he could already see that the communists were better disciplined and worked harder. Even the Communist officers participated in the training. Not so for the Nationalists Chinese officers.

"Sergeant Kalway," Sergeant Kerr of 4th Squad called, as Isiac approached his group of trainees. "We have a problem with 2 of our trainees. I had to send them to the hospital. They were beat up by a group of Nationalist soldiers."

"Tell me what happened, Sergeant Kerr," Isiac said.

"Six Nationalist Chinese collapsed the tent over my two boys and used clubs and kicked them while they were trapped under their tent. Some of the other Communist trainees heard the noise, but, by the time they got out of their own tents, the Nationalists were running away."

"Were they able to recognize anyone," Isiac asked?

"No. It was too dark, and they were too far away," Sergeant Kerr answered.

"What's the condition of your 2 trainees," Isiac asked?

"I don't know," Sergeant Kerr said. "They are still in the hospital."

When Isiac got to the hospital, Captain Doa Chan and two of his officers were with their injured men. Isiac asked the Chinese doctor, who also spoke English, about the condition of his patients. The Chinese doctor then responded in English,

"One has 2 broken fingers and a broken arm. The other one has a broken ankle and broken ribs. Both have massive bruising and symptoms of a possible concussion. Neither one of these men will be able to continue training."

Isiac's Chinese lessons were progressing well, but he wanted to make sure that Captain Chan didn't misunderstand him, so he asked the Chinese doctor, "Will you translate for me? I have a message for Captain Chan." The doctor nodded, yes, and Isiac began,

"There will be no retaliation. I know the Nationalists are responsible for the attack. But I also know they will deny it." Isiac waited for the doctor to translate. When Captain Chan made no response, Isiac continued.

"When I suggest that it must have been the work of bandits, I'm sure the Nationalists will agree. Then I will tell the Nationalist Captain that I am giving my MPs orders to shoot anyone, not authorized by me, who enters the training camps. I'm going to see the Nationalist Captain right now. Please ask Captain Chan if he will wait for me to come back. I have more to say."

"Captain Chan will wait," the doctor said.

With a slight bow to Captain Chan, Isiac left to find the Nationalist Captain.

"Excuse me, sir," Isiac said when he found Captain Kwang. "Some of your men beat up some communist trainees last night. I am here to arrest them."

The Nationalist Captain spoke English quite well and responded to Isiac's accusations,

"I assure you, Sergeant Kalway," Captain Kwang said, "None of my men were involved."

"The Communists must be mistaken, then," Isiac said. "Do you think it could have been bandits, sir?"

"Most certainly it was the work of Bandits," Captain Kwang said.

Isiac continued, "In that case, for everyone's protection, I'm going to give my MPs orders to shoot anyone in the training camps that is not authorized by me to be there. To avoid any possible accidents, it would probably be a good idea for you to warn your men not to accidently wander into the training area. I assure you, Captain Kwang, that all our young trainees will be protected so they can help us drive the Japanese out of China. If you feel the need for more protection, Captain, I'll arrange for some of the Communist veterans to stand guard around your tent each night. They have a lot of experience dealing with bandits."

No longer smiling, Captain Kwang said, "That won't be necessary, Sergeant Kalway."

With that, Isiac returned to the hospital. Again, the doctor translated for Isiac. When the doctor's translation was done, Captain Chan nodded, indicating his appreciation of Isiac's actions. Isiac then had the doctor tell Captain Chan that tonight he would have 4 of his MPs stand guard over the training camp, and tomorrow he would move the communist trainees inside the perimeter of his Company's Command Center.

When training was finished for the day, Isiac found Chao Lin and gave him instructions.

"No Chinese lessons tonight and no training for you tomorrow. Tonight, you and Lena are going to help my MPs patrol the Communist training camp."

"Yes, Sergeant," Chao said.

"And Chao Lin, carry your .45," Isiac added.

Isiac had the Communist trainee's move their tents and equipment, which wasn't much, into the southeast corner of his Company's compound before training began for the day. As the move was taking place, Captain Chan, with Lieutenant Ping, approached Isiac.

"Captain Chan and I joined your guard detail last night," Lieutenant Ping said in English.

"I heard," Isiac responded in Chinese, as his Chinese continued to improve.

Then Lieutenant Ping continued in English,

"Chao Lin gave us a demonstration of Lena's abilities as a guard dog last night. Captain Chan would like to buy Lena."

Isiac turned to Captain Chan and said, in Chinese, "Chao Lin would never sell Lena."

"I am sorry to hear that," Captain Chan replied in Chinese, "but I was expecting that answer." Captain Chan then watched Isiac to see if he understood.

Shaking his head yes, Isiac said, again in Chinese,

"Chao Lin is a good teacher; he can teach dogs and people."

"Yes, he is," Captain Chan said. "And your Chinese is improving rapidly. I could understand you perfectly."

Chao Lin, heading for Isiac's barracks, was intercepted by Captain Chan.

"Sergeant Kalway told me you would never sell your dog," Captain Chan said.

"Never," Chao confirmed.

"Would you train a dog for me," Captain Chan asked?

"I'll help you train a dog," Chao answered.

"Good, good. I'll find a dog," the Captain said.

"Young dogs are best, but not puppies," Chao said. "Between 6 months and 2 years is best."

"I'll find a dog," Captain Chan repeated.

February 25,1943

During training, Chao had seen Captain Chan with a big, yellow, curly-haired dog. After training, Captain Chan was waiting for Chao Lin.

"I found a dog, Chao Lin," the Captain said. "A little over a year old."

Chao knelt down, and even though Captain Chan had his dog on a rope, the dog moved closer and licked Chao's face. Chao asked, "What's his name?"

"Linga," Captain Chan said.

"Almost like Lena," Chao said.

"Both good names," Captain Chan said, and they both laughed.

Chao took the rope and used it to hold Linga so that he touched Chao's leg as they walked. Every time Linga

285

tried to pull ahead or move to the side, Chao gave the rope a quick jerk to bring Linga back to the proper position. When Linga planted his feet, Chao dragged him until he started walking again on his own.

"You have to show him that you are the boss," Chao said. "If Linga tries to be stubborn, you must never hit him. If he gets stubborn or wild, just hold him until he submits, then release him and start over. If he is really wild, lay down on him until he stops struggling. Now you try it."

Chao handed Captain Chan Linga's rope. Linga required short tugs to keep him in position as Captain Chan walked, but he didn't put on his brakes and refuse to walk. That was a good sign.

"As you walk," Chao said, "Repeat the word HEEL, and say HEEL each time you have to tug on the rope. Each time you stop, say the word SIT, and, as you pull up on his rope, push down on his hind end. Then say HEEL as you start walking again. If you can, take Linga everywhere with you. Play with him several times a day, and then let him sleep near you and play with him again each morning. If you can, bring him back tomorrow after my training is over, and we can work with him some more."

"I'll be back tomorrow, Chao Lin. Thank you," Captain Chan said.

February 26, 1943

Every evening after Chinese lessons, Isiac had been teaching Chao Lin Judo. When hand to hand combat training began today, it was clear that Chao Lin had a significant advantage over the other trainees. After training, but before Chinese lessons, Chao Lin continued to work with Captain Chan and Linga. You could say that Chao Lin was a busy boy, but that would not be completely accurate because Chao Lin had become a man.

India-Burma Border, February 28, 1943

The Ledo Road reaches the India-Burma border at milepost 36.

China, March 8, 1943

Linga had mastered heeling without a leash, sit, come, stay, and no; and each evening, right before sundown, Captain Chan and Chao Lin could be seen walking their dogs around the perimeter of the camp.

After their walk, Chao said, "Tomorrow we begin the commands, WATCH, ATTACK, and GUARD."

March 14, 1943

Isiac's cast is removed.

March 23, 1943

Isiac and Fritz watched as Captain Chan and Chao Lin were taking their evening walk around the camp. They knew that a new performance had been added to the nightly routine of the 2 men and their dogs. Behind the company office, where it was bright enough for an audience to witness the performance, Chao Lin and Captain Chan put on a demonstration of WATCH, ATTACK, GUARD. In addition to Isiac, Fritz, and a dozen other men from the Company, about 20 men from other parts of the base had come to watch. No one was disappointed.

India, March 24, 1943

A supply depot is created at "Hellgate" which provided a rest area, a refueling station, and a temporary storage facility for supplies.

Burma, March 28, 1943

Merrill's Marauders attack the Japanese at Shaduzup in Burma.

China, March 28, 1943

Captain Carter's cast is removed.

April 1943

The monsoons halt all work on the Ledo Road.

China, April 26, 1943

Basic training for the Chinese ends.

April 27, 1943

With orders from Captain Carter to establish an intelligence network in the surrounding area, Corporal Lang and Corporal Linder, along with Chao and Lena, leave in one of the Company's jeeps. They spread the word that a reward would be given to anyone who provided information about the Japanese or Japanese sympathizers. Because they were also looking for stolen goods and the bandits that stole them, a reward would also be given for information about any unusual movement of goods that leads to the recovery of the goods and the capture of the bandits that stole them. It was hoped that the possibility of being rewarded for information would keep Captain Carter's Company informed about anything unusual that happened around the base.

May 10, 1943

With a local intelligence system established, Chao suggests a plan to expand their intelligence network by using traders that travel more widely around the country. Captain Carter ordered Sergeant Woods and his team to take 3 jeeps with enough supplies for a week and help Chao put his plan in motion. After a week, they would evaluate Chao's plan; and, if it seemed to have merit, they would continue to develop it.

May 24, 1943

Chao and Lena had just returned from their second weekly trip into the surrounding area, and they had found a good prospect to become a permanent part of their intelligence network. Sergeant Woods had sent a message to Captain Carter asking for a meeting. When Sergeant Woods, Chao, and Lena arrived at the Captain's office, he was waiting for them.

"Come right in men, and lady," the Captain said, obviously referring to Lena. "I just sent for Sergeant Kalway. I also sent for the rest of 1st Squad. I wanted the whole 1st Squad to be in on this meeting."

Captain Carter was playing with Lena when Fritz and Isiac entered his office.

"Here comes my Michigan Marsh Sergeants," Captain Carter said.

Isiac and Fritz looked at each other and said, in unison, "Colonel Rodgers."

"Can't get anything past you boys," Captain Carter said.

When the rest of Squad 1 arrived, Captain Carter nodded for Chao Lin to start his report.

"Sergeant Woods and I found a young trader who already has a network of traders, all family members. They operate in areas south and west of Kunming."

"He frequently trades with the British," Sergeant Woods added. "So, most of his family speaks some English. Not as good as Chao, though. However, I did notice that his sister could use some help with her English, and I'd be willing to volunteer to spend some time with her to improve her English skills."

"I'm sure you would," Captain Carter said. "I don't remember any comedy classes being offered in MP school, but it seems that half of the Company is made of comics."

"Sergeant Heimlich holds special classes on comedy every Wednesday night," Sergeant Woods replied.

Everyone was already laughing when Captain Carter said, "What time on Wednesday?"

With the laughter continuing, Sergeant Woods said, "It looks like you've already attended some of Sergeant Heimlich's classes, Captain."

More laughing. It continued until Captain Carter held up his hands and said,

"Go on Chao, finish your report."

With the laughter subsiding, Chao continued.

"Jinn Wu and his family have a warehouse in Kunming. And his family also has small storage shacks that serve as warehouses in 6 cities to the south and west of Kunming. Sergeant Woods has them marked on his map."

Sergeant Woods spread out his map on Captain Carter's desk. His map had 7 cities circled. In addition to Kunming, Sergeant Woods had 6 other cities circled: Dali, Huxiong, Yuxi, Chengjang, Tonghai, and Kaiyuan.

"These cities form a line between Kunming and the Japanese positions in Burma," Sergeant Woods said, as he used a pencil to connect the 6 cities.

"Did you mention OSS to Jinn Wu," Captain Carter asked, Chao?

"No, Captain Carter. But I did offer him a discount on US Army Surplus goods, and favored trading status with my trading company after the war," Chao said and handed Captain Carter a business card that he had printed when he was in Ledo.

HSC Trading Company

Hong Kong, Shanghai, Calcutta
Current financial arrangements handled by Charted
Bank of India, Australia, and China.
Owners: Shawn McGregor and Chao Lin

After Captain Carter had taken Chao's business card, Chao continued, "I also told him that he would have to swear an oath of secrecy, and that violation of the oath would result in serious consequences and possibly death, not only for him but for any member of his family that chooses to join our organization. He agreed to meet with the 'secret sergeant' on June 7 at his home in Chengjang. He will have all his family members, who are willing to swear to an oath of secrecy, at the meeting."

"Do you think his family members will be as interested in your proposition as Jinn Wu," Captain Carter asked?

"Yes, Captain Carter," Chao Lin said. "Discounts and favorable trading status are powerful incentives for any trader. But to make it perfectly clear that they work for us, it would be wise to include a monthly payment for each person who joins our organization. That would make them obligated to us, and Chinese understand obligation."

"How much of a payment are we talking about, Chao Lin," Captain Carter asked?

"Five American dollars per month, just for watching and listening, would be a dream job for any Chinese, even without trading incentives," Chao answered.

"Having them obligated to us is worth 5 dollars per month. You can add that to their package of incentives," Captain Carter said. Then, speaking to Sergeant Woods, Captain Carter asked, "Are you the secret sergeant?"

"No sir. Chao and I have been traveling together, so I'm no secret. We thought Sergeant Kalway would make a good secret sergeant."

"It seems like the choice has already been made. Sergeant Kalway, you will accompany Sergeant Woods and Chao Lin to the meeting and administer the oath of secrecy. Any questions?"

When no questions followed, Captain Carter said, "Meeting is over, dismissed."

India, June 1943

In June of 1943, Ledo road construction was temporarily halted, and the Engineers were used to construct an airfield at Assam, India.

China, June 7, 1943

Sergeant Kalway, Sergeant Woods, and Chao Lin left camp early for their meeting with Jinn Wu and his family. Jinn Wu only lived about 50 miles from Kunming, but the roads were bad. Less than 2 hours after they left the base, Sergeant Woods pulled to the side of the road. An old man was sitting in the road, crying, with his arms around a dying donkey. A dozen feet away lay the lifeless body of a young Chinese girl.

"What happened," Isiac asked the old man in Chinese?

"My granddaughter was riding my donkey. An Army truck hit them," the old man answered.

"American or Chinese," Isiac asked, again in Chinese. In just a little over 4 months, Isiac had become fluent in Chinese.

"Chinese soldiers," the old man said. "They were laughing when they drove away."

"Why are you crying over your donkey, when your granddaughter is lying dead in the road," Isiac asked?

"I have 4 granddaughters and only one donkey," the old man replied.

Shocked by the old man's answer, all Isiac could say was, "Let's go."

For Sergeant Woods, Chao translated what the old man had said, and as they continued toward Jinn Wu's house, the silence seemed to last forever. Finally, Chao Lin broke the silence.

"The value of life is looked at differently here in China than it is in the West," Chao said, feeling a need to explain. The quaver in his voice clearly indicated that Chao was just as upset as the sergeants. Chao then tried to explain a situation that truly defied reason.

"The old man knows that his children can make him more grandchildren, but his donkey cannot be replaced. And without his donkey, he no longer has the means to support himself or his family. I think the views of the younger generations are changing, but some Chinese traditions go back thousands of years. I am so lucky to be a British Subject."

Jinn Wu's house, made of rough-hewed timber, looked little different from the surrounding houses, except it was larger. And instead of a dirt floor, Jinn Wu had a raised wooden floor. Before approaching Jinn Wu's house, Chao tried to further explain Chinese traditions.

"Bowing shows respect. Business will not be discussed until after dinner. If you see any of the men spit chicken bones on the floor, you must do the same, or they will be offended. Spitting out the bones shows that you are enjoying your meal."

As soon as Jinn Wu saw the men approaching his house, he hurried out to greet them. Jinn Wu's wife gave each man a small container of water and a towel so they could clean up after their journey.

"Dinner will be ready soon," Jinn Wu's wife, Biyu, said, in English, before she turned to reenter the house.

Jinn Wu introduced his Uncle, older brother, and cousin to Chao-Lin and his friends. The 7 men then squeezed in around the small table. The small talk, which was being conducted in English, was interrupted when Biyu began serving dinner. And quite a dinner it was: chicken, fish, rice, carrots, and peas, all covered in a cream sauce. Each man was also given a pickled egg and a cup of tea. Jinn Wu's Uncle was the first one to spit out a chicken bone. All the other men at the table soon followed suit, showing their appreciation of the meal just served.

Jinn Wu's wife and 3 children had eaten their meal at a temporary table that was formed by a board that was hinged to the wall. When it was needed, it was lifted and held in place by a stick at each end. After dinner,

Jinn Wu's wife gave each man more tea and rice cake covered in honey. Then, she and the children left the men alone to conduct their business. Jinn Wu had already explained the benefits of joining Sergeant Kalway's secret organization and about the necessity of taking the oath of secrecy.

"This is the secret Sergeant," Chao said, nodding toward Isiac. "He will administer the oath and explain the consequences of breaking it."

"You already know the benefits of joining our organization," Isiac began, "There are also dangers involved. If the wrong people discover that you are working with us, the results could be just as deadly as they would be if you broke the oath. Secrecy is a protection for all of us. Anyone not willing to take these risks should leave now."

Isiac looked each man directly in the eyes. When no one left the table, Isiac administered the oath. As they were preparing to leave, Isiac pulled four American 5-dollar bills from his wallet and gave one to each man.

"Congratulations," Isiac said, "You are now members of our secret organization. In addition to your other benefits, you will each be paid 5 American dollars each month for your eyes and ears."

Surprised by this additional and unexpected benefit, all 4 new members stood up smiling and bowed. Chao

Lin, Isaac, and Sergeant Woods returned the bows as they left Jinn Wu's house.

June 8, 1943

Captain Carter receives a message from Colonel Rodgers: Staff Sergeant Heimlich promoted to Sergeant First Class.

Isiac, along with Fritz and the rest of Squads 1 and 2, were waiting for their transport when it landed. Captain Peer watched as Isiac and his men transferred the cargo from the transport to one of the Company's trucks. Ten of the crates were unmarked. They contained scoped rifles and High Standard .22's with silencers.

June 11, 1943

Captain Chan found Chao Lin walking Lena and said, "Chao, I have a message for Sergeant Kalway, do you know where he is?"

"Yes," Chao answered, and they walked away together, both heeling their dogs.

When Chao and Captain Chan found Sergeant Kalway in Captain Carter's office talking with the Captain, Chao spoke,

"Captain Carter, Captain Chan has an important message."

"Bring him in, Chao Lin," the Captain said.

Captain Chan had already told Chao Lin his story. All Chao had to do was repeat it for Captain Carter and Isiac. Chao began,

"During the civil war, most of the Chinese Triades in the areas that the Nationalists controlled aligned themselves with the Nationalists. But in the northern and western parts of China, the Triades have an arrangement with the Communists. The Triades in these areas know that the Civil War will resume as soon as the war with Japan ends. And they believe the Communists will win."

Captain Carter had already sent that message to the OSS via Captain Goodman. Chao continued.

"The Nationalists brought some Triade leaders from Eastern China in an attempt to convince their Western colleagues to join with the Nationalists. When the Western Triade leaders refused, the Eastern Triade members, with help from Captain Kwang's troops, kidnapped the leaders of the Western Triades. If the Eastern Triades kill or torture the Western Triade leaders, it will start a war between the 2 groups. So, the Nationalists, who have been stealing supplies from the base and selling them to the Eastern Triades, made a plan to kill one of the Western Triade leaders, and leave his body behind the next time they steal American supplies. That way the Western Triades will be blamed for the thefts."

"How did you find out about this," Isiac asked in Chinese?

"Not all of the Eastern Triades like working with the Nationalists," Captain Chan answered.

After Isiac had translated for Captain Carter, Captain Carter said,

"One of Colonel Hardy's men was killed last night when someone broke into one of his warehouses. Was that the work of Captain Kwang's men?"

When Isiac translated Captain Carter's question, Captain Chan nodded 'yes.'

Captain Carter was fuming. It took a few moments before he was able to continue.

"Captain Kwang deserves a firing squad, but like you, Captain Chan, the Nationalists are our allies. If I try to arrest him, the politicians will make sure that I am the one facing a firing squad."

"Sir," Isiac said to Captain Carter, "The Eastern Triades can't kill their Western rivals for political reasons, and we can't kill Captain Kwang for political reasons. What if the Eastern Triades and Captain Kwang killed each other?"

That silenced the room. Captain Carter could tell that one of his Michigan Marsh Sergeants was beginning to form a plan.

"Go on Sergeant Kalway," Captain Carter said.

"If we could rescue Captain Chan's Western Triade allies, and kill their Eastern rivals, we could turn Captain Kwang into the hero who found and killed the bandits who murdered an American soldier. Captain Kwang also prevented the bandits from stealing supplies that were scheduled to be delivered to Nationalist Chinese troops. Unfortunately, during the gun battle, Captain Kwang was mortally wounded and died shortly after."

"Sergeant Kalway, that's an interesting story. Do you think there is a way to turn fiction into reality," Captain Carter asked?

"With Captain Chan's help, I think we can," Isiac answered with Chao Lin translating for Captain Chan. Then in Chinese, Isiac said, "Captain Chan, do you know where the Western Triade leaders are being held?"

"They are being held in an old farmhouse outside of town. And the stolen supplies are hidden in a barn close to the farmhouse," Captain Chan answered.

"How many Eastern Triade members are in the area," Isiac asked.

"Twelve," Captain Chan said, "But 2 of them are my informants."

"Are they all at the farmhouse," Isiac asked?

"Yes," Captain Chan said.

"Can your informants be trusted," Isiac said, still asking questions and gathering information.

"I'd trust them with my life," Captain Chan answered.

You could almost hear the ideas bouncing around in Isiac's head when he said,

"That gives us even better options."

No one else in the room said a word. They all seemed to be waiting for one of Isiac's ideas to bounce out of his head as a fully formed plan. They didn't have long to wait before Isiac, again, asked another question.

"Who is the leader of the Eastern Triades?"

"Wan Tan," Captain Chan answered.

Isiac began to lay out his plan.

"What if Wan Tan sent a message to Captain Kwang that they had kidnapped you and planned to kill you and leave your body with the body of one of the Western Triade leaders at the American warehouse after their next robbery. This would show that the Western Triade leaders and the communists are working together to steal supplies. And Wan Tan was hoping that this would prove to the other Western

Triade members that working with the Nationalists was a better option."

"Captain Kwang hates communists, and he hates me," Captain Chan said, "I think he would really like that idea."

"Would you be willing to be kidnapped by your 2 informants and be delivered, along with Captain Kwang, to the farmhouse," Isiac asked? "By then, the Western Triade leaders will be freed, and the Eastern Triade leaders killed."

"It would be my pleasure," Captain Chan said. "Seeing the look on Captain Kwang's face when he realizes that the plan has been reversed will be priceless. The only thing I ask is that I am the one to act as the firing squad that Captain Kwang well deserves."

Everyone looked at Captain Carter, waiting.

When Captain Carter nodded, Isiac said,

"Then that's the plan."

It was late afternoon when one of Captain Carter's trucks pulled into their warehouse. Captain Carter, Isiac, and all of Squad 1 were watching as Captain Chan pushed aside the canvas that covered the back of the truck and stepped out with his 2 informants. Captain Chan had a bruise on one cheek and a scratch on the other. His pants were dirty, and the right knee was ripped, and there was blood on his shirt. But he was smiling.

"Do I look like a kidnap victim," he asked?

When Chao translated, everyone laughed.

"You look perfect," Captain Carter said.

"Everyone take a good look at Captain Chan's two friends," Isiac said. "And don't shoot them."

When Chao translated, everyone was laughing, but the laughter of the two Triade members was only token laughter. As the possible targets, "Don't shoot them" didn't seem all that funny. The two Triade members felt much better when they found out that, by the time of their arrival, all the Eastern Triade members would be dead, except them, of course.

Captain Chan spread out a diagram of the farm. The farmhouse had only one door and two rooms. The front room had a window on each side, with an inside door leading to the back room. The back room also had a window on each side with an additional window in the back. The 6 kidnapped Triade leaders were on benches in the back corners of the room, 3 on each side. They were tied to the walls. A guard was seated in a chair on each side of the door that led to the front room.

In the front room of the farmhouse were a table and 4 chairs. Four guards would be in the front room, either playing cards at the table or sleeping on the floor. This early in the evening, they would probably still be playing cards. Outside, there were two men on the porch guarding the door. There was another guard at the back of the farmhouse, between the farmhouse and the barn. The forth outside guard was at the far end of the barn.

There were 10 Triade guards, and each guard was designated with a number. A member of the Squad was assigned to each number. If any of the guards were in a position different from the diagram, the Squad member assigned to that number would have to make any adjustments necessary to maintain his target.

With the details of the plan finalized, Captain Chan and his 2 informants left the base in the same truck that delivered them. Squad 1, with Isiac following in a jeep, left in another Company truck. The truck carrying Captain Chan dropped its 3 passengers off just outside the base, while the other truck delivered Squad 1 to take up its position around the farmhouse.

It was now dark, and one of Captain Chan's informants found Captain Kwang and informed him of the change in plans. Captain Kwang and the Triade member, who Captain Kwang mistakenly thought was his ally, left in the Captain's Jeep. Captain Kwang was given directions, and when he arrived at a secluded area not far from the base, he found another Triade member standing over Captain Chan. Seeing Captain Chan tied, gagged, and lying on the ground, Captain Kwang said, with sarcastic concern,

"You look a mess, Captain Chan. Let me help you up."

Captain Kwang and one of the Triade members, not so gently, helped Captain Chan into the Jeep.

"We're going for a ride, Captain Chan," Kwang said, "Unfortunately, you won't be coming back."

The truck carrying Squad 1, with Isiac following in a jeep, stopped a little less than half a mile from the farmhouse. Although not part of the original plan shared with Captain Chan and his two Triade compatriots, the four jeeps that had been following Isiac stopped as well. Isiac had brought along Squad 2 as backup. Two members of Squad 2 stayed with the truck and jeeps. The rest of the men headed toward the farmhouse.

When Isiac's MPs reached the farmhouse, all the Triade guards were in their expected positions, except one. The guard at the back of the barn had moved between the barn and the farmhouse. He and the guard at the back of the farmhouse were talking and smoking cigarettes. The MP assigned to the guard at the back of the barn adjusted his position to adapt to the slightly altered situation. Meanwhile, 8 members of Squad 2 had taken up positions about 60 yards from the farmhouse forming a perimeter. All members of both Squads were armed with their rifles and .45's. In addition, each man had a High Standard .22 with a silencer attached.

The 2 guards outside the front door and the two guards in the back were the initial targets. The cough of the silencers that eliminated the Triade members guarding the front door was the signal for the other MPs to dispatch their assigned targets. After the 2 guards in the back had been eliminated, the MPs assigned to each window moved into position. The coughing sound was then repeated as the MPs assigned to the windows found their targets.

After a second or two, 4 more silenced shots could be heard, then nothing. As Isiac opened the front door, a final shot from a side window was fired into the last moving Triade member. In Chinese, Isiac said,

"We are friends of Captain Chan. He will be here soon."

Then, stepping over bodies, Isiac moved to the back room and untied the captive Western Triade members. Isiac's whistle was the signal for Squad 2 to return to their jeeps and depart the area before Captain Chan's arrival. Isiac didn't want Captain Chan to find out that he only knew part of the plan.

When Captain Kwang arrived at the farmhouse, he got out of his jeep and said to his 2 Triade companions, "Bring Captain Chan."

The 2 Triade members, each one gripping one of Captain Chan's arms, removed him from the jeep. Even in the dark, Captain Kwang could see two guards smoking under a tree in front of the house, and a third guard sitting on the front steps.

"End of the line for you, Chan," Captain Kwang said, intentionally dropping Chan's title of Captain, as a sign of disrespect. "You will be with your ancestors soon."

Then Captain Kwang turned his back on Captain Chan and his escorts and walked toward the front door of the farmhouse. The guard that had been sitting on the front steps had moved away from the door and stood in the shadows at the end of the porch. As Captain Kwang reached for the door, he could hear Captain Chan being dragged up the steps behind him. The light was dim as he stepped into the farmhouse, but not so dim that Captain Kwang couldn't see 3 of the Western Triade leaders, that he had kidnapped earlier, sitting at the table; and 4 MPs, one in each corner, pointing their .45's at him. On the floor, where they had fallen, lay 4 of his Eastern Triade allies.

Before he could recover from his shock, Captain Kwang felt the barrel of a gun in his back and heard Captain Chan's voice.

"My ancestors will have to wait a while before I join them."

With Captain Chan now in control of the situation, Isiac's 4 MPs left the farmhouse. A few seconds later, they heard a single shot. By the time Squad 1 had returned to the farmhouse with their truck, Captain Chan and the kidnapped Triade members had disappeared. Isiac, with Captain Carter sitting beside him, drove back to headquarters to inform Colonel Hardy that Captain Kwang had found the stolen supplies and the Eastern Triades that had stolen them.

"Colonel Hardy," Isiac said, "Captain Kwang killed 10 Eastern Triade gang members. They were the ones who murdered one of your soldiers at the warehouse 2 days ago. Unfortunately, Captain Kwang died during the gun battle."

Then Captain Carter asked, "Colonel Hardy, should we inform Lieutenant Hura that Captain Kwang died a hero?"

"Good idea, Captain," Colonel Hardy said. "It's always nice to find something good to say about the dead."

By his tone, Isiac could tell that Colonel Hardy didn't hold Captain Kwang in high regard.

"I'll take care of it, Colonel," Isiac said.

"Thank you, Sergeant," Colonel Hardy said, "Anything else?"

"Yes, sir," Isiac said. "I have some of my men guarding the supplies that Captain Kwang found at the farmhouse. I'll bring the supplies back as soon as Captain Carter and I show Lieutenant Hura where and how his Captain died."

With a nod indicating agreement, Colonel Hardy said, "Take care of it then."

Captain Carter and Isiac left the Colonel's office, and when Captain Carter informed Lieutenant Hura of his Captain's death, it was apparent that he, like many other people, wasn't overly impressed with his own Captain.

June 13, 1943

Jinn Wu, accompanied by Chao Lin, left on a trading mission to areas farther from Kunming than Jinn Wu normally traveled. Because some of his goods were provided free of charge by Captain Carter, Jinn Wu's trading sojourn was profitable even before it began. While trading, Chao Lin was constantly watching for traders that might make good additions to their intelligence network. Once selected, and after taking the oath of secrecy, the new traders were given free supplies with the promise of a bonus anytime they provided useful information. Chao also gave each new trader that joined their intelligence network one of his business cards, offering preferred trading status after the war.

June 14, 1943

In gratitude for their rescue, the leaders of the Western Triades offer Captain Carter, Isiac, Fritz, and Captain Chan good friend status. And for information about Japanese troop movements, Japanese spies, and Japanese collaborators, Isiac and Fritz would arrange for guns and other supplies to conveniently fall off the Company trucks at certain places at certain times. Another link is added to the Company's intelligence network.

India, July 6, 1943

"Hellgate", (Milepost 34.5), which is the last section of the Ledo Road still in India, becomes the road construction headquarters.

China, July 25, 1943

After 6 weeks of trading with Jinn Wu, Chao returns to camp with the names of 4 new traders to add to their intelligence network.

Burma, July 1943

Work on the Ledo Road resumes, and, by the end of July, the road reaches Milepost 49.75.

August 1, 1943

Jinn Wu sends word to Isiac that a strange Chinese man is asking questions about the Army base.

August 2, 1943

Isiac, Chao, and Lena, along with the 2 boys who provided Jinn Wu with information about the possible Japanese spy, began to covertly watch the man. When Isiac hears the man relay information about the base to another Chinese man, Isiac has Chao, and the other two boys follow the new man. After the new Chinese agent leaves, Isiac grabs the other agent.

After returning to the base and delivering the spy to Captain Carter, Isiac found Captain Chan.

"We captured a Japanese spy, and Chao and two boys are following another spy," Isiac told Captain Chan.

When Captain Chan heard this, as Isiac had hoped, Captain Chan offered to take 6 of his best men and help Chao with his surveillance. Then Isiac continued,

"Captain Chan, you are a good friend. Thank you for your offer to help Chao Lin. Captain Carter asked if you would help with the interrogation of the spy, but I'm sure he would understand if you assigned one of your men to help with the interrogation. We all like Chao Lin and your concern for Chao Lin's safety will be appreciated by every man in our Company."

"Chao Lin is also my good friend," Captain Chan said to Isiac, "I will go with my men to help him. Lieutenant Ping can help with the interrogation."

To Lieutenant Ping, Captain Chan said,

"Lieutenant, help Sergeant Kalway and Captain Carter with the interrogation. And while I am gone, you are in charge of the men."

"Yes sir, Captain Chan," Lieutenant Ping said.

Captain Chan wasted no time. As Sergeant Kalway and Lieutenant Ping headed to Captain Carter's office to help with the interrogation, he was already assembling the men he wanted to help Chao with his surveillance.

The Japanese spy was tied to a chair in Captain Carter's office. The Captain and Fritz had tried to communicate with the spy, but either he didn't speak English or he was pretending not to speak English.

"Can we take a break, Captain," Fritz said, "I need a cigarette."

"Sure Sergeant," Captain Carter said. "I'll go with you. I could use a smoke myself."

Neither man smoked. As they closed the office door behind them, Captain Carter said,

"Let's hear it, Sergeant."

Now that they were out of hearing distance of the prisoner, Fritz said,

"I have an idea. If he doesn't speak when we go back in, you can pretend to give up. Then I'll suggest that we send him to the communists and let them conduct the interrogation."

"Good plan," Captain Carter said. "I'll start, and then you can use your already perfected acting skills to set the hook."

Back in the office, Captain Carter, once again, tried to engage the spy in conversation, still with no success. Waving his hands at his sides, Captain Carter did a little acting himself. With a look of disgust, Captain Carter said,

"I give up, Sergeant Heimlich. We'll never get anywhere with this man. We don't speak Chinese, and he doesn't speak English."

"We could turn him over to the Chinese, Sir," Fritz said. "They have more experience in interrogations than we do."

"Do you suggest the Nationalists or the Communists," Captain Carter asked?

"The Communists, sir," Fritz answered. "They don't seem to have any rules about interrogations. I think they will get results much more quickly."

"All right, Sergeant," Captain Carter said. "Go find Captain Chan and ask him if he will take over this interrogation."

"Wait," the prisoner said, as Fritz headed toward the door. "I speak English."

"Then you better start answering questions," Captain Carter said, practically spitting out the words.

"And remember, you are not a soldier. You are a spy. I could have you shot right now. And you were worried about the Communists. You are in a room right now with 2 men who were in a transport when it was shot down by your friends, the Japanese."

The change in Captain Carter's attitude from near complacency to anger and aggression had the desired effect on the spy. Captain Carter suddenly became calm again and asked the spy,

"What's your name?"

"Bin Teal," the spy answered.

"Bin Teal, sir," Captain Carter shouted, immediately reverting to anger and aggression.

Bin Teal was so scared that he probably would have fallen out of his chair if he wasn't tied to it. But somehow, Bin Teal got the words out,

"Bin Teal, sir."

Just then, Isiac and Lieutenant Ping entered Captain Carter's office.

"Just in time, gentlemen," Captain Carter said. "If this spy doesn't give us any useful information, we're going to take him outside and shoot him. He already lied about not speaking English. How can we trust him to tell us the truth about anything else?"

Turning back to Bin Teal, Captain Carter finished with,

"Now you are in a room with another man who was shot down by your friends, the Japanese."

"Captain Carter, may I speak with Bin Teal for a moment," Fritz asked?

"Go ahead, Sergeant Heimlich," Captain Carter said. "Bin Teal doesn't have many moments left in his life."

"What were your instructions, Bin Teal," Fritz asked?

"To gather information about the Army base," Bin Teal answered.

Turning his back to Bin Teal and facing Isiac and Lieutenant Ping, Fritz winked at Isiac to let him know that he and Captain Carter were in the middle of another one of their slyly developed schemes. Then Fritz addressed the 2 recent arrivals.

"Sergeant Kalway and Lieutenant Ping, before you arrived we threatened to turn Bin Teal over to Captain Chan and his Communists. He was so afraid of the Communists; he suddenly remembered that he could speak English. I think Bin Teal finally realizes that he is bargaining with men that would like to see him dead."

Turning back to the prisoner, Fritz continued.

"No more evasive answers, Bin Teal. There is no sympathy for a Japanese spy in this room."

With a slight quiver in his voice, Bin Teal became more specific.

"I was ordered to find information about the number of soldiers at the base and their patrols and other patterns of movement. I was also told to get information about flight schedules of the transports, both into and out of the base, so the Japanese fighters could set up ambushes instead of relying on luck to find the American planes."

"Are the Japanese planning to attack the base," Captain Carter asked?

"No sir, Captain Carter," Bin Teal said, remembering to add 'sir' to the Captain's name. "They are planning only sabotage and guerilla actions. They believe the base is too strong to capture with the number of troops that are currently available."

"Can we speak outside, Captain Carter," Isiac asked, speaking for the first time.

Leaving the spy tied to his chair, the 4 men left the room.

"I can see that you two are developing some kind of plan," Isiac said. "Can you share it with Lieutenant Ping and me?"

"With the information that Bin Teal has finally provided, I think we might be able to use him as a double agent. It all depends on how much he values his life," Fritz answered.

Seeing by the nods from Isiac and Lieutenant Ping that they liked the idea, Captain Carter spoke.

"I believe it's time to come up with another one of our nefarious plans."

With his cerebral wheels turning, Isiac began the planning.

"We could give Bin Teal accurate but useless information about the base and airstrip. Along with that information, we add inaccurate information as well."

"If Bin Teal tells the Japanese that most of our soldiers are being transferred back to India and that only a skeleton crew will remain on the base to service the transports, that might be too tempting for the Japanese to resist and give us an opportunity to set up an ambush," Fritz said.

"I agree, Sergeant Heimlich," Captain Carter said. "Capturing and controlling the Burma road to cut off the supplies that were being sent to Allied troops in China was an essential part of the Japanese war plan. Capturing the airstrip here would prevent the airlift of supplies from India, as well. That would be a major blow to the resupply of the Allied troops remaining in China. The Japanese would find it difficult to ignore an opportunity to further isolate the Allied troops in China. My only concern is that, if we let Bin Teal go, he might disappear."

"Lieutenant Ping, could you arrange for some of your men to covertly follow Bin Teal and monitor his movements," Isiac asked?

"I'm sure that can be arranged," Lieutenant Ping answered.

"What if Bin Teal gives the Japanese the flight schedules of our transports and our fighter planes show up instead," Isiac asked?

"Where do you two come up with these ideas," Captain Carter asked?

"It must be something in the Michigan water," Fritz answered.

"It must be," Captain Carter agreed.

"I have one more idea before we present our proposal to Bin Teal," Isiac said. "Can we take a 20-minute break, sir?"

"Another surprise," Captain Carter said. "I can hardly wait."

When the men reassembled outside Captain Carter's office, Isiac and Fritz were each carrying a scoped rifle.

"What's that for," Captain Carter asked. "I thought we decided not to shoot him. Did you change your minds and decide a firing squad would be a better idea?"

But everyone could tell that the Captain was really anxious to hear the explanation.

"Do you know the story of William Tell," Isiac asked? "So far, no one else knows about Bin Teal. I don't want to take him outside where he might be seen by another spy, but I'd like to give him a demonstration of what will happen if he ever tries to double-cross us."

"So, you plan to shoot an apple off his head," the Captain asked?

At this point, they had to explain the story of William Tell to Lieutenant Ping. It was clear that the Lieutenant enjoyed the implications suggested by the story. Isiac then answered Captain Carter's question.

"Actually, two apples. One held against each ear."

Like magicians, Isiac and Fritz each displayed an apple. When they finally reentered the Captain's office, Isiac asked,

"Do you mind if we untie Bin Teal's hands, Captain?"

"It's your show, Sergeant," the Captain said.

Isiac and Fritz, one on each side of Bin Teal, lifted Bin Teal's chair, with him in it, and moved it in front of the window, with Bin Teal facing outside. Then, they untied his hands. Isiac and Fritz each took a sharpened pencil from Captain Carter's desk and poked the pencils into their apples.

Handing Lieutenant Ping his baton, Isiac said, "If he doesn't cooperate completely, give him a tap on the shin."

"My pleasure, Sergeant Kalway," Lieutenant Ping replied with a smile.

Then Isiac and Fritz each handed their apples on a stick to Bin Teal. Bin Teal's eyes showed his fear and confusion.

"Captain Carter," Fritz said, "You realize that this demonstration will leave 2 bullet holes in your wall, if we don't miss, that is."

"No problem, Sergeant Heimlich," Captain Carter assured Fritz. "They might be useful the next time we need to have a discussion with a spy."

"Hold the apples against your ears," Isiac said.

When Bin Teal hesitated, Lieutenant Ping lowered Isiac's baton to leg level and pulled it back, preparing for a swing. Immediately, both apples were pressed against Bin Teal's ears. As Isiac and Fritz left the room with their scoped rifles, Isiac said,

"See you later, Bin Teal."

"Maybe," Fritz added, and everyone laughed, except Bin Teal.

Following the movement of Isiac and Fritz through the window, Bin Teal's nervousness and fear increased as they continued to move farther away. By the time Isiac and Fritz stopped, Bin Teal was shaking so hard it was difficult for him to hold the apples steady.

"It would be a good idea to hold the apples still," Captain Carter said. "Hitting a moving target is much more difficult."

With all his effort, Bin Teal finally managed to hold the apples still. Both apples splattered. A second later the rifle shots could be heard. By the time Isiac and Fritz returned, Lieutenant Ping had already retied Bin Teal's hands, not an easy job because they hadn't stopped shaking.

"You have a choice to make, Bin Teal," Captain Carter said. And, after explaining what would be expected of him as a double agent, Captain Carter asked,

"Firing squad or double agent?"

"Double agent, sir," Bin Teal said without hesitation, again remembering to say, sir when he addressed the Captain.

"When you return here and confirm that you have delivered the misinformation to the Japanese," Captain Carter said, "And if the Japanese act upon that misinformation, you will be given 50 American dollars and released. Your first act as a double agent is to give me the names of the men on the base who are supplying you with information."

Captain Carter then had Lieutenant Ping again free Bin Teal's hands. Captain Carter then handed Bin Teal a pencil and paper and watched as Bin Teal wrote down 3 names. Taking the pencil and paper from Bin Teal, Captain Carter ordered 4 men to guard the prisoner, two outside his office and two inside the office. Once outside the office, Isiac said,

"Sir, Captain Chan, with some of his men, is on his way to help Chao Lin watch the spies. Sergeant Heimlich and I need to catch up to Captain Chan and inform him of the change of plans, so he doesn't attempt to capture any of the spies under surveillance."

"Go, Sergeants," Captain Carter said.

After his two Sergeants had left, Captain Carter handed the note Bin Teal had written to one of his MPs and said,

"Arrest these men, and answer no questions."

After dark, Bin Teal was released so he could leave Captain Carter's office unseen.

August 10, 1943

Bin Teal entered Captain Carter's office after dark and informed the Captain that he had delivered the false information to the Japanese:

"Most of the troops in Kunming were being transferred back to India to reinforce the troops there. The base would be left with a skeleton crew until October, when reinforcements were expected to arrive. Ten transports with over a thousand men, and escorted by only 2 fighters, were scheduled to leave just before sunrise on September 8."

"You will remain as our guest, Bin Teal," Captain Carter said, "until we see how well you have deceived the Japanese."

Burma, August 1943

By mid-August, Ledo Road construction reached Milepost 50.7 as the 45th Engineer Regiment averaged 3/4 of a mile per day in August.

The 5307th composite unit (Merrill's Marauders), a jungle combat unit, is formed.

India, September 1, 1943

The 823rd Engineers begin the construction of an airstrip along the side of the Ledo Road at Milepost 7.5.

China, September 4, 1943

Captain Chan's scouts locate the Japanese troops that are attempting to execute a surprise attack on the Army base and airstrip in Kunming. Captain Chan sent a message back to the base:

"150 Japanese soldiers accompanied by 100 Burmese soldiers, rifles and mortars only, no vehicles and no artillery."

With that information in hand, Captain Carter, Isiac, Fritz, and Colonel Hardy begin to develop a plan to surprise the unsuspecting Japanese.

Burma, September 5, 1943

The lead bulldozer reaches Milepost 53.4. Then heavy rains halt new road construction.

September 8, 1943

Just before daybreak, instead of 10 transports and 2 fighters, 10 American fighters took off from Kunming following the path typically used by transports flying over the hump to India. Shortly after that, 10 more American Fighters left their base in India and followed a route that would put them behind the Japanese fighters that were expected to leave the Myitkyina air base for an attempted surprise attack on the 10 American transports that they believed were headed toward India.

Shortly, thereafter, the 6 Japanese fighters, that were circling the area where they expected to ambush the American transports, found themselves being attacked, instead, by 10 American fighters. The initial surprise resulted in 2 Japanese fighters being shot down.

The 4 remaining Japanese pilots, realizing they were outnumbered, tried to retreat to their airbase in Myitkyina. But again, to their surprise, the Japanese found their retreat blocked by the other 10 American fighters that had come from India. This second surprise resulted in two more Japanese fighters being shot down. The remaining two Japanese tried evasive action, but with the odds now 10 to 1 against them, it took only a few minutes before the last two Japanese planes erupted in flames. All 20 American fighters returned to their bases unharmed.

China, September 8, 1943

By noon, two Japanese scouts returned to report that the base was practically deserted. The Japanese commander, assured that his information was accurate and that his surprise attack was still undiscovered, ordered his men forward. He wanted them in position to attack before sunrise tomorrow. Two hours later, one of Captain Chan's scouts reported to Colonel Hardy that the Japanese had resumed their advance.

The base, that was supposed to be practically empty, erupted with activity. Eight hundred of Colonel Hardy's men advanced toward the Japanese. A little over a mile southwest of the base, Colonel Hardy and his men set up 2 howitzers on a hilltop. About a mile in front of the hill was a low ridge that ran for about 4 miles from the northeast to the southwest. Behind that ridge, Colonel Hardy deployed 400 of his infantrymen. He then deployed 200 men at each end of the ridge resulting in a u-shaped formation.

Captain Carter and Captain Chan had earlier taken 50 men each and moved behind the unsuspecting Japanese. The Nationalists had graciously volunteered to stay behind and guard the base.

September 9, 1943

Just before dawn, Colonel Hardy's front-line troops spotted the advancing Japanese. They waited until the Japanese began their accent of the ridge before they opened fire. The first sound of gunfire set several things in motion. The two howitzers on the hilltop opened up on the Japanese. Simultaneously, Colonel Hardy's men on each flank moved in to tighten the trap. At the same time, Captain Carter and Captain Chan closed the distance between them and the Japanese rear position.

With the two howitzers pounding them and receiving fire from all sides, the Japanese realized they were trapped. Wasting no more time, the Japanese sent a group of soldiers and tried to breach the left flank. Over a dozen men were killed in the attempted counterattack, and the rest of the attackers were pinned down.

Next, the Japanese tried to break through the troops that were attacking their rear and blocking their retreat. The Japanese spearheaded the attack with all 100 of their Burmese allies. Captain Chan's men, and Isiac's MPs, with their scoped rifles, killed over half of the Burmese soldiers before they retreated to the middle of the box. So far, the Japanese had suffered 80 casualties while the Americans and Chinese suffered none and didn't even have a man wounded.

The sun was now above the horizon, and Colonel Hardy came over the loud speaker, "SURRENDER, YOU ARE SURROUNDED."

He was answered by mortars being fired into his position which resulted in the first 2 American casualties. The howitzers answered the mortar fire, and rifle fire was now pouring in from all sides. The 10 American Fighter planes that had returned unseen by the Japanese scouts to an airstrip north of the base, now entered the fight, as well. By the time the fighters had finished strafing the Japanese, the Americans had tightened the box even more. Now, rifle fire was having a deadly effect on the Japanese. With over half of the Japanese force killed and over 50 wounded, the white flag was finally raised.

The battle lasted only 30 minutes. In that time, 138 Japanese soldiers were killed, and 52 were wounded. Two Americans and three Chinese were killed by mortar fire. One American and two Chinese were killed by rifle fire. The Allies lost 8 men and had 2 men wounded during the battle. Before they could be removed from the battlefield, an additional 17 wounded Japanese died.

By 2 PM, all of the captive Japanese were secured, some in the Brig and some in 2 empty warehouses. The wounded Japanese were under heavy guard in the hospital.

When Captain Carter returned to his office with Sergeant Kalway and Sergeant Heimlich, he said, "Take care of the spy, Sergeant Heimlich."

When Fritz pulled out his knife, Bin Teal's eyes widened like saucers. Approaching Bin Teal with a knife in hand, Fritz could smell the odor of urine. Before Fritz could cut his ropes, Bin Teal peed his pants.

"Bin Teal," Captain Carter said, as he approached, "We have already made it known that you are the one who led the Japanese into 2 traps. There are men on this base that would like to save the Japanese the trouble of killing you."

Captain Carter handed Bin Teal 50 American dollars and continued.

"You are free to go. I suggest you find someplace to hide where you are unlikely to meet any Americans or Japanese. And one more suggestion. Change your pants."

September 10, 1943

Now that they had no more use for Bin Teal's spy network, Captain Chan, with some of his men, went to round up the other known spies. Of the 6 spies previously identified, Captain Chan brought 4 back to the base. The other 2 had disappeared.

September 12, 1943

Colonel Rodgers and Captain Goodman make a surprise visit to Kunming.

"Captain Carter," Colonel Rodgers said, "General Donovan is pleased with the intelligence network you have established here and the information you have collected. And everyone in the Army has heard about how you used one of their own spies to trap the Japanese army and to plan an ambush on the Japanese fighters over Burma. General Donovan believes promotions are in order. Chao Lin will now receive Sergeant's pay. Corporals Lang and Linder are being promoted to Sergeants. And Sergeant Woods is being promoted to Staff Sergeant."

Colonel Rodgers saw the worried look on Captain Carter's face, and asked, "What's the matter, Captain?"

"I hope you are not going to promote the 2 best Sergeants in the Army to Lieutenants," Captain Carter answered.

"General Donovan and I did discuss that very thing," Colonel Rodgers said.

"Then you better promote them both to Majors, sir," Captain Carter said. "Anything less would be a waste of talent."

"We also discussed that, Captain," Colonel Rodgers said. "But you forget that I've known Sergeant Kalway and Sergeant Heimlich just as long as you have. I told the General that you would be devastated to lose your two best Sergeants, so we decided to promote them both to Master Sergeants, instead. You have been so busy that the General and I decided that you needed two Master Sergeants. As far as your suggestion of a promotion to Major is concerned, we also agreed with you there. Congratulations, you are now Major Carter."

It was hard for Major Carter to respond. Finally, he just said,

"Thank you, sir."

"Your promotion comes with new orders, Major," Colonel Rodgers said. "General Donovan wants you to set up an intelligence network in Burma and India. In order to do that and still maintain your current network in China, your Company will need to expand. Kunming will continue to be your Headquarters. I assume that you would like to take your entire Company with you to India, but that won't be possible. You need to leave one Squad here to maintain your Headquarters and to manage the intelligence network that you have already established."

"I brought a hand-picked squad of my MPs, already sworn to secrecy, to assist the Squad that you chose to remain here. As more qualified MPs become available, I intend to send you another Squad. I also brought 2 Lieutenants with me, again, both sworn to secrecy, to help you manage your growing Company. Notice that I said manage, not lead, your Company. I expect you to continue to rely on your two Master Sergeants for advice and leadership."

"You can count on that, Colonel," Major Carter said.

"I knew I could, Major," Colonel Rodgers said. "That's why you are now a Major. Start making plans. You leave here for India on September 21st."

September 13, 1943

Colonel Rodgers returned to Ledo, India; but Captain Goodman remained to help Major Carter with his upcoming move and to help the 2 new Lieutenants adjust to their new duties. Lieutenant Tomlyn was going to remain in Kunming and would be in charge of the Company when Major Carter was away. Lieutenant Tomlyn also needed to become familiar with Major Carter's intelligence network. For that reason, Captain Goodman spent most of his time working with Lieutenant Tomlyn. Captain Goodman also had to make sure that Lieutenant Tomlyn understood how to send any new information that he received, back to Ledo.

Major Carter decided to keep Squad 5 in Kunming. Squad 5 was ordered to help the new Squad, now called Squad 6, adjust to their new camp and new duties. At the same time, Major Carter made it clear that he expected Lieutenant Tomlyn to rely on Squad 5's experience, and to seek their advice when needed. Meanwhile, Major Carter was working with Lieutenant

Treadway and his Sergeants to prepare for their departure to India and Burma.

September 18, 1943

"Your accomplishments have not gone unnoticed Captain Chan," Duc Feng, a high-ranking Communist Party leader, said. "Eliminating the corrupt Captain Kwang, capturing spies, and defeating the Japanese that tried to attack Kunming speak well for your abilities. For that reason, you are now promoted to Major Chan. We are sending you reinforcements. You will soon be in command of over 100 men. And your Lieutenant Ping is now a Captain."

"Your new orders are to watch and gather information about any Nationalist troops that you come in contact with. You are also ordered to help defeat the Japanese in Burma. But you must remember that you are the commander of your troops, not the British, and not the Americans. You may cooperate with them to defeat the Japanese, but they do not give you orders."

"Yes sir," Major Chan said, "I understand my orders. I have worked well with the American MP Company commanded by Major Carter. Should I continue to work with them?"

"Major Carter is the one who discretely helped you eliminate Captain Kwang. I think you could continue to work with Major Carter," Duc Feng answered. "But remember, the Nationalists are our enemies. After the war with Japan is over, we go to war with the Nationalists."

"I'll remember, Duc Feng," Major Chan said.

September 19, 1943

Major Carter's and Major Chan's first meeting as Majors took place in Major Carter's office.

"I understand that you are moving the bulk of your Company back to India," Captain Ping said, acting as interpreter for Major Chan and Major Carter.

"We leave on September 21st," Major Carter said. "We are leaving 2 Squads here to maintain our Headquarters. We have been ordered to set up observation posts to help monitor Japanese troop movement in Burma and to conduct policing duties in India."

"We have been ordered to engage the Japanese in northern Burma," Captain Ping said. "As you know, Major Carter, the Nationalists are our enemies and working with them would be nearly impossible. But Major Chan received permission to work with your Company. Since you have to leave two Squads here in Kunming, Major Chan thought that you could use some extra men. And our men have worked well together in the past. We were strictly forbidden to be bound by any orders from your Company, Major Carter, but we were given permission to work on any cooperative missions that you and Major Chan can mutually agree upon."

"Tell Major Chan that I accept his gracious offer," Major Carter said.

"We will not be able to depart by September 21st," Captain Ping said. "We are expecting reinforcements soon. If you can arrange transport for us to India, we can join you as soon as our reinforcements arrive."

"I'll tell Lieutenant Tomlyn that scheduling your transport to India is his top priority," Major Carter said.

"Thank you, Major Carter," Captain Ping said, "We will see you soon in India or Burma."

India, September 21, 1943

Major Carter and his Company depart Kunming and arrive in Ledo, India. In a clandestine meeting, Major Carter, accompanied by Sergeant Kalway, Sergeant Heimlich, and Chao Lin, conversed with Colonel Rodgers and Captain Goodman.

"The information you have gathered in China has been of immense value to the Army," Colonel Rodgers said. "High-ranking officials agree with your assessment that the Chinese Civil War will resume after we defeat the Japanese. But even though you have provided information that the Communists will most likely win the Civil War, and I also agree with that assessment, the politicians are continuing to support the Nationalists."

"Sir, do these so-called politicians realize that the Communists have been dependable and trustworthy allies while most of the Nationalist officers have proven to be unreliable and corrupt," Isiac asked?

"Sergeant Kalway," Colonel Rodgers responded, "I think our politicians believe that corruption is an integral and acceptable part of politics and that it belongs in every successful politician's bag of tricks. All we can do is give them the best information possible, and then hope they use it to make wise decisions."

"Unlikely," Fritz said.

By the laughter that followed, it was clear that everyone agreed with Sergeant Heimlich.

Colonel Rodgers continued,

"Sergeant Heimlich, since you know the route from Ft. Hertz to the Salween River, I want you to take Chao Lin and establish another intelligence network there."

"Yes sir, Colonel," Fritz replied.

Then speaking to Chao Lin, Colonel Rodgers said, "While you are establishing an intelligence network along the Salween River, I have assigned another squad of MPs to Major Carter's Company, and instructed the

Major to set up another intelligence network here in India. Before you leave for Ft. Hertz, I want you to help Major Carter develop plans for the intelligence network here in India?"

"Yes sir, Colonel. I know an Indian trader who speaks English. I'll send him a telegram to expect a visit from Major Carter regarding trading opportunities available in Ledo."

"Good." Colonel Rodgers said. "Take care of it, then. Dismissed."

September 27, 1943

With reinforcements, Major Chan, now commanding over 100 Communists troops, arrives in Ledo. In a meeting with Major Carter, Major Chan, using Captain Ping as his interpreter, explains that his orders are to harass and engage the Japanese in northern Burma.

"We have new orders as well, Major Chan," Major Carter said. "To prepare for the deployment of General Stillwell's and General Merrill's troops in northern Burma, we were ordered to set up supply centers and observation posts. We will also be collecting information about the location and strength of the Japanese 18th Division. Recruiting Kachin guerillas to join in the upcoming attack on the Japanese is also part of our mission. In addition, we will be using snipers and guerilla tactics to harass any Japanese advance units that we locate."

"Our orders seem to fit perfectly," Captain Ping said. Listening to Major Chan's response, Captain Ping continued, "I believe that our orders will allow each of us to collaborate in the performance of our duties."

"I agree," Major Carter said, "And if it is your desire, Major Chan, I can pass on information to General Stillwell and General Merrill that you would like to participate in the upcoming attack."

"The Major likes that idea very much," Captain Ping translated for the smiling Major Chan, "And he likes the way you worded it. Very Diplomatic."

September 28, 1943

The plan, developed by and agreed upon by Major Chan and Major Carter, was to split their forces into 3 groups. Sergeant Heimlich, Chao Lin, and Lena, accompanied by Squads 2 and 3, would fly to Fort Hertz. From there they would retrace the same route followed after they rescued the downed pilot, only in reverse. Squad 2 would set up an observation post on the Salween River about 75 miles north of the Japanese positions in northeastern Burma. Squad 3 would move 30 miles west and set up another observation post on the east branch of the Irrawaddy River.

Each man would carry 2 rifles and extra ammunition. The extra rifle and ammunition were to be given to any Kachins who agreed to be guides and help man the observation posts. Other incentives were waiting at Fort Hertz for any Kachins who would go there to join General Stillwell's and General Merrill's forces. What wasn't revealed to Major Chan was Chao Lin's plan to use Kachin traders to replicate the intelligence network that he had already established in the area around Kunming, China.

Sergeant Woods and Squad 1, accompanied by Captain Ping and 30 of his men, would also be flown to Fort Hertz. Sergeant Woods would retrace the same route, in reverse, that he followed after their plane crash. An additional Squad of Colonel Rodgers' MPs would accompany Sergeant Woods to the crash site and return with the bodies of the 3 Americans that had died on the crashed transport plane.

The soldiers, led by Captain Ping and Sergeant Woods, would also carry extra rifles and ammunition to be given to any Kachins that agreed to join their force. The plan was to establish an outpost about 75 miles south of Fort Hertz and 50 miles north of the nearest known Japanese encampment. This outpost would be about 30 miles due west of Squad 3's outpost.

Sergeant Kalway, with Squad 4, and Major Chan, with 70 of his men, would leave the Ledo Road and proceed south down the Chindwin River. They planned to establish an outpost on the river about 30 miles south of the Ledo Road and about 30 miles northwest of the nearest known Japanese encampments. They would be about 80 miles from Sergeant Woods outpost. Sergeant Kalway's group would also carry extra rifles and ammunition with the hope of recruiting Kachins willing to participate in probing attacks and hit and run tactics against the Japanese in the area.

Isiac realized that he and Major Chan had a sizable force even before the possible addition of any Kachin guerillas. Before leaving the Ledo Road, Isiac procured as many boats, as possible. Most of the boats were what the men called 'Kachin canoes.' They would be needed to supply his outpost and to stockpile supplies for the eventual arrival of General Stillwell's forces.

Burma, September 29, 1943

As they started down the Chindwin River, Isiac spoke to Major Chan.

"With the size of our force and the expected arrival of supplies, we need to be looking for a fort instead of a camp."

"I'll send word to my scouts to start looking for a secure area as soon as we reach the 30-mile mark," Captain Chan replied.

September 30, 1943

Finding a defendable place along the Chindwin River became more of a problem than Isiac had anticipated. They finally found a tributary deep enough for the Kachin canoes and also too deep to be waded by any attacking force. They placed their outpost on the inside bend of the tributary about 1/4 mile from the main river. Four Sentries were placed upstream of the tributary, and four more were placed where the tributary entered the Chindwin River. Four sentries were also stationed across the tributary on the outside bend of the tributary.

October 1, 1943

Sergeant Woods and Squad 1, with Captain Ping and his men, set up an outpost on the west branch of the Irrawaddy River about 75 miles south of Fort Hertz. During the journey, they recruited 24 Kachin guerillas that agreed to stay at the outpost with Captain Ping until General Stillwell sent some of his troops to engage the Japanese 18th Division.

Sergeant Linder and 2 Kachin scouts returned to Fort Hertz to report the location of their outpost, and to inform General Stillwell's officers that the outpost was secure and ready to start receiving supplies for his soon to be advancing army.

Burma, October 2, 1943

With the recruitment of 32 Kachin guerillas, Isiac and Major Chan had a total force of 112 men. Major Chan set up 3 groups of 10 men each that patrolled a 10-mile stretch along the eastern shore of the Chindwin River. Their patrols penetrated 2 miles inland. So far, no contact with the Japanese had been made.

Now that the outpost was fully fortified and functional, and with the supply route established, Isiac and Major Chan, with a force of 24 men, started moving farther down the river. They hoped to locate the Japanese without themselves being detected.

China, October 2, 1943

Sergeant Heimlich, Chao Lin, and Lena, along with Squads 2 and 3 and 12 Kachin guerillas from Fort Hertz, cross the Burmese Border and reach the Salween River in China.

October 4, 1943

Sergeant Heimlich and Chao Lin find Amin Shan on the Salween River.

"Hello my friend," Amin Shan said when he saw Fritz.

"Hello my friend," Fritz said, returning his greeting and handing Amin Shan 200 rounds of ammunition for his .45. "This is my friend Chao Lin and his dog, Lena."

After the greeting, Fritz explained his plan to establish an intelligence network and the secrecy that would be required. He also explained the risks that were involved. After being sworn to secrecy, Amin Shan said, "Now I am an American spy. Too bad no one can ever know." Amin Shan began to laugh at his own joke, but when Fritz gave him 8 rifles, and 100 rounds of ammunition for each rifle, the laughing stopped, and he became serious, again.

"You will receive soldiers pay until the end of the war," Fritz said.

"We plan to recruit traders for our intelligence network," Chao said, "But they must be trustworthy and agree to take the oath of secrecy."

"I know traders that can be trusted, and they hate the Japanese," Amin Shan said. "They won't have a problem taking an oath of secrecy. Our culture is very clear about the consequences that occur to those who cannot be trusted."

Before Fritz and Chao discussed more details with Amin Shan, Fritz sent Squad 3 and the 12 Kachins from Fort Hertz to establish an outpost about 10 miles farther down the river.

Burma, October 5, 1943

Thirty miles south of their outpost, Isiac received information from a Kachin woman fishing in the river that the Japanese had been to the river almost every day to get fish. Sometimes they paid for the fish, and sometimes they just took the fish. Last week they beat up 2 old men and took their fish.

"How many Japanese come to the river," Isiac asked?

"Always 6," the woman answered.

"Do they have a camp nearby," Isiac asked?

"Small camp nearby, big camp farther away," the woman answered. That was all the information they were able to get.

Isiac and 2 of the Kachin guerrillas crossed the river in an attempt to find the Japanese camp. It wasn't hard. The camp was less than a mile from the river at the base of the foothills, and the path from the river led directly to it. Isiac and the 2 Kachin scouts spent the entire day watching the camp. The Kachin scouts circled the

Japanese camp and found the position of 2 sentries and another trail that led in a southerly direction. Isiac used his 20X spotting scope to watch the camp. Including the sentries, there were 14 Japanese soldiers. Isiac watched the sentries change three times, and each time they used the same location as their guard post.

After returning with the information about the Japanese camp, some of Major Chan's new recruits were anxious for battle.

"Wait until you hear the Plan Major Chan and Sergeant Kalway come up with," one of Major Chan's veterans said. "Those two men work magic together."

"Yeah," another veteran said. "We might not even have to attack. I wouldn't be surprised if the Major and the Sergeant talked the Japanese into shooting each other."

While his men were talking, and joking, Major Chan sent 2 of his men and 2 Kachins back to their outpost with orders: Bring back 68 men, leave 20 to guard the outpost.

China, October 6, 1943

With the outpost on the Salween River established and manned by the 12 Kachins from Fort Hertz, Squad 3, along with 20 Kachin guerrillas, that agreed to join

General Stillwell's army, began their return trip to Fort Hertz.

Burma, October 6, 1943

Before daylight, Major Chan and Isiac, with the same two Kachin scouts that accompanied him the last time he scouted the Japanese camp, crossed the river a mile downstream of the Japanese camp. They easily found the trail that led downriver; and with their small group, they were able to move quietly and quickly. By shortly after 10 AM they had covered 10 miles. Still no Japanese.

Isiac sent one of his scouts into the foothills and the other scout to the river. They were looking for any local people who might have information about the location of the Japanese camp. Just before noon, both Kachin scouts returned, and both had the same information. There was a large camp of Japanese about 6 more miles down the river.

Leaving the main trail, Isiac's small group moved into the foothills and followed an animal trail that led in a southerly direction, parallel to the river. They covered slightly less than 5 miles when they saw the Japanese camp. They continued moving south until they were directly east of the Japanese camp. Then, carefully, they crept closer.

It was a large camp. Too big to get an accurate count of the number of Japanese soldiers; but by using his spotting scope, Isiac estimated that the camp contained between 4 and 5 hundred Japanese soldiers. And that was a surprise. The Japanese were not expected to be this far west.

"Well," Isiac thought, "We'll just have to create a surprise of our own." And he did.

October 11, 1943

Reinforcements arrive from the newly created outpost. Major Chan and Isiac now have a force of 92 men. After dark, Major Chan added 18 of the reinforcements to his original group of 24, and crossed the river.

October 12, 1943

Before daybreak, Isiac had 2 of his men, with silenced .22's, stationed at each of the 2 Japanese guard posts. His other 5 men had moved into the foothills and got within 100 yards of the camp. They had scoped rifles. Isiac remained with Major Chan and 6 of his men. They also kept the 6 Kachin guerillas with them. Isiac was concerned that the Kachins would kill all of the Japanese soldiers. And Isiac wanted to capture some of them if he could.

Twenty of Major Chan's men surrounded the camp. They were waiting for Isiac's rifle shot which would be their signal to fire one shot into the air. Isiac wanted the Japanese to know that they were completely surrounded. The Kachins were ordered not to fire. Isiac's 5 snipers were ordered to fire one shot each at their selected targets, also using his rifle shot as their signal to fire.

When Isiac heard the muted sound of the silenced pistols, he used his rifle to kill the Japanese soldier that was closest to him. As planned, 25 other shots rang out. Then silence. Two of Isiac's snipers had targeted the same man by mistake which left 5 men dead in the Japanese camp.

Breaking the silence, in Japanese, Isiac said, "Your two guards are also dead, and you are surrounded. My Kachin friends want to kill the rest of you, but I'm going to give you one chance and one chance only to surrender. In 5 seconds, anyone not standing with their hands on their head will be shot."

All but one of the remaining Japanese soldiers were standing with their hands on their head as ordered. The one that fired his rifle at targets that he couldn't see had over a dozen bullet holes in him. Isiac knew that the 6 Japanese that remained would never second guess their decision to surrender.

The 6 Kachin guerrillas were left to set up ambush positions around the now empty camp, just in case any Japanese came to check on the men that had been stationed there. The rest of the men, with their 6 Japanese prisoners, crossed the river. When Captain Chan ordered 6 of the Kachin guerrillas to escort the Japanese prisoners back to their outpost, Isiac whispered in his ear.

"The Kachins will kill the Japanese before they even get close to the outpost." Then out loud, Isiac said, "Major Chan, I think our Kachin friends would much rather come with us and kill some Japanese."

Watching the Kachin guerrillas nodding, Major Chan said, "I believe you're right, Sergeant Kalway. I'll send some of my men as escorts for the prisoners."

That left 80 men to execute the rest of the plan. Staying on the opposite side of the river, they began moving toward the large Japanese base located downriver. As they moved south, Isiac and Major Chan began formulating a plan for the pending attack. They decided to keep it simple. Use the element of surprise, then retreat before the Japanese could locate them and return fire.

Major Chan gave the men their orders, "Choose a target before the shooting begins. No one shoots until they hear Sergeant Kalway's snipers open fire. Now, Sergeant Kalway has something to say."

"Thank you, Major," Isiac said in Chinese. "The maximum shooting time before retreat is one minute. To delay pursuit, 8 men will be chosen to continue firing for an additional minute before retreating. And retreat means run because dead Chinese soldiers can't kill any more Japanese."

Major Chan's men reacted positively to Sergeant Kalway's speech.

"Plans don't always work out as anticipated," Isiac continued. "We haven't had time to study the patterns of the Japanese camp. We've located the position of three Japanese sentries and will send two men with silenced pistols to each location. But we don't know if they use the same positions each day. And there are sure to be other sentries that we haven't located."

"Plus, we don't know the routine of the camp at or near sunrise. If everyone finds a target, we could kill 80 Japanese. But at the time of our attack, there might not be that many targets available. If there are no targets available after your first shot, shoot into the tents, vehicles, fuel supplies and anything else that will impede their ability to fight."

"If we are discovered before we are in position, or if any shots are fired early, that will be our signal to start firing. But the rest of the plan stays the same. Our major objective is to cause as much damage as possible without any of our men getting killed, even if that means only killing one Japanese soldier."

Major Chan continued, "We will attack in 3 groups. Kachins from the south, Sergeant Kalway will attack from the east, and we will attack from the north. We regroup at our outpost. Any questions?"

"Yes, Major," one of Major Chan's soldiers responded. "How will any soldiers that disobey orders and get killed be punished?"

The reaction that followed clearly showed the high morale of the Major's men. It took a while before it was quiet enough for the Major to respond.

Finally, he said,

"I'll think of a way."

The pandemonium resumed.

It was still light when Isiac and Major Chan neared the Japanese camp. They found a place of concealment and watched. After dark, they crossed the river.

October 13, 1943

It was still over two hours before predawn when all the troops were in position. Now came the hard part. Waiting. Every minute that passed without shots being fired meant that, as of yet, they were still undiscovered.

For 80 men to work together, while under 3 different commands, in 3 separate groups, was a testament to the discipline of all involved.

Finally, the sky began to lighten. Now the waiting was even more difficult. When Isiac was able to discern movement, he made a quick survey of the Japanese camp. Not much action yet, but some. Isiac could clearly make out at least a dozen targets, but still, he waited. When another group of 6 Japanese approached the area where the trucks were parked, Isiac said to his snipers, "Pick your targets."

Knowing that time was short and that the men would be getting anxious, Isiac decided to wait another 30 seconds, hoping more targets would appear. When Isiac saw that a few of the Japanese were beginning to leave their tents, he put down his spotting scope and picked up his rifle. Isiac picked his primary target and then a secondary target. With 10 seconds remaining in the time he had allotted himself, Isiac fired his first shot. The surprise attack had begun. As sudden gunfire broke the stillness of the morning, more Japanese hurried from their tents increasing the number of targets.

In less than a minute the firing from the Kachins and from Major Chan's men significantly decreased, indicating that the retreat had begun. For the next minute, as planned, 8 of Major Chan's men continued to produce scattered gunfire. Then, the only gunfire was coming from the Japanese. As Isiac was waiting for the scattered gunfire of the rear guard to cease, he again returned to his spotting scope to access the results of the attack. Making a quick count, Isiac was able to confirm 28 Japanese dead. Then, it was time for him to retreat, as well. Taking gunfire from all directions and not knowing the size of the attacking force, it took the Japanese almost 20 minutes to access the situation and organize a pursuit. For Isiac and Major Chan, that was much better than anticipated.

A little past 10 AM, Isiac and his men arrived at the Japanese camp they had attacked yesterday. By then, most of Major Chan's men had already arrived. Major Chan had already sent the 6 Kachins that had remained at the now abandoned Japanese camp, to look for stragglers and to watch for approaching Japanese. By 10:15 AM, Major Chan had sent two of his men to retrieve the Kachins and to then function as the rear guard. By 10:20 AM, Major Chan had his group moving again.

The trail along the river was a good one, so they continued to move after dark. The Kachins that were scouting ahead sent word back to Major Chan that they had found two fishermen who were willing to ferry them across the river.

In addition to the two paddlers, the Kachin canoe could only carry 8 soldiers at a time. That meant 7 trips unless they could find another canoe. Since each round trip took almost an hour, the crossing would take about 7 hours. In addition to having four men missing, Isiac could see that Major Chan was worried about the length of time needed to make the crossing. Even though the crossing should be completed before dawn, a lot could happen in 7 hours.

"Major Chan," Isiac said, "I'm going to send 5 of my men to act as rear guard while we wait to cross the river. I'm going to take the rest of my men toward the foothills to find a secure place to defend in case the Japanese catch us before we can get everyone across the river. I'd like to take two of your men with me so that they know our location and will be able to lead you to it if it becomes necessary."

"Good idea, Sergeant," Major Chan said. "But tell your men on rear guard to watch out for the two men that I left on rear guard. And I still have four men unaccounted for. Watch for them, as well."

"Yes Major," Isiac said.

When Isiac returned from the established fallback position with Major Chan's two men, he saw Major

Chan and his men in a tight group, and they were excited. Listening to the conversation for a few minutes was all Isiac needed to understand the excitement. Major Chan's two rear guards had returned with the four missing men.

In the dark, as Isiac knew well, distances are deceiving. And now Major Chan's four stragglers knew that as well. When dawn arrived, they found that they had crept so close to the Japanese camp that they had to crawl to heavier cover before they could retreat. Their comrades were ribbing them pretty good until one finally said, "But we left 4 dead Japanese behind."

Then Isiac noticed that two canoes were returning instead of one. That just cut their crossing time in half.

Sergeant Woods and Squad 1 arrived in Fort Hertz where Sergeant Linder was waiting for them.

"Enjoy your vacation," Sergeant Woods asked?

"It was wonderful," Sergeant Linder said. "But it looks like I'll have to go back to work now."

Sergeant Woods was shaking his head, yes, but he had a smile on his face.

Later that day, Squad 3 arrived at Fort Hertz with 20 Kachin Guerrillas that agreed to join General Stillwell's attack on the Japanese 18th Division.

October 14, 1943

It was after dark by the time Isiac and Major Chan returned to their outpost. They had fought a battle, and, without losing a man, had killed at least 28 Japanese. They then traveled 46 miles in two days.

October 17, 1943

Isiac and Squad 4, escorting 6 Japanese prisoners, arrived at the Ledo Road on the same day that Colonel Pick was appointed as Commander of Base Section 30 and put in charge of Road Construction. The arrival of 10 MPs and 6 Japanese prisoners temporarily halted work on the road. But not for long. As soon as Isiac found General Stillwell, road construction resumed.

"What have we here, Sergeant Kalway," General Stillwell asked as Isiac approached with the 6 prisoners?

"A scared group of prisoners that might be willing to talk to you, sir, if you guaranteed them protection from the Kachins," Isiac answered.

"Afraid of the Kachins are they," General Stillwell asked?

"And with good reason, General," Isiac said. "The Kachins hate the Japanese."

"So, I've heard," General Stillwell said. "You and your men can sit down and rest. I want to get as many of my officers and Sergeants here as possible before you begin your report."

When the General returned with a group of officers and Sergeants, Isiac began his report.

"We set up an outpost 30 miles down the Chindwin River on a small but navigable tributary. The supplies that you sent have already been delivered to the outpost. After we secured the outpost, Major Chan and I led a group of men downriver in an attempt to locate the Japanese."

"By these prisoners, we can see that your attempt to make contact was successful." General Stillwell said. "Go on, Sergeant Kalway."

"We found a small Japanese camp about 30 miles south of our outpost," Isiac continued. "That's where we acquired these prisoners."

"How many Japanese were in the camp, Sergeant Kalway," General Stillwell asked?

"14, sir," Isiac answered.

"What happened to the other 8?" General Stillwell said, still asking questions.

"They're dead, sir," Isiac said.

"What were your casualties, Sergeant," General Stillwell asked?

"None, sir," Isiac answered. "We surprised them."

"Continue, Sergeant," the General said, obviously pleased.

"We found a trail that led to a much larger camp located 16 miles farther down the river," Isiac replied.

"How large," General Stillwell asked?

"Between 4 and 5 hundred," Isiac said, answering another question. "We did a recon and then returned with more men and a plan."

"How many men were in your camp," General Stillwell said, asking another question?

"10 MPs, 70 Communist troops commanded by Major Chan, and 32 Kachin guerillas that we recruited on the way to our outpost," Isiac answered.

"You attacked 500 Japanese with only 112 men," one of General Stillwell's Captains asked?

"No sir," Isiac answered. "That was the total number of men we had at the outpost. We had to leave some of our men at the outpost to guard the General's supplies. We attacked with 80 men."

Then, tired of being continually interrupted by questions, Isiac continued quickly with answers to questions that were sure to be asked.

"Major Chan and I suffered no casualties, but the Kachins hadn't returned to the outpost by the time I left, so we don't know about them. In addition to the 8

Japanese killed in our first attack, we had at least 28 confirmed kills in our second attack."

As soon as Isiac took a breath, he was interrupted again, by another Captain, and Isiac was wondering if they were ever going to let him finish his report.

"How can you be sure of the number of kills," the Captain asked?

"I have a spotting scope, and I counted them myself," Isiac said, waiting for more questions. When no more questions followed, General Stillwell said,

"Thank you, Sergeant, unless there is something else you think we should know, that will be all."

With the prisoners delivered and his report finished, Isiac made arrangements for him and his men to return to Ledo.

Having already received reports from Major Carter's men on the Irrawaddy and the Salween Rivers, General Merrill spoke to General Stillwell.

"Three outposts established, 100 well-trained Communist troops and 90 Kachin guerrillas persuaded to join our Army, two battles fought with 36 Japanese killed and no allied casualties, all in less than 3 weeks. And all that after they decimated the Japanese force that tried to capture Kunming. If I had another soldier like Sergeant Kalway and another Company like Major

Carter's MPs, I'd be able to recapture all of Burma in 3 months."

China, October 18, 1943

With an intelligence network established in the area around Amin Shan's village, Fritz, Chao, Lena, and Squad 2, along with Amin Shan and 3 of his newly recruited OSS agents, head south along the Salween River to the outpost created by Squad 3. They intended to expand their intelligence network.

Burma, October 19, 1943

With the information provided by Major Carter's men, General Stillwell takes two divisions of American armed Chinese, Merrill's Marauders, the 90 Kachin guerrillas supplied by Major Carter's men, and Major Chan and his men, and proceeds to engage the Japanese 18th Division in northern Burma.

China, October 21, 1943

As Major Carter and Isiac return to their base in Kunming, China, Isiac made a suggestion to the Major.

"Major, with Squad 2 on their own for two more months, it might be a good idea to send them additional supplies and extra weapons for the Kachin guerillas in the area. Sergeant Heimlich will need their support if the Japanese decide to move north up the Salween River."

"I'll inform Captain Goodman and ask him to have the supplies delivered from Fort Hertz by Kachin Guerillas, and, if possible, to have some supplies airlifted to Amin Shan's village," Major Carter said.

Burma, October 22, 1943

By the end of October, 1943, the American Engineers reach Milepost 60.

China, November 21, 1943

The routine was well established at the outpost on the Salween River, and the intelligence network in the area was expanding. Previously, the closest Japanese penetration had been 40 miles south of their current position. When Chao Lin returned with information supplied by a newly recruited Kachin Agent, everything changed. A Japanese force of 50 men had been spotted less than 20 miles south of their outpost. The Japanese were attacked by 10 local Kachins. Although the Kachins killed 6 Japanese soldiers with only one casualty of their own, the Japanese, in retaliation, burned a nearby village and killed over 20 villagers that were either too old or too young to run away.

Fritz immediately sent 4 Kachin guerillas with orders to set up two observation sites with two men at each site. One observation site was established one mile south of their outpost. The other one was established one mile southeast of their outpost. If the Japanese were spotted, one man would stay as long as possible and keep the Japanese under surveillance, while the other man brought the information back to the outpost.

Fritz sent two more Kachins north to alert the villagers and to move them into the hills; then they were to return as quickly as possible with as many men as they could find that were willing to fight the Japanese. Leaving 4 men at the outpost to wait for reinforcements, Fritz left the outpost with Squad 3, Chao Lin, Amin Shan, and 5 Kachin guerillas, giving him a fighting force of 17 men. Nine more Kachin fighters might be waiting downriver if he could find them. In 3 or 4 days, reinforcements might arrive, maybe.

But Fritz knew that "ifs" and "maybes" didn't count. Fritz also knew that the biggest "maybe" would be resolved soon. Maybe he was chasing 44 Japanese with 17 men and a dog, or maybe the Japanese were chasing him.

November 23, 1943

Moving south along the Salween River in pursuit of the Japanese, Fritz made contact with two Kachins and received more bad news: reacting to the atrocities that the Japanese had inflicted upon their village, the nine Kachins again attacked the Japanese. But this time, they did so out of anger and without a plan. However, this time the Japanese were ready for them, and the tables turned. Only these two Kachins survived. Their seven companions were killed while the Japanese only suffered one additional casualty.

One "maybe" was resolved, however. The Japanese were retreating south down the Salween River. This presented Fritz with a "good news, bad news" situation. The good news was that the villages to the north were no longer in imminent danger; the bad news was that they were unlikely to catch up to the Japanese before they returned to the security of their base.

As bad as the new information was, it allowed Fritz to begin making plans. The first thing he did was to send two Kachins north with the news that the villages in the area were, at least temporarily, safe. If reinforcements were met on the way north, one of the Kachins would lead them south to join Sergeant Heimlich and his men.

"Sergeant Drake," Fritz said, "Take team 2, Chao Lin and Lena, and Amin Shan and his men and follow the Japanese south along the river. The two local Kachins will follow as your rear guard. In addition to watching for Japanese, they will also be watching for reinforcements. I will take team 1 and try to flank the Japanese on the left. Unless reinforcements arrive, we will use our scoped rifles and silenced pistols to pick away at the Japanese whenever opportunities arise. And by that, I mean, only opportunities that provide a high probability of retreat without casualties. Hit and run tactics only, no direct assaults. Any questions, Sergeant Drake?"

"No questions," Sergeant Drake answered.

"One more thing," Fritz added. "Rely on Chao Lin to advise you when and how Lena can be used to help."

"Understood, Sergeant Heimlich," Sergeant Drake said.

As Sergeant Drake followed the trail left by the Japanese, Sergeant Heimlich disappeared into the trees on the left side of the trail. Using Lena's ears and nose, Sergeant Drake had Chao Lin, Lena and one of Amin Shan's men in the lead as scouts. Sergeant Drake and his team followed, but always within sight of Chao Lin. Two of Amin Shan's men, each armed with a scoped rifle and a silenced pistol, were positioned, one on each flank, and again within sight of the Sergeant.

About two hours after Sergeant Heimlich and Sergeant Drake separated, Sergeant Drake and his team witnessed the value of Lena. Hearing a low growl and seeing the hair rise on Lena's back, Chao Lin slowly moved Lena and the Kachin scout into heavy cover. With a hand signal, Chao Lin indicated that Lena had located something ahead and to the left. Sergeant Drake then signaled the Kachin scout on the left flank and watched him disappear. The rest of Sergeant Drake's men waited.

Twenty-five minutes later, the Kachin returned with the dead Japanese soldier's weapons. As they continued to follow the Japanese trail, the same scenario repeated itself 10 minutes later with the same results, only this time on the right flank. Now Sergeant Drake had to make a decision. Not knowing how far the rear guard was from the main body of Japanese, Sergeant Drake, following his orders not to engage, decided to regroup with Sergeant Heimlich. He did not want to make contact with the main body of Japanese. Calling in his scouts and flankers, Sergeant Drake reversed direction. When he reached his two rear guards, Sergeant Drake left the trail in the same direction Sergeant Heimlich had taken.

When one of the Kachin scouts found Sergeant Heimlich's trail, they followed until sunset. Conferring with his Kachin scouts, Sergeant Drake was assured that they could follow the trail for another half hour. And then, if they traveled slowly, they could follow the trail by moonlight.

Back at Amin Shan's village, 8 Kachin guerillas arrived from Fort Hertz with enough rifles and ammunition to arm an additional 16 guerrillas. They also carried information that on November 25th an airlift would drop additional supplies.

November 24, 1943

At sunrise, after 4 hours of rest, Sergeant Drake again began following Sergeant Heimlich's trail. In less than an hour, the Kachin scouts found the place where Sergeant Heimlich and his men had spent the night. That meant that they were probably less than 4 miles behind Sergeant Heimlich. Increasing the pace, Sergeant Drake hoped to close the gap.

A little over an hour after sunrise, using his spotting scope from the top of a hill, Fritz located the Japanese base. Although the Japanese that he had been pursuing had already reached their base, Fritz carefully approached the base to see if any other opportunities to cause mischief presented themselves.

About 2 miles from the Japanese Base, Fritz located the position of a Japanese sentry. He then sent two of his men to the right, and two of his men to the left, to see if any other sentries could be located. If another sentry was found, one man would establish a shooting position with a secure path of retreat while the other man returned to inform Sergeant Heimlich. When Fritz was informed that both of his snipers were in position, his shot would become the signal for the other two snipers to fire. If possible, all 5 men would attempt to regroup at the base of a ridge a little over half a mile north of their current position. The base of the ridge had plenty of cover and was high enough to see any pursuit.

As soon as both of his men returned, Fritz sighted his target and fired. His shot was followed by a shot from his left and then by another shot from his right. Wasting no time, Fritz and his men were immediately on the run to their rendezvous point.

After a quick-paced mile, Sergeant Drake heard 3 shots in quick succession. Sergeant Heimlich had engaged the enemy. Pointing out a notch in a long ridge as a rendezvous point, Sergeant Drake ordered two Kachins to the top of a hill to the southeast, the same direction that the rifle shots had come from. From the top of the hill, they would make a quick survey of the area ahead and then move to the rendezvous point with whatever information they could obtain. Sergeant Drake took the rest of his men past the hills to the notch in the ridge to quickly establish a defensive position.

In less than 6 minutes from the time the first shot was fired, Sergeant Heimlich and his men had regrouped at their designated rendezvous point. Using his spotting scope, Fritz could already see three Japanese patrols in search of their attackers. As soon as contact was made, more Japanese would join the pursuit. If they tried to set up an ambush or a defensive position this close to the Japanese base, they would be quickly surrounded and annihilated. Retreat was their only option, and that's what they did.

By the time the Kachins reached the hilltop, Sergeant Heimlich could be seen continuing his retreat. The Kachins could also see the 3 groups of Japanese that were searching for Fritz and his men. Just as Sergeant Heimlich had, both Kachins realized that trying to set up a defensive position would be a mistake. Luckily for all concerned, the Kachins only followed orders if the orders made sense.

With one of the Japanese patrols approaching their position, one Kachin would remain to ambush the

Japanese, and then immediately retreat toward the river. During his retreat, he would fire sporadic shots in an attempt to draw at least one of the Japanese patrols away from the retreating Americans.

The other Kachin was ordered to return to Sergeant Drake to inform him of the situation. So much for lack of formal education; the Kachin guerrilla immediately calculated that the geometric intercept point of Sergeant Heimlich's retreat was closer than Sergeant Drakes position. He would intercept Sergeant Heimlich and then lead him to Sergeant Drake's position.

After Sergeant Heimlich and Sergeant Drake reunited, their retreat proceeded without incident.

Burma, November 25, 1943

On Thanksgiving Day, even before the Ledo Road reached the airstrip at Milepost 88.8 and before the airstrip itself is completed, the first allied patient is flown from the airstrip to the American hospital at Assam, India.

China, November 25, 1943

Although it took over a month for Major Carter's rush order of supplies to be delivered, as promised, Amin Shan's village and the guerillas in the area received presents from the sky.

November 26, 1943

It was late afternoon when the scouts from the Kachin outpost saw Sergeant Heimlich returning with his men. The news that 20 villagers and 8 Kachin guerillas had been killed before Sergeant Heimlich and his men arrived was devastating. The fact that the Kachins had killed 7 Japanese before they died and that Sergeant Heimlich and Sergeant Drake had killed 5 more Japanese without suffering any casualties, helped a little, but not much.

The Kachin spirit returned quickly, however, and Fritz could see why. The outpost, instead of being manned by the 4 Kachins that Fritz had left as guards, now contained 32 Kachin guerillas. They were armed with American rifles, and each guerrilla had two American grenades attached to his belt. With further observation, Fritz noticed 4 mortars and two small artillery pieces. Painted on the barrel of one of the artillery pieces was a message, "Compliments of Major Carter."

After the excitement of their arrival settled down a little, Fritz, using Amin Shan as an interpreter, asked about the position of sentries around the outpost.

"Two sentries are located on each side of the river a mile south of the outpost," Amin Shan said.

"Very good," Fritz said. "Now that we have more men available, I think we should increase the number of sentries. Especially since we now know how close the Japanese are to your village."

"I agree," Amin Shan said. "Give me your suggestions, and I'll see that they are implemented."

In addition to being in charge of the intelligence network on the Salween River, without objection, Amin Shan had assumed control of this newly formed guerilla force.

"You also need to post sentries around the village and in the hills on both sides of the river," Fritz continued. "If you pass out some of the binoculars to some of the boys, they could provide extra eyes for your sentries. Do young boys know how to take orders from your men?"

"All the children know how to take orders," Amin Shan said proudly. "They are Kachins."

Burma, November 30, 1943

Because of dry weather, new road construction averaged 3/4 of a mile per day during November, and the road reached Milepost 82.5.

China, November 30, 1943

Due to the limited amount of mortar and artillery shells, Fritz had to limit the training period with these new weapons.

"In two days, we have to return to Fort Hertz," Fritz said to Amin Shan. "In addition to the scouts already placed around your village and outpost, scouts should also be placed around the Japanese base to prevent them from organizing a surprise attack. Organized withdrawal from the village should also be practiced."

"Anything else," Amin Shan asked?

"Attacking the Japanese base with mortars at night would be very disruptive to the routine of the base," Fritz added, "and the resulting loss of sleep would be very irritating."

"What a nice thought," Amin Shan said. "Irritated Japanese."

December 2, 1943

Farewells were exchanged as Fritz and his men prepared to return to Fort Hertz.

"Goodbye my friends," Amin Shan said, and then it was repeated by the whole village.

In a parting statement to Amin Shan, Fritz said,

"With the size of your guerilla force increasing, I'm going to suggest that more weapons be delivered to your village."

Burma, December 27, 1943

Continued good weather in December allowed road construction to advance a mile per day. And on December 27, the Ledo Road reached Shingbwiyang (Milepost 103). The completion of this section of road helped supply the allied troops who were fighting the Japanese 18th division in northern Burma. As the Japanese were forced to retreat farther south, the Ledo Road could be extended.

End of December, 1943

Because of their success at guerilla warfare, Merrill's Marauders were increased from a few hundred men to over 3000 guerillas and were organized into 3 Battalions. By the end of 1943, although 200 of Merrill's Marauders were killed, they inflicted heavy damage to the Japanese 18th Division, with over 800 Japanese soldiers killed.

By the end of December, the construction of the airstrip at Ledo and the airstrip at Milepost 88.8, near Tagap, are completed.

February, 1944

The ground campaign intensifies as General Stillwell and Merrill's Marauders attack the Japanese in the Hakawing Valley and gain control of the valley.

India, March, 1944

The 10th Chinese Regiment is flown from Kunming to India to assist the American Engineers with road construction.

March 8, 1944

The Japanese attack India.

Spring 1944

B-29 bombers start arriving in India.

Burma, First Week of April, 1944

The Hakawing Valley is opened past Shadazup (Milepost 192).

China, April 17, 1944

The Japanese begin their last offensive in eastern China with an attack on US airbases there.

April 20, 1944

Colonel Rodgers sends Major Carter an additional squad of MPs.

Burma, May 11, 1944

Widening of the Ledo Road ceased as all the Engineers began to gravel the existing road.

May 17, 1944

Fighter planes from the Japanese airbase at Myitkyina were being used to attack Allied cargo planes flying "over the hump" to deliver supplies to allied troops in China. Those attacks stopped when Merrill's Marauders, using a surprise attack, captured the Myitkyina airbase. However, the unwillingness of the British to send additional troops prevented the Americans from capturing the city and resulted in a long, costly siege. American Engineers, who were not trained infantry men, had to be sent to man the siege line. By the end of May, Merrill's Marauders were losing 75 to 100 men per day to malaria, dysentery, and typhus.

May 26, 1944

Squads 1, 2, and 4 of Major Carter's MPs are sent to patrol the Ledo Road to replace the MPs that were sent to man the siege lines at Myitkyina.

June 12, 1944

Isiac and Fritz, along with Squads 1, 2, and 4 are sent to Myitkyina to join the siege line. Major Carter's newest Squad, Squad 8, remains in China with Squads 5 and 3, while Squad 6 is sent to patrol the Ledo Road. Squad 7, with Lieutenant Treadway in command, remains in India to manage the Intelligence network that was established there.

June 15, 1944

When Sergeant Kalway arrived at the siege line at Myitkyina, he was appalled at the condition of the men.

"Sergeant Graham," Isiac called. When Sergeant Graham arrived, Isiac could see that Sergeant Graham shared his concern.

"Anything we can do to prevent us from ending up in the same condition as these soldiers," Isiac asked?

"Probably not, Sergeant Kalway. Just keep using your insect repellent, and be careful with your drinking water," Sergeant Graham answered.

"Sergeant Graham," Isiac said, "Your orders are to monitor the health of our men, you and your medics included, on a daily basis. None of my men are going to die of sickness or disease. Make sure that your medics understand their orders."

"I'll make it clear to them, Sergeant Kalway," Sergeant Graham said.

"If we are all going to get sick, you make sure that the men are evacuated before their conditions become irreversible," Isiac said. "I've only lost one of my men in this war, and that was in our plane crash. I don't intend to lose any more. Discretely start making plans for our evacuation. If you have any interference in arranging for our evacuation, come to me immediately. In case our reputation isn't known to all the officers here, I might have to explain to them that any interference in the completion of our duty will result in arrest and court martial. Make sure that everyone in our company knows of the evacuation plan so they know that, as bad as it may be, their discomfort will only be temporary."

"Good idea, Sergeant Kalway," Sergeant Graham said, "That will be a great boost to their mental health."

"When the time comes," Isiac said, "We just add to our mystique and disappear."

At the end of the day, Major Jakes, as usual, met with General Merrill to report on the day's events. After listing the casualties and the number of men incapacitated with, malaria, typhus, and dysentery, Major Jakes gave the General the only good news of the day.

"General Merrill, the 3 squads of snipers from the 1st Independent Military Police Special Assignment Company had 22 confirmed kills today. Where did you find these guys, General?"

"That's not the way it works, Major," General Merrill said, "These guys find you. I've dealt with them before. They're the same MPs that were involved in the capture of the Japanese that tried to conduct a surprise attack on Kunming."

"Are they the ones that planned the surprise attack on the Japanese fighter planes," Major Jakes asked?

"The same ones, Major," General Merrill said, "And the same MPs that attacked the Japanese on the Salween and Chindwin Rivers, established 3 outposts in northern Burma, provided me with 90 Kachin guerrillas, and trained and then convinced 100 Chinese Communists to join me in my fight against the Japanese 18th Division."

"General," the Major continued, "I've also been informed that Sergeant Graham, of the MPs medical unit, on his first day here, has already started to arrange for evacuation of the MPs."

"Don't interfere, Major," General Merrill said, "In fact, I suggest that you make sure that they receive any assistance they require."

"Who gives them their orders, General?"

"Someone with a much higher rank than me," General Merrill said, "God, maybe. Anything else, Major?"

With bewilderment, Major Jakes shook his head no, and the report ended.

June 16, 1944

With the loss of 22 men yesterday to Isiac's snipers, the targets were not so easy today. To counter the extra caution being used by the Japanese, Isiac changed tactics. He organized his snipers in teams of 3 instead of 2 and moved a little closer. Each team was cautioned to never shoot from a position unless it had a secure path of retreat. They already knew that, but Isiac wanted to remind them just the same.

Depending on the target location, each team increased their separation by several yards, when possible. The increased separation enlarged the area and angle of each team's sight lines.

The approach and retreat route to Isiac's chosen snipping position was through a shallow ditch. By the time Isiac, Lang, and Linder reached their shooting position, they were covered in mud. Not very comfortable, but good camouflage. And a little discomfort is much preferable to being dead.

Each man had enough water to last the day. And regardless of how many targets appeared in their sight lines, the plan was to retreat from their sniping positions after dark, or sooner if circumstances dictated. Even before sunrise, Sergeant Linder was able to locate and dispatch a target. Then, for the next 8 hours, the three of them just laid patiently in the mud waiting for another target to present itself. It wasn't until late afternoon that new targets entered their sight lines. Then, within seconds, Isiac and Sergeant Linder each located a target and eliminated them.

Then more waiting. The mud and heat, along with the flies and mosquitoes, were making concentration difficult. Isiac had to continually refocus on his target area as he found his thoughts drifting toward Nedra, Jayme, Peg, and the rest of his family. Isiac was in Mouillee Marsh with Fritz and Peg when a shot from Sergeant Lang ended his daydream. Lang had found and eliminated his first target of the day.

Discomfort had now become so intense that the thoughts of the men started to be equally split between finding new targets and retreating from their mud pit. And this was only their second day at the siege. Isiac's decision to inform his men of their evacuation plans in advance, just as Sergeant Graham had predicted, turned out to be of immense value to the men's morale. By the end of the day, Isiac and his men had eliminated 9 more Japanese soldiers.

June 17, 1944

When Isiac first arrived at Myitkyina, he noticed that many of the men on the siege line had cut holes in their pants so that, when diarrhea struck, they didn't have to waste time pulling down their pants. Today, he noticed that several of his men had done the same. The countdown to evacuation had begun.

June 20, 1944

All of Isiac's men had dysentery.

India, Early July, 1944

The invasion of India failed after the battles of Imphal and Kohima. In early July, the Japanese retreated after suffering heavy losses. During the Indian campaign, the Allies lost over 12,000 men, while the Japanese casualties were over 50,000.

Burma, July 5, 1944

Sergeant Graham found Sergeant Kalway after he returned from his snipping position and gave Isiac the information he had been expecting.

"Almost half of our men are showing signs of malaria and typhus, Sergeant Kalway. You also have malaria. As you ordered, it is time for us to leave."

"Have all the arrangements been made," Isiac asked?

"Yes," Sergeant Graham answered.

"Then we leave tomorrow before dawn," Isiac said. "What is the condition of Sergeant Heimlich?"

"He also has malaria," Sergeant Graham said.

"If my condition and the condition of Sergeant Heimlich deteriorate to the point that we can no longer lead the men, you are ordered to assume command," Isiac said.

"Understood, Sergeant," Sergeant Graham said. "I'll monitor the condition of both you and Sergeant Heimlich very carefully."

July 6, 1944

Before leaving Myitkyina for hospitals in India, with Sergeant Graham in command, Major Carter's 30 MPs were credited with 98 confirmed kills in just 3 weeks.

August 3, 1944

Chinese troops, with the help of Merrill's Marauders and Kachin guerillas, capture Myitkyina as the siege finally ends. At the end of the siege only a few of Merrill's Marauders remained, and the cost in allied lives was high: 4,200 Chinese troops and 2,200 American troops were killed.

August 4, 1944

With the capture of Myitkyina, the Ledo road was now open and secure from Ledo to the Tanai River (Milepost 145.98) and from Sakan (Milepost 164) to Warazup (Milepost 191).

China, August 29, 1944

Isiac and his men that fought at the siege of Myitkyina, now, mostly recovered from their ordeal, leave India and arrive at their base in China. Major Carter, with most of his company reunited, organizes a celebratory dinner for his men.

Burma, End of August, 1944

By the end of August, 1944, most Japanese aircraft in Burma were destroyed. This further reduced the danger to American cargo planes flying over the hump. Road construction had advanced to the point that 4 Battalions were needed just to provide maintenance of the completed road from Ledo to Shingbwiyang.

Washington D. C. October, 1944

Roosevelt recalls Stillwell and General Wheeler is named Supreme Commander of all S.E. Asia Forces.

Burma, Late October, 1944

The use of the recently captured Myitkyina airstrip helps speed road construction.

India, January 12, 1945

Although the entire route is not completely cleared of all Japanese resistance, the first convoy of 113 vehicles, led by General Pick, leaves Ledo.

January 28, 1945

The campaign in India and northern Burma ends. The Burma Road is finally completed and secured. 15,000 American soldiers, 60% of which were black, and 35,000 local workers constructed the road, which stretched from Assam, India to Kunming, China. The road, which covered a distance of 1,079 miles, was constructed in slightly over 25 months, an amazing feat of engineering.

China, February 4, 1945

Major Carter supervises the increased security needed as the first shipment of supplies carried over the Ledo Road arrives in Kunming.

Washington D. C. April 12, 1945

Roosevelt dies, Truman becomes President.

Burma, spring, 1945

A national uprising in Burma results in the defection of the entire Burmese National Army. The Japanese are now trapped between the Burmese National Army and the advancing Allied Army.

Germany, May 7, 1945
Germany unconditionally surrenders.

Tibet, June 1, 1945
Captain Peer flies Squads 1 and 2, along with Isiac, Fritz, Chao Lin, and Lena, to Tibet for some rest and relaxation. In between the rest and relaxation, another intelligence network is established.

China, June 29, 1945
Captain Peer and the men in Tibet return to their base in China.

Burma, July 1945
The Allies reoccupy Burma.

End of July 1945
By the end of July, over 71,000 tons of supplies were delivered to Kunming, China by air from India. Only 6,000 tons were delivered via the Ledo Road. 26,000 trucks were given to the Chinese after their one-way trip over the Ledo Road.

Japan, August 6, 1945

The atomic bomb is dropped on Hiroshima. Truman warns Japan to surrender.

August 9, 1945

Another atomic bomb is dropped on Nagasaki.

The War Is Over

August 15, 1945

Japan Surrenders.

Hong Kong, August 30, 1945

The British reoccupy Hong Kong.

China, September 28, 1945

Chao Lin receives a telegram from Shawn McGregor.

"Noticed HSC account growing.
Ship and warehouse repossessed.
Are we back in business?"
Chao Linn answers Shawn McGregor's telegram.
"Yes, will arrive in Hong Kong, date uncertain."

October 1, 1945

The OSS is abolished. Until further notice, Major Carter is ordered to continue with his policing duties in Kunming, China.

October 10, 1945

With the war over, Major Chan is ordered back to Shanghai. As the preparations to leave for Shanghai began, so did the farewells between Major Chan's men and Major Carter's men. While walking their dogs, Major Chan told Chao Lin of his new orders.

"My official duties here are also over," Chao Lin said. "My plans are to go to Jinhua to find my sister and cousin. Then I plan to go to Hong Kong to restart my trading business."

"We will pass through Jinhua on our way to Shanghai," Major Chan said. "Can you be ready to leave in 3 days?"

"Yes," Chao Lin said.

"Then we travel together, my friend," Major Chan said.

October 11, 1945

After a special dinner arranged by the two Majors, they all gathered together in one of Major Carter's warehouses for a going away party, Army style.

"I understand you're traveling with Major Chan," Fritz said, speaking to Chao Lin.

"Yes," Chao Lin said. Then he explained his plans to Fritz.

"With your trading skills, I think that you will be a rich man someday, Chao Lin," Fritz said.

Fritz was right about a lot of things, but there was no way he could have imagined how accurate his prediction would become.

"How can someone invest in your company," Fritz asked? "Buy shares of stock?"

"Not exactly," Chao Lin said. "The HSC Trading Company is a private company. But my partner, Shawn McGregor, could handle the details of anyone willing to invest in our company. He just repossessed our ship and warehouse in Hong Kong that were confiscated by the Japanese."

Handing Fritz one of his business cards, Chao said,

"I'd welcome your investment and participation in our company."

Sitting across the table from Fritz and Chao, Major Carter and Isiac looked at each other and nodded.

"What about us, Chao," Major Carter asked?

"Equally welcome," Chao answered with a smile, handing out two more of his business cards.

Before the evening was over, Fritz, Isiac, and Major Carter, using the money that they saved from their OSS payments, each gave Chao Lin 1,000 American dollars to invest in his trading company.

October 13, 1945

Everyone on the base that was watching saw Major Chan's Company, along with Chao Lin, walking off the base; but Fritz and Isiac saw two friends walking their dogs.

Back to Civilian Life

Michigan, March 1946

Isiac is discharged from the Army in California. At the time of discharge, Isiac, with his body still recovering from the punishment inflicted by the war, weighed 145 pounds, 30 pounds lighter than when he entered the Army. But he was still able to make it home in time for Jayme's 4th birthday.

China, April 1946

The Chinese Civil War resumes.

Michigan, Fall 1946

It was opening day of duck season. Peg was now 14 years old. When Bud left for the Army, he never thought he would ever see his dog again. But, here he was, in his duck boat in Mouillee Marsh, with Peg standing on the Front seat and Fritz sitting on the middle seat. He was sitting on the back seat next to Jayme who had his hand on the tiller and was steering the boat… in the dark.

"Just like his father," Bud thought with pride, "Running the boat when he's only 4 years old. Bob and Deke Stovey were following close behind in their own duck boat. It was images like this that had helped Bud survive his time in the Army and the separation from his family.

Washington D. C. 1947

The Office of Strategic Services is restructured into the Central Intelligence Agency.

Michigan, January 1947

Jayme just makes the cut-off to start kindergarten in January. Children born after April 1 had to wait until September to start kindergarten.

February 5, 1947

When Jayme returns home from school, Peg is not there to greet him. She died shortly after he left for school that morning. With Jayme sitting in his lap, Bud's thoughts drifted back to last duck season, and they were bittersweet. Jayme was able to hunt with Peg in his first duck season. And he was able to hunt with Peg in her last duck season.

The end

www.ingramcontent.com/pod-product-compliance
Lightning Source LLC
Chambersburg PA
CBHW080526090426
42733CB00015B/2497

* 9 780099 814171 8 *